# BUILDING, MARKETING & OPERATING A PROFITABLE
# TAX PRACTICE

A practical, step-by-step, working guide to running a successful, efficient, & lucrative professional tax practice

*Fifth Revised Edition*

NATIONAL TAX TRAINING SCHOOL
PUBLICATIONS DIVISION

Training and Serving the Tax Professional since 1952

"This publication is designed to provide accurate and authoritative information in regard to the subject matter covered. It is sold with the understanding that the publisher is not engaged in rendering legal, accounting, or other professional service. If legal advice or other expert assistance is required, the services of a competent professional person should be sought."

*From a Declaration of Principles jointly adopted by a Committee of the American Bar Association and a Committee of Publishers and Associations.*

Published by:
National Tax Training School
Publications Division
POB 767
67 Ramapo Valley Road
Suite 102
Mahwah, New Jersey 07430

Telephone: 201-684-0828 / 800-914-8138
Fax: 201-684-0829 / 888-814-8140
Website: www.nationaltax.edu
E-mail: info@nationaltax.edu

Copyright © 2012
National Tax Training School
ISBN: 978-0-9821978-5-1

All rights reserved

No parts of this book may be reproduced in any form or by any means without written permission from the publisher.

# Table of Contents

A Word to the Reader .................................................................................................. v
Acknowledgements .................................................................................................... vii
Chapter 1: Introduction ............................................................................................. 1
Chapter 2: Tax Practice—What It Takes to Succeed ............................................. 9
Chapter 3: Establishing Your Office ........................................................................ 15
Chapter 4: PTIN Requirements per the IRS ........................................................... 33
Chapter 5: Updating Office Technology & Today's Tax Professional ................ 39
Chapter 6: Successfully Marketing Your Practice .................................................. 57
Chapter 7: Purchasing a Client or a Practice ......................................................... 89
Chapter 8: Expanding Your Practice ....................................................................... 99
Chapter 9: Tax Return Procedure ............................................................................ 115
Chapter 10: Streamlining Your Office Procedure .................................................. 123
Chapter 11: Hiring Staff Members ........................................................................... 139
Chapter 12: Fees and Billing ..................................................................................... 153
Chapter 13: Collecting Your Fees ............................................................................. 159
Chapter 14: Obtaining Additional Income from Clients ..................................... 165
Chapter 15: Ethical Responsibilities of the Tax Consultant ................................ 175
Chapter 16: Tax Audits and How to Handle Them .............................................. 185
Chapter 17: Assuring Your Advancement through Professional Self-Development ... 203
Chapter 18: Should You Consider a Tax Office Franchise? ................................. 215
Chapter 19: How to Profitably Sell or Merge Your Practice ................................ 223
Chapter 20: Niche Markets and Value-Added Services ........................................ 237
Chapter 21: Sample Portfolio Letter ........................................................................ 249
Chapter 22: Special Practice Builder Reports ........................................................ 269
Appendix: Average Tax Return Fees ....................................................................... 285

# A Word to the Reader

The original version of this text, BUILDING & OPERATING A PROFITABLE TAX PRACTICE, was first published in 1977. Since then it has appeared in several updated and expanded editions.

Initially, the book was designed to serve as a hands-on blueprint for new tax practitioners—mainly graduates of the National Tax Training School's basic and advanced tax training programs. But, to our surprise, the feedback we received indicated that even seasoned professionals with years of experience, found much useful and valuable information and a wealth of practical tips in its pages.

Accordingly, in later editions—and especially in this new revision—we took great pains to address the interests and needs of those readers as well. Whereas, originally, the primary goal was to guide the newcomer through the various steps of setting up a viable tax practice, we now focus extensively on providing proven ideas and know-how for developing an existing practice—with regard to both clientele and increased revenues.

If you are new to the tax field—or are presently working for an accounting or tax firm and contemplate going into business for yourself—you need not feel shortchanged. All the information, tips, and guidelines that have helped so many of your predecessors build flourishing professional practices are still here, along with a host of new ideas and strategies. But this manual will also show you how to take your business much further once you're firmly established. After all, isn't that what you're aiming for?

If you're an experienced professional with an up-and-running tax practice you may want to skip (or just skim) those portions of the first few chapters that deal with setting up a practice. However, the balance of the book, comprising the overwhelming majority of topics covered, is addressed to both novices and veterans alike. You'll find a goldmine of down-to-earth advice, proven strategies, and tested marketing methods—all designed to boost your bottom line.

To get the most out of this book, don't just read through the pages. Use it as a hands-on working manual. Make marginal notes, underline or highlight business-and profit-building ideas and techniques you wish to implement immediately, or at a later date.

Most important, try to formulate a clear, specific, plan of action to advance your practice from where it is now to where you want it to be. You can be assured that your efforts will be well rewarded.

Have a happy, productive journey.

# Acknowledgements

This work is dedicated to the thousands of National Tax students and graduates throughout the United States (and abroad) whose enthusiasm, professionalism, and success stories have been a constant source of encouragement and inspiration to us for over five decades.

We are particularly grateful to the many NATIONAL TAX subscribers and customers—the men and women, both students and non-students—who have supplied us with some of the material in this book.

They graciously shared with us their experiences, patiently answered detailed surveys and questionnaires regarding fees, marketing methods, promotional strategies, etc. Many went out of their way to submit innovative ideas, point out potential pitfalls or volunteer other valuable inside information…for no other reason than to extend a helping hand to their fellow professionals.

We are indeed proud to be in such good company.

# Chapter 1

# Introduction

*Three men were performing a similar task when a passerby stopped to observe them. After a few minutes he asked one worker, "What are you doing?" And the man answered, "I'm laying bricks."*

*He then asked the second worker, "And what are you doing?" And the man said, "Why—I'm building a wall."*

*Then he asked the third worker the same question, and the man looked up and replied: "I'm building a house of worship!"*

*It all depends on how you look at things: a lot of people may be performing a similar task, and one can think of it as menial, while the other sees it as inspiring—and the difference depends upon their outlook on life.*
**Author Unknown**

*The journey through life can be a pleasant and rewarding experience if we have the right attitude. A good attitude is like cork—it can hold you up. A poor attitude is like lead—it can sink you.*
**L. Kenneth Wright**

## General Introduction

Our system of taxation in America has a long and curious history. In many ways the evolution of the current tax system even mirrors the development of our country as a whole.

The early colonists rebelled against what they considered to be unfair tax legislation imposed by the British magistrates: a sugar tax in 1764, a stamp tax in 1766, and a tea tax in 1773. All of these events, of course, led up to the Revolutionary War, and finally, American independence in 1776.

It takes time for a country to grow, and it wasn't until 1861 that our first federal tax law was signed; that was to help finance the Civil War. With that as a base, income tax laws progressed, and with the advent of the First World War taxes and tax legislation increased dramatically. This trend naturally continued through World War II and thereafter.

As twentieth century life in America became more complex, so too, did federal tax legislation. The result, at present, is a body of federal law so intricate that few taxpayers can obey it without some kind of expert assistance. Consequently, a great many taxpayers find that tax practitioners and tax advisers are indispensable guides when it comes to planning and filing their annual tax returns. In fact, given today's market, it would be simply unwise to pursue many personal business transactions without first consulting with a tax expert to determine the best way of arranging one's financial affairs, both for compliance and maximum profit.

It's understandable, then, that as life and tax law in this new century become more complex, the tax professional will come into play as an even more important and ever-expanding role in the American business community.

## Tax Practice—An Overview

Income tax practice is an unusually satisfying, respectable, and profitable occupation. As a tax practitioner you provide a vital, professional service in the nation's economy and occupy a position of prestige and dignity. Whether you view this profession as a full-time career or as a happy supplement to your regular income by preparing tax returns during the tax season, you will, no doubt, find tax work to be stimulating, challenging, and enjoyable.

The tax practitioner is in a position to advise and assist people with many financial, and occasionally even personal problems, thereby saving them money, getting them refunds, devising tax saving strategies, and finding deductions that were overlooked or clients didn't even know existed. Sharing in the most intimate facets of a client's financial life, the consultant becomes a trusted friend and adviser. Compensations like these are rare in any line of work, but they are your privilege to enjoy as a tax consultant.

Also, in the course of your practice, you will come into contact with individuals from all walks of life. As a result, you will acquire first-hand knowledge of various trades, businesses, and professions, and gain insight into a wide variety of investment and other financial situations. The valued friendships, breadth of experience, and the detailed knowledge learned regarding various business practices—all of these are of tremendous value to many practitioners in their business as well as in their personal lives.

Furthermore, it is very unlikely that tax work will ever become obsolete; there is very little chance that the tax consultant will ever join the swelling ranks of the technologically unemployed. "Death and taxes" being the certainties that they are, an ever-increasing need for tax consultants seems equally as certain. As far as financial rewards go, few professions or occupations provide a quicker or greater financial return when compared to the relatively small amount of money, time, and effort required to enter the field.

While being a tax consultant is extremely rewarding, before we proceed to the next chapter let's briefly discuss a few commonly asked questions—some of which may be troubling you too.

1. **Isn't the computer and consumer tax software available today making the services of tax practitioners unnecessary? Why would anyone hire a tax professional, incurring a large service fee, when you can get inexpensive tax preparation software and do your own return for less?**

   Rest assured that in spite of all technological advances preparing any but the simplest tax return by computer is still quite a formidable task for the untrained. The primary market for the low-priced tax preparation software is that group of taxpayers who have relatively simple situations and have always prepared their own tax returns. Even many of these individuals, after a few disastrous attempts, give up and turn to professionals. They realize that the hassle of dealing with both the complexities of tax law and the often-confusing computer tax program just isn't worth it.

2. **What good is my professional training at setting me apart for tax services? Why can't anyone with a computer and tax software just set up shop and grab my clients, perhaps by offering lower fees?**

   Tax preparation software is an excellent tool yet, like all professional tools, it is worthless, or worse, if you don't know how to use it properly. At best, and if you are willing to spend the necessary time and effort, tax software may help you prepare your own return, but anyone who thinks that it can be used on a professional basis for different taxpayers and different situations is in for a rude awakening.

3. **What about the large tax preparation chains and their enormous advertising budget? What chance do I have competing against them?**

   There's no doubt that the big tax preparation chains—especially H&R Block or Hewitt—have taken over a large share of the potential tax return preparation market. However, their strength—quick, but impersonal, assembly-line tax return preparation by low-paid employees with a high turnover rate—is also their greatest weakness.

   First, the large-scape tax preparation business model pretty much restricts clientele to the less wealthy taxpayer class, mainly lower-income wage earners with fairly simple returns. More complex returns take too long and cut into the bottom line. These businesses need people to come in, pay the fee, and move out quickly. It's the only way they can remain profitable supporting so many retail offices and personnel, even just during tax season.

   Secondly, development of a more personal business model makes it relatively easy for small tax consultants to attract many of the mega chain's clients by offering superior, personal service. Indeed, statistics show that the tax preparation chains have not gained market share in recent years. Apparently, whatever gains they have made came primarily from natural population growth.

   Later in this book we will discuss in detail how you can capitalize on this inherent weakness and turn it to your advantage. We will describe proven methods and techniques that alert tax practitioners effectively use to cope with the competition. Plus, we will show you how to build your business by weaning clients away from the chain tax services.

4. **I read that the coming FLAT TAX or other tax-simplification measures will do away with current income tax returns entirely, or—at most—call for a "post card" size tax return, is that so?**

   Have no fear! The Flat Tax idea (and similar ones) has been around for decades. Though it's politically appealing it has gone nowhere and, according to most experts, is unlikely to be seriously considered in the foreseeable future. One reason for this is that to make such a system equitable and workable in our complex national economy Congress would have to enact so many new rules, exceptions, and special provisions that the resulting tax system would be nearly as complicated as the current income tax system. Given how hard it is to get normal legislation through the process, aside from partisan bickering and the influence of lobbyists getting involved, a flat tax proposal is very unlikely.

   Further, the flat tax could actually reduce national tax revenues. Much of what is paid in taxes comes from those with above $60,000 a year incomes. The majority of filers earn less, don't typically pay anything and frequently receive a refund for all the withholding taken out of their paychecks. The fear of a flat tax actually generating less in taxes from the higher incomes raises a specter of what programs would have to be cut. Special interests are far too involved in Congress to let that happen without objection. As a result, any kind of tax overhaul with a flat tax would be in for a bruiser of a fight just to see the light of day.

As far as the siren call for "tax simplification" is concerned, you know what has happened every time in recent memory when Congress has tried to simplify the law? It became only more confusing. In fact, the 1986 Tax Reform Act, which was termed at the time "the most complex tax law ever," has become immeasurably more complicated as a result of all the 'simplification' amendments added since.

In summary, we can safely assure you that the independent tax professional is alive and well, and—with the help of Congress—doing better all the time. Based upon our intimate association with the field, we're convinced that tax practitioners will continue to prosper well into the future.

## Tax Practice for Now and for the Future

The tax profession has undergone some changes since this book was first written and for a number of reasons, which include:

- Frequently changing tax legislation,
- Advances in technology and the ongoing information revolution,
- A more complex economic climate, and
- More complex business practices and procedures.

Consequently, tax practice as a career opportunity has opened up and the demand for qualified tax practitioners is growing as well.

However, as the economic picture changes and as career prospects improve, new demands are being made on tax practitioners as well. In order to be a successful, developing tax practitioner today, you must structure your career around something more than technical competence alone.

Of course, it goes without saying that technical skills and tax knowledge are absolutely indispensable to our discussion; without these essential skills there is nothing further to talk about. But as important as technical knowledge is, there are other skills you have to develop that are also very important ... skills that relate to your general business sense and overall effectiveness as a person over- seeing your own business. This is primarily what this text prepares you for.

**Building, Marketing and Operating a Profitable Tax Practice** may not make you a better qualified tax practitioner in the narrow sense of the word, but it will show you how to take the technical skills you have acquired—and continue to acquire—and convert them, employ them, channel them, in a way that can make you a more successful practitioner.

**Building, Marketing and Operating a Profitable Tax Practice** may not necessarily provide you with a better understanding of tax law and tax law application, for its overriding concern is to coach you in how to utilize your acquired skills to your best advantage. The text aims to help you effectively structure and manage your career. You will find chapters containing timely and practical advice on how to organize, manage, and communicate your skills; how to handle yourself and how to deal with others; and how to promote your services, along with suggestions on how to make full use of your technical know-how—and all for the sake of successfully advancing your career.

Again—technical competence is paramount, but the fact that you are a qualified tax professional indicates that you already have the basic skills necessary for a productive career. To use a metaphor, your tax skills are like a well-tuned engine: the task is now to steer that engine properly in a desirable direction. That calls for implementing the information gathered and presented in this text.

Basically, the picture that emerges for tax practitioners in the coming years is of a practice built around client contact: not only more contact, but also more quality, multidimensional contact between client and practitioner. And this, in turn, calls for better communication and relationship skills: being able to inform, explain, and instill confidence in clients. Therefore, in addition to being technically proficient you also have to be able to listen, manage, and advise. In order to help you meet these challenges we have revised, expanded, and updated our original text.

This text contains a wealth of information, advice, practical suggestions, and examples—but don't be overwhelmed by it all. It is not meant to be read and implemented in one night, or one month, or even a year. You can review the text, or read it from cover to cover to get an overview of the material, but it is designed primarily as a guide and reference work—for you to turn to as the need arises. There are chapters that may or may not—practically speaking—concern you right now. You may read them for their information value, and then study them more carefully when you are ready to actually make use of the information. In other words, the text is designed as a guide—to use the information as the need arises and to accompany you as your practice begins, changes, develops, and grows.

## A Final Thought before We Begin

Some things, of course, change, but some matters of principle do not change. The following excerpt (with minor changes) taken from the introduction to the first edition, still holds true today:

> *"It is important to establish firmly in your mind that you are not a technician or robot trained to put the right number into the right space on the right form. Your duties, opportunities, and responsibilities as a tax consultant go far beyond the procedure of merely filling out a tax return. If you really want to do justice to yourself and your clients you will apply your expertise, experience and ingenuity to assist them in paying the lowest legal tax possible. Also bear in mind that preparing tax returns means dealing with the lives of people, and not just with facts and figures. And finally, as you will be pleasantly surprised to discover, you will derive an enormous amount of satisfaction from delivering a professional, quality service. As the various forms and schedules take shape and fall into a pattern you will begin to feel a sense of achievement—heightened by the fact that you have not only done your best to work out the lowest possible tax liability for your client, but have also helped him or her comply with the law. At this point you will begin to take pride in your work, in your respected and ongoing association with clients, and you will be truly grateful you chose this honorable and satisfying profession."*

One thing is certain: tax law is fascinating, intricate, and ever-changing. And as long as that remains the case, taxpayers—be they individuals or business firms—will be in need of professional assistance and advice to properly manage this vital aspect of their lives.

Since this volume is intended to help the beginning tax novice as well as the seasoned practitioner, we will now proceed to the basics of how and where to establish your practice. Those of you who are already in business may want to skip the next few chapters (except the PTIN section in Chapter 4), but we feel a quick review of the covered material will provide valuable ideas that every one of you will, sooner or later, find beneficial.

# Chapter 2

# Tax Practice—What It Takes to Succeed

*Success is discovering your best talents, skills, and abilities, and applying them where they will do the most amount of good.*
**Wilferd A. Paterson**

*According to the theory of aerodynamics, and as may be readily demonstrated through laboratory tests and wind tunnel experiments, the bumblebee is unable to fly. This is because the size, weight, and shape of its body in relation to its total wingspread make flying impossible. But the bumblebee—being ignorant of these profound scientific truths—goes ahead and flies anyway... and even manages to make a little honey every day.*
**Author Unknown**

# Today's Practitioner: Taking Steps to Success

This chapter did not appear in the first edition, but we thought that before we focus on outer furnishings and preparations—such as location, and marketing strategies, etc.—we should devote a few words to the subject of "inner preparation." In today's ever-changing and competitive marketplace, it's worthwhile developing a mindset that promotes personal success rather than one that undermines it. This chapter is far from exhaustive but it will highlight a few key attitudes and personal traits that are certainly worth mentioning.

The idea of running one's own business has long been part of the American dream. In fact, in many ways America's entrepreneurial spirit epitomizes that dream with its unique system of free enterprise, whereby anyone with some capital, some skills, and some fortitude can pursue any business endeavor that he or she desires. This is a noble freedom that millions of Americans continue to take advantage of, and rightfully so. No wonder, "going into your own business" is a phenomenon that is definitely on the rise.

Nevertheless, transforming this dream into reality calls for the practical implementation of certain skills, insights, and attitudes that we will now discuss. A better understanding of these "components of success" will be of help to you in your own development as a tax professional.

Nutritionists often say, "You are what you eat!" If this holds true in a biological sense then it probably holds true in a psychological sense in that you essentially are what you think and believe. In fact, this has proven to be the case; it is a well-established fact that your attitudes—about yourself and about life in general—have a lot to do with your measure of success. By firmly believing that you will succeed you improve your very chances of success. So to begin, you have to believe in your own potential for success and that you have what it takes to succeed. Even if you don't have all that it takes just yet, you at least know that you can develop, acquire, or learn the necessary traits or skills that contribute to personal success. Everything that follows in this chapter relates to this fundamental belief in your own potential.

Beyond this basic belief in oneself, those who go into business for themselves tend to exhibit the following attributes in some measure—and if not all of them, then at least some of them—depending upon what their particular task or work situation demands of them.

### 1. A drive for independence

A desire for personal working autonomy coupled with an ability to work well alone seems to be an essential attribute of those who go into business for themselves. Of course, as a tax practitioner, opportunities abound for client and social contacts, but in a predominantly one-person venture you have to appreciate your independence while you effectively make good use of it.

We should quickly point out that independence here does not mean "free to do whatever you wish." It's independence from direct supervision over you, but you still have to make use of that independence to fulfill your various responsibilities. Therefore, being a good **self-starter** is critical to success. Since you don't have your own boss watching over you, you have to be your own boss—to get up, get going, and get the job done!

## 2. A willingness to sacrifice

Especially when you begin a new practice and are seeing if off the ground, you have to be willing to give it the time and attention it deserves. This calls for hard and steady work. Of course, you don't have to abandon your other interests and associations, but you have to be willing to "put in that extra hour" or "go that extra mile" if it is necessary to do so. This is certainly the case when you are opening a new practice, and it will also hold true at various times of the year—such as at tax season and the weeks leading up to it.

It's also important for an entrepreneur to keep in mind that he or she is not the only one who will likely need to make a sacrifice for a new business. Many times his or her family and close friends will be impacted as well. In the beginning almost all will be supportive, but over time balancing the business with personal time needs will be very challenging. Even the best entrepreneurs admit a new business can cause significant strain and stress at home.

You will have to find a way to balance what the business needs if you are to become successful while also still meeting your personal commitments. This can be extremely hard at times, resulting in instances where fairness takes a backseat to necessity.

## 3. A willingness to take chances

Managing your own professional tax practice means that you must be willing and able to take occasional calculated risks. To be sure, there are a number of things you can always do to minimize the risks involved—such as planning, research, and careful consideration of all essential factors—but as in any business, an element of risk remains and you have to be able to deal with it.

Along with this trait goes the ability to make decisions. As a sole practitioner, you have to be able to gather the information you need and analyze your choices in order to make sound and accurate decisions. Developed skills in this area will certainly help your practice to expand and grow.

### 4. An ability to persevere

One of the most commonly-cited reasons for failure in a one-person venture is simply giving up far too soon. You have to be persistent in your endeavors and not let minor setbacks or negativity sway you from your goals. Naturally, all this is easier said than done, but the importance of perseverance cannot be overestimated. Don't let yourself be overcome by impatience or the fear of failure.

An extension of this principle is the idea that not only do successful people persevere, but they also possess a healthy, productive outlook on failure as well. They tend to see failure in a more positive light. It's an opportunity to stop and assess one's motives and abilities, as well as a chance to sharpen one's skills and resolve. A temporary setback can also be instructive in terms of what to do and what not to do next. The ability to weather a failure can make you stronger, smarter, and better prepared for your next round in the business world—but all this holds true only if you are willing to examine the setback in this way.

Therefore, being successful means having the courage to meet failure without being defeated and refusing to let a current loss interfere with your genuine long-range goal.

### 5. A sense of enthusiasm

Successful practitioners are basically optimistic and enthusiastic, not only about their work, but about life in general. Therefore, they are able to look upon their endeavors as exciting, adventurous, stimulating, and creatively challenging. This outlook, in turn, enables the mind to see the possibilities in every encounter, to visualize solutions to daily concerns, and to ultimately look upon problems and setbacks—not as obstacles, but as stepping stones—to further growth.

### 6. A willingness to learn

Formal schooling is one way—but by no means the only way—to gather facts, accumulate knowledge, and gain insight into the ways of the business world. However, beyond any of the means at one's disposal, we are referring here to a deeper openness and willingness to learn and go on learning whatever is necessary to ensure the proper running of your tax practice. Make use of community resources, libraries, lectures, seminars, and updates. Be an avid reader—of books, newsletters, and journals—to keep in touch with current events, business trends, and financial affairs. And of course, don't forget the internet. We are dealing here with a healthy curiosity, with being a student of life, with keeping your eyes and ears open so you can creatively learn from all that you see and hear around you. As a result, the more you learn the more confidence you acquire, and the better prepared you are to serve your clients. You thereby enhance your chances of both financial and personal success.

## 7. An ability to plan and prepare

Going into business for yourself—opening a professional tax practice—calls for planning, preparation, and a good deal of forethought. Planning and researching forces you to think, look ahead, and weigh alternatives.

You should have some concrete idea of what goal you are aiming for, and then do whatever you can to reach that goal. Your planning should take into account as many pertinent factors that you can think of (many of which are discussed in this text), factors that will affect your actions. Then with all your preparations set before you like a road map you are in a better position to advance in the direction of your own success.

You may compare this entire planning stage to the task of an archer aiming his arrow at a specific target. The clearer he is on the location of his target, the more skilled he is in the use of a bow and arrow, and the more careful he is about taking aim (considering all the conditions around him), the more likely he is to succeed at finally hitting the mark. The same holds true in your approach to your tax practice. With your skills in hand, with your goal in mind, and with proper aim and preparation, you increase your chances at success. That is what this book is primarily about… increasing your chances of success as a tax professional.

Few people possess all of the valued traits of a perfect business-starter, and fewer still possess them to any degree of perfection. Fortunately, however, as you develop your practice you don't have to be the epitome of all these attributes. You only have to be willing to learn about them, cultivate them, and draw upon them as the need arises. This determination to do what is right will help you and your practice to flourish.

The possibilities are great, the journey promises to be an exciting one, and what awaits you as you proceed is most exciting of all: an opportunity to live a flexible and expansive personal life; to play a larger, more influential role in your community; and to gain financial satisfaction and true personal fulfillment by contributing to your community in a meaningful way.

# Chapter 3

# Establishing Your Office

*A journey of ten thousand miles begins with a single step.*
**Confucius**

*If you want to be successful, it's just this simple: Know what you're doing. Love what you're doing. And believe in what you're doing.*
**Will Rogers**

It is possible to operate a tax preparation office out of a briefcase, but if you are at all serious about getting into tax work on a more than incidental basis you should have some sort of an office—even if it is in your own home—and acquire a minimum of office furnishings, supplies, and equipment.

This chapter will help you locate, outfit, and equip your office or workspace.

## Location

Selecting a good location for your tax practice is one of the more important decisions you will have to make, because your location will strongly affect other aspects of your business including:

- Your operating hours,
- Overhead, and
- The amount and type of clients you attract, and much more.

Therefore, it pays to do some careful research into the question of location. After all, it's a decision you do not want to make too often. Moving around can quickly get expensive. In the long run a well-considered location could actually save you time, energy, worry, and money.

To begin with, you may not even be in a position at first to select the best possible location for your practice. In the beginning of the business you may want—or need—to work out of your home. Or perhaps your limited finances will dictate the location of your office. Then again, you may be purchasing someone else's practice and the transaction may include a predetermined location. So there are many factors that may automatically keep you from choosing an optimum location. But if you have any control over your location, and to the extent that you do, here are some points worthy of consideration:

### 1. Identify possible neighborhoods for your tax practice

A common saying in real estate is "location, location, and location." The physical, geographic address of your office can make a big impression on customers. Begin by asking yourself: Who are my prospective clients and where are they located? You may identify this target market in various ways: by age, economic status, or vocational characteristics. Your answer may include various types of people but list them and determine approximately where they work and/or reside.

By the way, the study of populations and their make-up is a science of its own called demography, and a great deal of sophisticated statistical research data is available to you in this field. For example, a lot of big businesses study, in detail, the demographics of a specific region before opening an office or business there. As a tax practitioner you can take advantage of this available research when considering your own office location. If you want to pursue this avenue further the following community resources are good places to begin:

- Your local library will have much of this information available as reference material, including detailed neighborhood maps from government agencies indicating population and business shifts and trends. For example, your library should carry Statistical Abstracts of the United States. This annual publication from the United States Census Bureau contains ample information on population density, growth, incomes, occupations, and similar data. The city or town hall is a good resource, as well as real estate firms or banks.

- Your local Chamber of Commerce has data on different sections of the city and can be of help. Make a point of speaking to state, county, and town officials as well as people in business and business organizations in the area. They should know about business trends and the population potentials in a given neighborhood.

Incidentally, it's all too natural to think of starting your tax practice in your own hometown, but you shouldn't assume that where you live now is necessarily your best choice for a tax practice. Your research may uncover some other pleasing and promising possibilities in other communities. Don't overlook these findings. Check them out.

## 2. Other neighborhood considerations

Once you have selected a number of possible areas that represent a rather high concentration of your potential client population, you can then examine these neighborhoods from other worthwhile perspectives.

Also bear in mind that in determining a location you are primarily trying to meet your clients' needs and not necessarily your own. For example, you may favor an office building perched on a hill with an impressive view overlooking the bay below, but if it is too difficult to access for most of your prospective clients then it could actually drive them away. In fact, try to think in terms of two major concerns when weighing any of the following aspects of office location:

a) Maximum convenience for your clients, and

b) Maximum operating effectiveness for you.

Also consider:

- Consider traffic and accessibility, asking: Is the location in a well-traveled area or an isolated one?

- Think about transportation, asking: Is there public transportation to where you are? Is the office easily reachable and easy to find, by car or on foot? On the other hand, is the area overly congested, noisy, and dirty?

- Think about parking, asking: Is adequate parking readily available? Is it free or is there a cost?

- Consider locating near compatible businesses and services; i.e. banks, real estate firms, insurance agencies, and other professional service-oriented occupations.

- Consider the competition: Is the area saturated with tax consultants, or is there room for one more? Or perhaps there are practitioners in the area, but the quality of the service is disappointing, leaving room for better service.

- Try to avoid blighted, run-down areas. Ask yourself: Is this neighborhood improving or deteriorating? How pleasant are the surroundings? Is the area clean or full of litter? Is the area well lit and safe at night? Would you go there yourself and feel safe in that location to hire a service?

### 3. The particular building and your office space

After considering the population of the neighborhood, the prospects for business there, along with some of its physical attributes, it's time to examine the building and office space you intend to occupy. Here are some questions to consider. Again, remember to view each office site as if you were a prospective client.

- What is the age and condition of the building?
- Is it clean and attractive, or shabby and hazardous?
- Is there adequate lighting outside and inside the building? Are the grounds well kept?
- What kind of traffic patterns do you see around the building, and what kind of people do you see in and around the building?

When you check out the prospective office itself, consider:

- How many rooms or how much space do you have?
- What is the condition of the office's mechanical systems: electric, plumbing, heating, and air conditioning? Is there a restroom available? Is it clean and well kept?
- How are the floors, windows, walls, and ceilings? Check the acoustics. Is it necessary to remodel or paint the office? At whose expense?
- What type of lighting is provided?
- What are the terms of the lease, and what are the terms for renewal or cancellation of the lease?

In general, don't bother going into neighborhoods, buildings, or offices that are definitely unsuitable. Unless you need an office immediately don't settle on the first site that seems adequate either. Shop around and try to find an office that has as many positive features and advantages as possible.

## Opportunity for Expansion

It may seem premature to you now, but if you use common sense and follow the guidelines and suggestions presented in this volume, you may soon find yourself in need of more space. Moving an established business is always costly, traumatic, time consuming, and may even result in the loss of some clients. Therefore, see if you can make some provisions in advance, in order to avoid—or at least postpone—the necessity of relocating.

For example, try to initially obtain more space than you need. This may be expensive, but if you are renting an office your landlord might be willing to insert a clause in your lease giving you the option to take on additional, adjacent space when it becomes available. Or, you may be able to lease more space than you need, and sublet it until you actually need to make use of it for your own needs. Doing so allows you to grow when necessary without having to immediately change your business address.

If you build an addition to your home to house your office, you can also probably incorporate provisions for future expansion into the current plan at little extra cost.

As a general rule, try to envision your business needs three to five years from now, and see if you can obtain a space that is both adequate now and that can also accommodate your future needs.

### Checklist—What to Look For and Ask When Office Hunting

- Access to building—mass transit, any other; check parking facilities.
- Access within building—elevators or stairs.
- Condition of building—inside and out.
- Office space—number of rooms or size of available work area.
- Number and location of electrical outlets/type of wiring.
- Terms of lease and monthly rent—length of lease and conditions of lease.
- Are any repairs or alterations needed: paint, doors and locks, security, floors and carpets, windows and walls, ceilings, drapes and curtains, etc.
- Who pays for maintenance, utilities, repairs, and other services (cleaning, trash removal, etc.)?
- Are office signs allowed—inside the building and/or outside?
- Traffic conditions: How easy or difficult is it to get to the office?
- Noise levels—inside the office and out. Is it tolerable or intolerable?
- Restrooms: Are restrooms easily accessible and are restroom conditions adequate?

- Exits and/or fire escapes.
- The lighting situation inside and outside the building, as well as inside and outside the office: Is it sufficient? What type of lighting is it?
- Heating and cooling systems: What type of system is it and is it working properly?

## Office Arrangement

For a tax professional, creating an office environment that is effective, efficient, yet congenial, is an important consideration. Your office should be set up in a way that enables you to get your work done; at the same time the arrangement should allow clients to feel physically comfortable and psychologically at ease.

To operate effectively most practitioners need a work area that can accommodate a desk and chair from which you can do paperwork and make phone calls; suitable space for electronic equipment—be it a computer or other office technology; space for storage—a filing cabinet, bookshelves and reference materials; and some space for storing supplies and other equipment (which may even be in a different room).

If you have more space to work with you can utilize the extra room as necessary: a conversation or meeting area, a waiting area for clients, or a work space for such activities as assembling, producing, or mailing materials.

Of course, all of these considerations depend upon the amount and configuration of your available space. If you only have one room to work with and you need a waiting area then room dividers, partitions, or screens are helpful; even bookcases and file cabinets can help section off one area from another. And while room dividers can provide some degree of privacy, curtains can help close off storage areas where you keep supplies and accessories that don't fit into cabinets.

One possible solution to layout problems in tight quarters is movable furnishings. Many furniture units—chairs, files, desks—come on casters or locking wheels. This allows you to easily transform your room arrangement contingent upon your needs. You can keep computers, printers, or copiers on a movable stand and roll them away when not in use. Also, if you have a lot of books you can use tall bookcases and make better use of vertical space. Furthermore, manufacturers today are designing office furniture and equipment that enable you to make optimal use of your limited space. For example, there are compact office file cabinets that fold out to become a full desk, and that can roll into any corner of a room. Spend some time checking out your options in stores and online.

When it comes to designing and arranging whatever space you have, you should try to strike a balance between practical and aesthetic considerations—bearing in mind personal preferences, client needs, as well as your professional goals.

## Office Decor

As you plan out the interior of your office, think of making it as pleasant a setting as possible—for yourself and for your clients. While some managers like to put up their own taste in art, it could turn off a customer who doesn't share the same taste. Keep your décor relatively neutral. Also remember that pleasant for yourself means creating a setting wherein you can effectively and efficiently spend many hours of time, and this means (among other things) cutting down on disturbances such as excessive noise, movement, and poor lighting.

### Noise Control

Noise can be a serious distraction for you and your clients. Fortunately, there are a number of things you can do to make your work area more effective, from a "sound" perspective:

- Carpets, curtains, and drapes are not only attractive, but they can help reduce extraneous noise. Furthermore, they are excellent insulators, keeping out both summer heat and winter cold.

- High ceilings from which sounds reverberate can be lowered with acoustical tiles or other sound absorbent material.

- Weather stripping on doors and windows, padded furniture, cushions and rubber pads under office equipment and room dividers can also help reduce noise.

Some people find that not only is too much noise an interference, but that too little is also disturbing. If you fit into this category then you might consider installing low volume music or a fish tank to alleviate the situation. If you live in an area where you plan to have open windows for much of the year you can consider exterior features such as a small, bubbling pond or fountain. Such natural sights and sounds may help you to work better, make your office more pleasing, and may help screen out noises that can't be masked in any other way.

### Minimizing Movement

The best way to handle disruptive movements, such as people coming and going, is to be in a separate room. If this is not possible then decorative room dividers may be helpful. If this is also not a practical consideration, then try arranging yourself and your furnishings in such a way that you don't have to look up every time someone passes by. Do this by considering which way to face your desk (towards a wall, open room, window) and how you arrange bookcases and such.

## Lighting

Lighting has a lot to do with comfort and productivity. Good lighting reduces fatigue, promotes accuracy, and can provide a cheerful working environment, so you should consider this matter carefully.

The best light for your office, of course, and the cheapest, is natural sunlight—through windows and even a skylight, if possible. It's impractical, however, to rely entirely on daylight, so you will have to supplement with artificial lighting.

- For more general illumination you should have some form of overhead fixture—either fluorescent or incandescent lighting. Each has its distinctive advantages, and you will have to assess which works best for you.

- For more task oriented lighting—to get specific jobs done—you should have some sort of adjustable desk, swing-arm, or floor lamp that you can use for more focused lighting needs.

- With whatever lighting you choose be on the lookout for eyestrain, glare, or other light-related conditions, and try to make adjustments accordingly. The light may be too weak or too strong, you may need frosted bulbs instead of clear, or better shading, or you may not react well to fluorescent lights. Bear in mind, too, that people working long hours on computer screens need subdued, glare-free light.

## Walls and Accessories

Office walls can be functional—with calendars, bulletin boards, notices, and news clippings, or decorative—with paintings, pictures and tapestries, or both—depending upon what works best for you. Of course, with whatever you put on your walls, try to maintain a professional décor and avoid over-cluttering.

If you have to refinish walls, paint, wallpaper, or paneling are among the more common ways of changing the appearance and character of your wall space. Just bear in mind that the colors you choose can have an impact—both on mood and work efficiency. Basic, traditional, earth-tone colors are more conducive to a professional setting than loud, vibrant colors and patterns. Use bright colors mainly to accentuate your surroundings.

The colors and color combinations you employ should be pleasing, and yet enhance your ability to function. Furniture and accessories should also be tastefully selected—with concerns of comfort and professionalism in mind:

- In addition to whatever essential furniture you need, introducing some natural elements is always appropriate: plants, flowers, dried flowers, or a fish tank, if there's room.

- Paintings, prints, or photographs (but not too many) can do a lot to enhance the appearance of a room. Other wall decorations may include small rugs, tapestries, or even a mirror.

- Displaying evidence of your professional accomplishments, competence, and expertise, certificates of achievement, other awards and credentials, or expressions of interest and personal concern can be appropriate as wall, desk, or table ornaments. Such displays can include professional licenses, diplomas, trophies, a family photograph, or social involvements such as a photograph of a little league team you coach. Not only do such items personalize your office; they also instill clients with a sense of confidence—in you, your abilities and values.

- If you have a separate waiting area be aware that this will be the first visual impression visitors will have of your office procedure. Have some comfortable furniture available, and a magazine rack or table with a variety of interesting reading material. Make sure the lighting is adequate, and have some interesting things on the walls—even a decorative clock. Waiting won't be such an irritating experience if there is something interesting to read or look at.

- Remember, too, that even if you have no more than a small work station to operate from you can make the most of it: personalize it, decorate it, and make it as welcome and as comfortable an area as possible, so you can effectively spend as much time there as is necessary. Too often, people make the mistake of only seeing the limitations of their work area and fail to modify it to meet their working needs.

## Selecting Office Furniture

When you look for office furniture, try not to get carried away by gimmickry and sleek design. Such offerings at furniture stores tend to be easy ways to sink a lot of money without any direct return. Instead, examine a piece of furniture and ask yourself these questions: Is it practical, useful, durable, and easily maintained? Is it worth the expense? Will it help me perform better at work?

## Desks and Chairs

It's no exaggeration to say that you may be spending more than half of your working day in your chair—at your desk—so these are items that must serve you well.

Look for a sturdy chair that gives your body as much natural support as possible. Your chair should be comfortable and encourage you to sit with good posture. A high quality, adjustable posture chair can go a long way towards reducing fatigue and increasing productivity. With adjustments in seat height, back height, and back tension, you can perform a variety of tasks without inviting unnecessary aches and pains. Padded seat, back, and arms, being able to swivel around, and having strong casters that enable you to roll around from one area to another are further considerations in the purchase of a good desk chair.

Since you will spend so much time in your office chair, it pays to put some extra money there. If you skimp on your chair and sacrifice your health, the saved money may just go to doctor bills instead. Despite the close relationship that you will develop with your chair, do remember that the human body was not meant to stay put in one spot for too long; it's a good idea to periodically get up, walk around, and get some fresh air and sunshine. The same goes for your eyes when you are working on a computer, remember the 20 / 20 / 20 rule: every 20 minutes, take 20 seconds to look 20 feet away.

Choose your desk with function and practicality in mind. Desktops tend to be loaded down occasionally—not just with papers but also with heavier equipment—so your desk should be sturdy and able to carry the load. To be normally functional your desk should have a file and supply drawer, and the drawers should lock. Depending upon how much space you have, try to get a desk with a reasonable surface area so you can sort things out and have enough room to maneuver.

**Storage Systems**

A good filing system is essential to good office organization. You will almost immediately have to "put things away" and you will have to know where these things are so you can easily retrieve them. Therefore, a good file cabinet is an early purchase for your office. It doesn't matter if it is a two or four drawer file, just be sure it's sturdy, with drawers that slide easily, because it undergoes a lot of steady use. Buy an ample number of hanging files and manila folders, and since you carry confidential material, locks are essential.

You may also want to consider an electronic filing system. Much of the paperwork you will handle will include items that over time will take up space and are only used for occasional reference. These documents can be scanned and saved on a computer hard drive. If a paper copy is needed again, it can simply be printed out. This approach can save a lot of space, but you will need a set procedure to make it work effectively. Paper can't just be piled up to magically become scanned. As documents come in, an office will need to digitize it to avoid a pile of filing workload at the end of the month.

In some cases hard copy documents with original signatures will still be necessary for filing. A scanned copy should be made anyways for backup purposes, and then paper copies can be filed in the folder storage space. This preserves cabinet space for essential paperwork and digitizes what's left.

For additional storage space, you may want to consider buying a credenza to place behind or alongside your desk. This is a useful piece of furniture equipped with file drawers, box drawers and shelves—and with casters, so you can easily roll it from place to place.

If you have subsidiary items that you need only rare or occasional access to then cardboard or plastic archive boxes may suffice. Of course, what does not fit into a filing drawer or cabinet may go on a shelf. Making good use of vertical shelf space is especially effective in a small office setting.

Depending upon your office needs and what space you have available, here are some other furnishings to consider:

- Additional tables, even folding tables, can add to your surface working area, support equipment, and even double as a conference table if need be. End tables or coffee tables can enhance your waiting area.
- Extra padded chairs (or even sturdy folding chairs) in case you have a conference or meeting.
- A wall clock and mirror can be nice additions for appearance and utility by you and your clients.

If you don't have a closet you will also need some sort of coat rack where these and other personal client accessories can be stored temporarily.

## Office Supplies

Whereas office furnishings and other equipment are, for the most part, a one-time investment, office supplies always need replenishing and are therefore a more constant drain on your operating budget. In addition, office supplies tend to be expensive. Therefore, it pays to shop for these items with thrift in mind:

- Be sure to compare prices. There can be a significant difference in prices between one office supply store and another. Very often a discount outlet will carry just what you need—at substantial savings.
- Office supply items are generally less expensive when purchased in quantity, so if there is something you know you will be making constant use of, try to buy as much of it at one time as you can, provided you have the storage space.
- Keep an eye out for quality as well. Try to buy items that are durable and that will serve you well. A cheap stapler that will soon need a replacement is not a source of savings. On the other hand, if you need pads for scribbling lists or notes, there's no need to buy high gloss, heavy-duty paper. So the quality of an item can reflect its use or function.

- Take advantage of coupons. Why pay more than you have to? Many supply stores provide online or newspaper coupons that can be utilized regularly. Frequent use of such marketing offers can save anywhere from 10 to 20 percent, and more, on the cost of supplies over time.

**Checklist of Office Supplies**

You may or may not need all of the items listed below but it is a basic list of common office supplies that most office personnel tend to use at one time or another.

- Accordion files
- Bulletin board and push pins
- Business cards
- Calendars: desk, wall, date book, or appointment calendar
- Dictionary and directories
- Envelopes: small, business size and large manila envelopes
- File folders, labels, and tabs
- Hole puncher
- In/out trays
- Index cards
- Paper: pads, message pads, "Post-it" notes, notebooks, and computer or typing paper
- Paper clips
- Pens, pencils, pencil sharpener, erasers, and markers
- Postage stamps or postage meter
- Rolodex type name, address, and telephone number file
- Rubber bands
- Rubber stamps
- Rulers
- Scissors
- Stapler, staples, and staple remover
- Stationery: letterhead and billhead
- Tape and tape dispenser
- Wastebasket and trash bags

Of course, computers, mobile apps and smart phones, and other office technology may have replaced some of these items. At the same time, many offices carry both—a standard and computerized version of some of these supplies.

## Chapter 3: Establishing Your Office

**Tax Forms**

It is absolutely essential that in addition to your list of general office supplies you are well-stocked with a broad array of tax forms, particularly those that are not allowed to be printed from electronic samples on the IRS Internet website, such as 1099 forms.

If you prepare your returns by computer (this topic will be discussed later), your software package will generate most of the tax forms and schedules you need. If you prepare returns manually you'll need specific paper tax forms. Since the IRS no longer supplies forms in quantities, you can order a few copies of each of the major forms from the IRS and reproduce them on your copier as you need them. Or, you can purchase them in bulk from an office supply retailer or one of the accounting supply houses. If you rely on the IRS make sure to get your order in early and check carefully to make sure that you receive everything (errors and omissions are not uncommon).

As your practice grows, you'll often need some of the less common forms and schedules—forms your software does not include, that you did not order from IRS, or that you haven't yet received —because there's no way to anticipate all your requirements. While you can order the desired forms from the IRS as you go along (and hope you'll get them in time), not having the right forms or instructions when you need them can tie your office up in knots. There are two ways to handle this problem:

1) You can download them from the IRS Internet website.

2) You can purchase a CD-ROM tax forms service (not to be confused with a tax preparation program) that will give you just about every tax form in existence, together with instructions. The better services are frequently updated during the tax season and give you the choice of printing out blank forms, or filling them out on screen.

Basically, the same applies to state tax forms in that they are available online. All states have their own websites, and with access to the Internet you can retrieve them online.

## An Office in Your Home

Home-based business ventures are definitely on the rise and for a variety of reasons. For one thing, numerous changes have occurred in contemporary society that have made working at home a great possibility: the computer revolution, the rising costs of office space, the increasing amount of time and money spent going to and from work, and a shifting emphasis in our economy to one of service and information exchange.

Of course, working at home is still not for everyone. Whereas an office is strictly a work area, a home is primarily a shelter for you and your family. The question is, if your practice is at home, how will you handle the many activities that take place on the premises that are not business-related? If you're the type that can develop the discipline and the strategies necessary to handle the distractions, then working at home may be good for you. But if you cannot clearly separate your work from your home life, then you may be better off in a straightforward office setting—away from home.

**Some advantages to working at home…**

1) Financial—You can save money on commuting, fuel, parking, office expenses, and take some tax deductions too.

2) Time—You can save time preparing, waiting, commuting; these hours saved can be spent productively in your practice.

3) Flexibility—In terms of life style and commitments, you can be more flexible in how you manage your time—working as early or late as you wish, and taking breaks as you need them.

**… and some disadvantages…**

1) Interruptions and distractions—Both home and family needs, the expected and the unexpected, may keep you from giving your practice the time and attention it deserves.

2) Loneliness—Many people need a work environment around them—offices, workers, the hustle and bustle of a business atmosphere—to bring out the best in them, and they just don't function well in isolation.

There are others who may find it counterproductive to be at home all the time—both for purposes of living and working. It may also put a strain on family relationships, which can be a serious problem—especially if both spouses work at home.

If you do choose to operate out of your home, here are some tips to help you along:

1) If possible, try to keep your office or workspace physically separated—even closed off—from your living area.

2) Try not to use your office space for anything other than your tax practice. Keep regular office hours, and get into the routine of treating your day in a professional manner.

3) Take breaks as you need them, and be in touch with professional colleagues.

4) Politely inform or re-educate family, friends, and neighbors regarding your new routine, practices, and policies.

5) If possible, have a separate business phone for use during business hours. Use an answering machine, or answering service, during non-working hours.

6) Although you can certainly personalize the decor in your home office, you should still try to maintain an image of professionalism so that visiting clients see that you take your business seriously.

## Full-Time or Part-Time

One other matter worth mentioning that might affect your choice of office arrangement is the degree to which you are committed to your practice.

Generally, tax practitioners fall into one of three categories:

1) There are independent tax consultants who work part time during the tax season though they may do some individual tax work throughout the year.

2) Others work full-time during the tax season, and continue on a part-time basis the rest of the year.

3) Still others work on a full-time basis throughout the year. Since there is rarely enough individual tax work available during the off season to be fully occupied, these practitioners devote the rest of the year to business tax returns, financial and tax planning, bookkeeping, social security practice, and similar activities. We will discuss this in detail in a later chapter.

The question is: To which group do you belong? And to a great extent the answer to this will depend upon your current situation plus your future plans and aspirations.

If you are now fully and gainfully occupied in a job or business, are pleased with your work and earnings and future prospects are good, then you probably look to tax work primarily as a second income: a lucrative source of seasonal, part time earnings. The same reasoning would presumably apply if you are an active homemaker with some time to spare; or perhaps you are semi-retired and are looking to creatively occupy some part of your day.

In these and in comparable situations, you would probably fit into the first two categories mentioned above. It is also quite possible that you are in a period of transition, trying to shift from the first two categories into the third. If, in fact, any of these descriptions relate to you, then you might want to look more seriously into one of the following office arrangements.

1) A home-based office (as described above) to begin your practice—provided that your home is easily accessible to clients.

2) Going to your client's home or place of business: Very often clients are willing to pay a higher fee for the convenience of you visiting them, and it is often advisable for the beginner who is breaking into the field and acquiring a clientele to employ this method. Many large and successful tax practices have started

this way. In fact, visiting clients has taken on a new slant in this age of computers. If you are proficient with computers, then laptop or notebook computers that weigh just a few pounds are worth your consideration. They come with handles, are portable, can fit into a briefcase, and can run any of the software programs you currently use. This relatively new and exciting category of office technology can turn client visits into a busy and lucrative practice.

3) Office rentals: You can rent a vacant store or office with a street entrance, in a good business district—preferably in an area with a lot of pedestrian traffic. A store or office in a shopping center is also an excellent choice. Such locations can attract a lot of walk-in clientele. However, this is not always a practical choice for the beginner because of the high rent such prime locations usually demand. Furthermore, if you expect to be open during the tax season only, it may be difficult finding such a location, and you may have to look for new office space every year. As your practice grows, however, it may be worth your while to pay rent on such space for the entire year, just to keep the office on a permanent basis and to remain clearly visible to the public. You may even be able to sublet the office during all or part of the off- season months, in order to cut your expenses. Another option is to rent a small office in an office building. Rent is bound to be considerably lower, but you may get very little walk-in business. Here again, the same off-season drawbacks apply. But if you do rent in an office building, make sure that you are able to display a prominent sign at the building's entrance or in the lobby.

4) Renting desk space: You might also consider securing desk space in a store or office, preferably in an insurance, real estate, or similar office setting. In most cases such arrangements work out to the mutual satisfaction of all concerned. Just make sure the office is located in a good business area, is visible to the public, easily accessible from the street, and that you can make use of the space evenings and on weekends. Most part time practices operate evenings and weekends because clients generally prefer to meet after business hours when they are more at ease. Also, consider your need for privacy in such an arrangement, so you can engage in confidential discussions if you do meet with clients during business hours.

Leasing your own space in a larger office setting whileusing central facilities and services has recently developed into a popular concept in office design. Tenants pay a proportionate share for a receptionist, secretary, and other services used. Very often such centers provide access to copiers, printers, fax machines and other forms of office technology. Again, you pay proportionately for what you use. Check into the overall cost of such services. Such a setting may be an ideal solution for a practice just getting off the ground.

If you happen to be "in transition"—moving your way up from a part-time into a full-time practice—proceed gradually. Rarely, is the average beginner fully occupied in the first two or three years. Tax practice, like almost any other profession, is a growing, evolving business. It takes time and perseverance to develop a lucrative practice, though it is time well spent when you consider the invaluable experience you gain while building up your practice.

The information above is merely intended to provide you with a general outline of what you can expect as you begin to develop your practice. You may find that the pattern varies in your own personal circumstance. Above all else, do not be discouraged if business is slow at first. You are sure to become busier as the tax season progresses, as your reputation grows, and you become better known—both in your neighborhood and in your community.

## A New Frontier: Internet-Based Work

For those who still want to keep their tax work limited as a second-income, Internet-based tax work is becoming far easier. Through various work-for-hire forums and per diem relationships over the Internet, quite a bit of work is available to those who are creative and able to take advantage of these resources.

### The Job-Bidding Forum

One of the most viable new technologies is the job-bidding forum. The most established of these work forums is E-lance (www.elance.com). Setting up an account is free both for employers and contractors; you can choose to be either with the same account. Once established, a contractor uses the forum's search engine to find tax work being offered on the website. The projects can vary from basic individual tax returns to business returns and S-corporation returns. In some cases, tasks can even involve tax research. For those who are flexible, there's quite a bit of work to be had which can fill in gaps during slow times.

On E-lance, once a job is awarded, the contractor pays a fee as a commission for using the forum. The fee ends up being about 8 percent of the total earnings paid on E-lance, for example. Other sites vary depending on their particular details.

Internet-based work is ideal for the part-time tax preparer working from home because it tends to be very flexible. As a result, it works well for a tax preparer who still has a day job to consider but wants to make extra earnings on the side.

### Classified Ads

An alternative source tends to be Internet-based classified ads. The most commonly used is Craigslist (www.craigslist.com). However, much of the work on this site tends to be very general and actual tax work can be hit-and-miss. That said, tax work does appear during the tax season, and the site offers both advertising as well as ad searching by local region.

Local newspapers will have their classifieds on the Internet as well, but these are detail listings only and usually don't include a connection link to the client. However, some newspapers are starting to modernize their ads so it depends on the region and particular periodical.

**Local Trade Groups and Networks on the Internet**

Tax preparers and professionals have various trade groups organized by regions and frequently connect with each other both for resources and work. Many such networks provide opportunities for shared work. Where one preparer may be overwhelmed with a sudden flood of projects, she can connect with others nearby via an Internet group and task out the overload. This creates gap opportunities for other preparers available in the network to take advantage of the offers. The approach does take a bit of personality and connecting with others but once solidified an opportunistic tax preparer can find additional work through this resource as well.

**Social Media Networks**

Both Facebook (www.facebook.com) and LinkedIn (www.linkedin.com) are becoming a young generation's go-to place for more and more business as well as networking. Tax preparers who are savvy enough to realize the potential can generate new work and customers through these two resources, as well as networking connections with others in the tax field. Both resources take time investment to generate feedback and customer attention, but they are free to join and provide an additional avenue for business marketing.

**Your Own Website**

Of course, creating and maintaining your own website is a very important part of any business. A website can serve to attract new customers, inform potential customers and service existing customers. A good website is attractive to look at, easy to surf and quick to load. In today's world a website is paramount. If a person sees your advertisement in the paper or somewhere they are likely to want to go to your website to learn more about you before they call. You can also use your website to provide tax advice and information to current clients. Perhaps most valuable of all, your website can earn you business by being an information source that people find when they are searching for tax advice. One great way to do this is to fill your website with valuable articles and information so that people stumble onto your site when surfing the web.

# Chapter 4

# PTIN Requirements per the IRS

*Training is everything. The peach was once a bitter almond; cauliflower is nothing but cabbage with a college education.*
**Mark Twain**

## The Preparer Tax Identification Number

Beginning in the summer of 2010, the IRS initiated a new program that created a better tracking system of professional tax preparers. Done in response to many concerns with unscrupulous preparers who would apparently run scams and illegal tax shelters and then disappear, as well as a need for the IRS to track who was preparing claims, the federal government passed authorization to create the program. As a result, all tax preparers who operate as a business providing tax return preparation for federal returns must register with the IRS.

Known as the Preparer Tax Identification Number (PTIN) program, preparers are required to both be certified by the IRS and licensed accordingly in order to practice tax preparation. This applies in all 50 U.S. states and territories. Given the way the program is designed, a professional tax preparer must maintain a PTIN when working, and renew the PTIN as necessary, paying appropriate filing and update fees to the IRS. In turn, the PTIN allows the IRS to track transactions and records associated with a specific preparer by cross-referencing the PTIN number on file.

The fees associated with the PTIN are set by the IRS with a graduated approach. The first year of PTIN for a preparer was initially $64.25 per preparer filing. This charge includes a $50 component associated with system cost recovery from a new entry. The remaining cost goes to the vendor the IRS has contracted to maintain the electronic PTIN system. The renewal fee for preparers is charged annually and will fluctuate, depending on what the IRS determines in the future is necessary for cost recovery.

There is no distinction between tax return preparers who already work electronically with the IRS and those starting up for the first time. All preparers are required to apply for a PTIN to be able to submit a compensated tax filing for another party. This rule applies even to those who only occasionally prepare compensated tax filings and are not required to maintain ongoing professional development or education. This rule does not apply to family members or private friends who help out a party on a volunteer basis to file their tax return properly.

The program was originally operated as a paper application, but this version ended in August 2010 when the IRS converted to an electronic registration via the agency's website. Now all tax preparers who need to register are required to go through the electronic application process, including those who applied prior to August 2010 but weren't approved yet.

The PTIN was made a requirement so that the IRS could easily track a tax preparer to a series of tax returns prepared by that particular professional. This makes it easy and quick for the IRS to pull up all affected returns should they find an issue with a particular preparer or return submitted by that preparer. Often the IRS looks to see if the same issue appears in other returns to see if there is an intentional pattern of illegal tax sheltering or fraud occurring as a business. This search was often stymied by paper filings having no easy way to connect to each other. Now with e-filing of returns as well as PTIN numbers being linked to those returns, the linkage is as easy as running an identifier search in the IRS database and pulling up all the related hits on file.

Additionally, the licensing scheme helps the IRS pay for its tracking system and any new costs associated with electronic tracking. By transferring the cost to tax preparers, the IRS reduces its own agency costs to make the program happen. Tax preparers then have a choice whether to pass the cost on to their customers or not. The IRS has left it open-ended how the fee will be managed or if it will increase, simply stating the fee will be adjusted as system costs occur in the future. As a result, the fee has the potential for being a new revenue stream for the IRS on an ongoing basis.

Those concerned about tax preparers being singled-out somehow by the new PTIN system shouldn't be. The approach of the IRS with the PTIN program is the same thing the agency has always done to find issues with incorrect tax liabilities being reported. However, because the PTIN makes the search electronic and easier, tax preparers who have

Chapter 4: PTIN Requirements per the IRS

been bending the rules somewhat should be on alert that it be easier to catch such behavior now. For those like you, following the rules and maintaining an ethical office, there should be no worries aside from a minor fee to pay and a license to maintain annually.

Because the program is still in development, it is being rolled out in phases. Phase 1 has already occurred to date, with future steps to come.

**Phase 1: PTINs for Everyone**

Beginning January 2011, every tax preparer professionally working and receiving compensation for preparing someone else's tax return to the federal government must have a Preparer Tax Identification Number before preparing returns. Also, all enrolled agents are required to have a PTIN. You can sign up for your PTIN online at the IRS' Internet website. It costs $64.25 per year. For those who previously had a PTIN, a renewal is required for the 2012 and future years.

**To renew your PTIN online, just follow four easy steps:**

- **Access Your Account**—If you don't remember your password or user ID, click the Forgotten Password or Forgotten User ID buttons.

- **Renew Your PTIN**—Complete the online renewal application. You must verify your personal information and answer a few new questions. It helps to have the information ready ahead of time to answer quickly. Keep in mind as well that all returning federal tax return preparers and enrolled agents must have a current year PTIN. Before you begin your PTIN renewal application, be sure you have the following available:
  - Personal information (name, mailing address, date of birth),
  - Business information (name, mailing address, telephone number),
  - Explanations for felony convictions (if any),
  - Explanations for problems with your U.S. individual or business tax obligations (if any),
  - Credit or debit card as an electronic payment tool for the $63.00 PTIN user fee, and
  - If applicable, any U.S.-based professional certification information (CPA, attorney, enrolled agent, enrolled retirement plan agent, enrolled actuary, certified acceptance agent, or state license) including certification number, jurisdiction of issuance, and expiration date.

- **Pay Your Fee**—Pay the $63 renewal fee via credit card or direct debit. Yes, it is slightly less than the applicant who receives a PTIN for the first time.

- **View Your Next Steps**—Review your next steps, including any testing and continuing education requirements. Remember to renew your PTIN each calendar year.

While the IRS generally wants applicants to file electronically and people are encouraged to do so, paper applications can still be made despite previous restriction statements. Those who are establishing a PTIN account online for the first time can do so by filing paper Form W-12 marked "renewal". Phone assistance is available as well by calling the IRS at 877-613-PTIN (7846). This phone number provides an online activation code and instructions for creating an online account and linking it to your existing information. The call method is probably faster since it generally only takes about 15 minutes to sign up or renew online and receive your PTIN. This is in comparison to the paper application, which can take anywhere from 4 to 6 weeks to process and approve.

### Phase 2: Additional Requirements for Some Preparers

Some preparers have additional requirements beyond obtaining a PTIN due to their professional status. If this applies to your office, you want to pay special attention to these requirements.

- **Attorneys, Certified Public Accountants, and Enrolled Agents** who are active and in good standing with their licensing agency have no additional requirements other than to:
    - Renew their PTIN annually.
- **Supervised Preparers and Non-1040 Preparers**** need to:
    - Renew their PTIN annually.
    - Supervised Preparers are those who do not sign returns and who are employed by attorney, CPA or EA firms and are supervised by an attorney, CPA or EA. Non-1040 preparers are those who do not prepare any Form 1040 series returns. Note: Form 1040-PR and 1040-SS are not considered Form 1040 series returns for this purpose.
- **All other preparers** need to:
    - Renew their PTIN annually.
    - Pass the Registered Tax Return Preparer competency test.
    - Take continuing education courses annually.

Those who have a provisional PTIN have until the end of 2013 to take and pass the RTRP test, **but the continuing education requirement begins in calendar year 2012.**

# The Registered Tax Return Preparer Competency Test

The test is $116 and must be paid at the time the appointment is scheduled. The test fee is non-refundable and not transferrable. Please bring with you one unexpired U.S. government issued photo ID that includes your name, photo, and signature. Paper and pencil, a calculator, and reference materials will be provided at the test site. Personal items are not allowed in the test room and must be stored in a locker. Persons not scheduled to take a test are not permitted to wait in the test center.

Tests administered beginning April 16, 2012 are based on 2011 tax law. Likely, each year's test will rely on the previous year's tax laws. You may take the test at any time during the year except during the annual black-out period from April 1—April 15. During this time the test is unavailable while the system is updated.

There are 120 questions. The test is timed at 2 ½ hours and your appointment will average 3 hours. You should plan to arrive for your test appointment at least thirty minutes early to check in. Once you are seated in the test room, you will receive a personalized introduction to the testing system. You may also take a short pre-test computer system tutorial. Following the test, you will have the opportunity to participate in a customer satisfaction survey.

Test questions are weighted in value to arrive at an overall pass/fail score. There is no exact number of questions to obtain a passing score. The test's potential scaled scores range from 50-500. Scaled scores of 350 and above are passing scores. If you fail the test, you will receive diagnostic information to assist you with future examination preparation.

You will receive your test score at the test center immediately after taking the test. Scores are automatically shared with the IRS and IRS records will be updated accordingly. If you have an online PTIN account, the test information will be updated on the "Next Steps" page in your account in 7-10 business days.

Those individuals required to take the Registered Tax Return Preparer competency test that already have a provisional PTIN have until December 31, 2013 to pass the test. Your provisional PTIN enables you to continue to prepare all types of tax returns and claims for refund through December 31, 2013, provided you complete any continuing education requirements and renew your PTIN on time each year.

Those provisional preparers who do not pass the test by December 31, 2013 will be contacted by the IRS proposing to deactivate their PTIN and remove them from the list of authorized preparers.

You will be able to prepare any Federal tax return or claim for refund if you pass the RTRP test unless the IRS develops additional competency tests for other tax returns in the future.

You may not hold yourself out as a Registered Tax Return Preparer unless the RTRP exam is passed. You must pass the test and a tax compliance check before obtaining the Registered Tax Return Preparer credential.

## Studying for the Exam

A number of resources are available for studying for the PTIN IRS Exam both from the IRS and from private tutorials. Those looking into these options outside of the IRS' samples should do a bit of research before signing up. Some operations will offer a free exam sample while others offer the first parts of their courses for review. In many cases these are just rehashes of what the IRS has already put out for free on its own website.

The above said, there are some good training programs out there. New practitioners considering the exam for the first time would be best served by talking to other practitioners in the area and asking for referrals to programs that worked for them. This avoids blind sampling, especially with fly-by-night website type courses that promise the moon but don't deliver much.

Alternatively, there are also a number of software packages now available for download or ordering over the Internet. These software programs are designed to train a person on his own schedule how to pass the RTRP Exam. The success or failure of these programs is unknown, so buyers should do their research first before buying. However, some of the programs available may be approved, in some way, by the IRS itself, so that at least can be used as a filter.

## Background Checks

The IRS is also considering requiring certain tax return preparers to undergo a background check as part of PTIN requirements. This criterion has not been implemented yet but it is likely to happen soon, especially given the ease with which individual information data can now be generated through linked government databases. When the requirement is put into place, the IRS will notify specific tax preparers if they are required to undergo a background check in the future.

## Additional IRS Resources

PTIN Requirements for Tax Return Preparers
http://www.irs.gov/taxpros/article/0,,id=210909,00.html

Requirements for Tax Return Preparers: Frequently Asked Questions
http://www.irs.gov/taxpros/article/0,,id=218611,00.html

# Chapter 5

# Updating Office Technology & Today's Tax Professional

*Be not afraid of going slowly; be afraid of standing still.*
**Ancient Chinese Proverb**

*Don't watch the clock. Do what it does. Keep going.*
**Sam Levenson**

*Find something you love to do and you'll never have to work a day in your life.*
**Harvey Mackay**

## Introduction

Tax preparation has taken place year in and year out, even before there were computers, fax machines, cell phones and copiers. However, despite this well-beaten history most tax professionals today want to avail themselves of the many advantages offered by modern information technology. That said, there is an important line that needs to be drawn.

Having the appropriate office technology can make an important difference in the growth of your practice. At the same time, as important as technology is, it doesn't mean you always have to have the latest and most elaborate equipment. You have to be able to realistically evaluate your needs and purchase accordingly. Hopefully, the guidelines in this chapter will help you discover that happy medium.

There are still some tax consultants who operate with little more than a desk, a typewriter, a calculator, and a filing cabinet, along with the necessary forms and papers, and it can be done. But typically, today's office will include any of the following:

- A personal computer, perhaps a laptop;
- A printer, fax machine, modem,
- An answering machine,
- Copy machine,
- Scanner, along with
- A variety of specialized telephone features.

To be competitive in the field today, you must be able to utilize technology. Moreover, computer proficiency creates confidence and credibility with your clients. The public, for the most part, is accustomed to the fact that this is how most businesses are run today—and they will very likely expect this same degree of professional competence from you.

## Why So Much Technology?

Well, for one thing, the price of all this equipment keeps coming down, making it more available to more consumers. If you shop carefully, you can get all the items discussed below for under $2,000.00—and who knows how much less it will be by the time you read this page. Second, office technology keeps coming in smaller and smaller packages—more compact—making it easier to install this array of items into a small workspace. And finally, most tax professionals are discovering that access to such technology goes a long way in helping their business grow.

So what do you need? One thing you certainly don't need is to get everything all at once. You don't want to frustrate and overwhelm yourself. If you're not familiar with current office technology, you may want to step into it gradually, slowly working your way up to a level where you can operate effectively and efficiently. Among the items to at least consider are the following: a personal computer—desktop and/or portable, a two-line cordless phone, answering machine or service, voice mail, pager or cell phone, fax or fax/modem, printer, copier, and a scanner.

Bear in mind, too, that office technology is constantly and rapidly changing, so the information presented here may be somewhat dated by the time you read this. This will include cost, features, size of equipment, and more. It's all subject to change. So when it comes to making your purchases, try to get a hold of the most current information available. For example, it's quite common today to call, print, copy, scan, and fax from one compact machine. With this in mind, let's take a brief tour around a contemporary tax consultant's office and see what we find.

## Your Personal Computer and Attendant Software

It would be impossible to cover, in this text, the subject of computers as it relates to tax practice primarily because the technology is so extensive and changes so rapidly. Nevertheless, certain guidelines are in order.

A computer can carry out a wide variety of office functions and seems to operate best at those tasks a person finds most tedious and time-consuming. A computer can perform these functions more rapidly and with greater accuracy—from maintaining accounts and files, to budgeting, typing personal and business letters, addressing envelopes, and of course, tax research, and a great deal more. The time you save on these jobs can be spent doing more creative, productive work to advance and enhance your practice.

So the first thing you have to do is sincerely determine just what your computer needs are. Precisely what do you want a computer to do for you? What general office tasks, and what specific—tax related—office tasks? Then find the software that does just that. Of course, you have to purchase the hardware that can accommodate that program or set of programs. Remember to focus on the requisite hardware and software, and not all the attendant bells and whistles. That said, it is fairly easy today to find a basic desktop computer that has enough power to handle most tax and office software, running up to five programs at the same time without a hiccup.

However, it doesn't hurt to do a bit of research as well on how to use a computer in a tax office. Since a computer system is a major decision in relation to your practice, and since it calls for a considerable investment of time and money, it is to your advantage to think clearly and examine your possibilities well. Before you reach any decision, be sure you do at least some of the following:

- Consult with friends, relatives, or fellow tax practitioners who are familiar with the technology.
- Do some reading on your own—books, magazines, journals, newsletters, and online resources.
- Take a course in computers or attend a related seminar before you purchase anything if you are unfamiliar with them.
- Consider hiring a well-informed consultant for a few hours of professional advice.

Once you make your purchase, you may still need some training to attain a working level of proficiency and confidence in tax software management. For training opportunities you can check the business section of your local newspaper for specialized courses and seminars or contact the following resources: local colleges and universities, technical schools, business schools, courses offered by computer dealers, computer consultants, computer manuals—and don't forget to speak with relatives and friends who are in the field.

As you may well know, there are two major kinds of computers available today: the PC or personal computer utilizing the Windows operating system; and the MAC, or Apple Macintosh personal computer. At present, the PC continues to be the standard tool in the realm of business preferences and business software. That's not to say an Apple system can't be used, it can. However, if your tax business will be exchanging files a lot with other PC systems you're better off having a compatible system. Keep in mind, too, that software running on one system will probably not run on the other, although interfaces and exchanges between the two are easier now than ever before.

Select the system that best suits your needs and try to get the best computer you can afford…realizing that technology is ever evolving and enhancements are bound to appear every few months or so.

In the past, when buying a computer a business owner needed to make sure that what he bought today would allow him to expand and upgrade if and when the need arose; most good computers manufactured at the time were built to be generally useful for at least three years. Today a system can become obsolete within a year, at least to those worried about keeping up with changing technology. You're buying today, but thinking about tomorrow. By extension, it's better to get too much memory than too little, and better to get a faster processing speed than a slower one. If you can afford to spend more you should; a more expensive system will last longer.

If finances allow, get a good computer monitor. Here, too, bigger is probably better—for entering data as well as for visual reading. A large screen is simply easier on the eyes—especially when you're looking at the screen for hours—filling out forms and working with numbers.

Another point worth mentioning in the way of a warning: make sure you have a system in place whereby you always back up your electronic files. Make this as common a regular practice as turning on the lights and going to the bank. One of the most disastrous experiences you may ever have is to lose the data on your hard drive. It can occur for any number of reasons, and your work is then suddenly gone. It's as if someone simply walked off with your office, never to return again. To avoid such a catastrophe performing a regular backup is essential, and this can be done in a number of ways involving "remote storage facilities."

# Chapter 5: Updating Office Technology & Today's Tax Professional

- You can back up your data onto recordable CDs or DVDs, which is a basic type of backup system. Unfortunately, this approach typically keeps the CDs in the same location as the primary computer. If the office itself is damaged or vandalized, the CDs as well as the computer could both be wiped out at the same time. Even as of the printing of this book, CDs were considered antiquated as far as data storage, but some people do still use them.

- You can employ the use of a cloud storage service. There are a number of such services that start out with free accounts for small storage service and then begin to charge for space needs above 2 or 5 gigabytes. These services basically allow a user to upload files and sync online folders with the home computer folders via an Internet connection. A broadband connection (cable or satellite) is required to use this kind of service effectively. The downside, however, is security. Unless a user does some research, she doesn't really know where her files are being kept. They could be sitting on a server physically sitting in some remote, foreign country. The upside is that these are relatively cheap, can back up automatically, and can truly save your data from loss.

- Dedicated backup storage is also possible via the Internet. These services are secured via a subscription payment scaled to the size of storage needed. The services tend to be the same companies that produce anti-virus and firewall software, so the storage is dependable and secure. However, some of these services require some technical knowledge to install and operate. They have the same benefits as cloud storage.

- Backup tapes have always been a reliable recovery tool if kept in a remote location from the office. This tool essentially makes a full copy of a system onto a data tape. The tape is then stored in a separate physical location to be retrieved in the future should a data wipeout occur. You would need a computer professional to set-up such a system for you.

- Flash drives make an easy, quick backup tool for small offices. While they won't restore software, they make great repositories for files. These drives are becoming smaller in physical presence but larger in storage size every day; as of the printing of this book you could purchase a drive smaller than a stick of gum that could hold up to 80 gigabytes. They are easy to carry and keep in a different location outside the office. However, due to size, flash drives are also easy to lose. Thus, if used, the files should be encrypted with a password. This makes the drive useless should it be found by someone other than the owner.

Whatever backup method you employ make sure to follow through regularly—at least each day.

We've touched upon some of these, but among the features you will want to carefully weigh when purchasing a computer are the following:

- **Processor speeds:** This is measured in megahertz. The higher the number the faster your computer will run. You will need a faster processor to carry out many of the business related tasks you will want your computer to perform. Your office computer should be running with at least 1.6 MHz to manage today's office software.

- **RAM capacity** refers to a computer's ability to store information. You'll need 2 gigabytes of access memory to be comfortable.

- **Disk drives** are the computer's "file cabinets" where a variety of storage devices are available. While computers still have the old "floppy" drives, they are practically useless. The better drive to have is a CD/DVD drive. This is standard in all new computers that are desktop size and in most laptops. Some smaller units such as netbooks or lightweight laptops are now relying on Internet software loading for flash drive connections for data transfer. With a good size flash drive you can pack entire libraries of tax related information into the space normally occupied by a few small books; you'll need all the current information you can get to provide your clients with the best and most up- to-date information available.

- **The Internet broadband connection** is another essential component to access the Internet; when hooked up to a network it lets your computer communicate with another computer. Here, too, speed is an important factor: it will cost a slight bit more, but faster speeds enable you to upload and download files more rapidly. A good broadband connection is indispensable for filing tax returns electronically. For the IRS, electronic filing means less paper to deal with and faster returns. In addition, professional preparers are now required to file returns electronically—for your client, it can mean a faster tax refund. In some cases a refund can be had within two to four weeks versus paper returns which can take up to three months. Additionally, almost all tax preparation software now contains an electronic filing utility.

Of course, there are other factors to consider, so unless you are personally familiar with computer technology you will have to rely on the advice and guidance of an expert in the field.

## Tax Preparation Software

Income tax returns can be prepared manually or by computer. Preparing taxes manually does not call for investment of time or money into computer technology, but preparing returns by hand is slow, and there is a greater likelihood of error given the complexity of today's returns.

The overwhelming trend therefore is definitely toward computer and electronic tax preparation. This will save you precious time, and increase your efficiency, accuracy, and productivity. It also allows you to spend more time developing your practice—both qualitatively and quantitatively.

There are currently dozens of professional tax return software packages available, and though they share some fundamental features, they differ distinctively as well in various features, price, ease-of-use and more. What it boils down to is this: each practitioner must take the time to evaluate and compare various software programs to determine which will best suit the needs of his or her practice.

At present, you'll find that tax preparation software appearing on CD-ROM or DVD disks contain tax laws, regulations, and instructions keyed to the tax form displayed on the screen. These programs are regularly updated with periodic Internet updates. Many of these programs come with good technical support and other accessories. You may find it helpful to speak with colleagues about which tax preparation software they use; you can get demonstrations, test several software products, and then decide. It's a good idea to take these precautionary steps because this is an important and worthwhile investment. Don't rush your decision.

## The Office Internet Connection

As was noted before, a good, high-speed Internet connection is a must for a functioning tax office. Not only will you be able to access quickly many tax resources, both free and paid, over the Internet, the format also provides a convenient way for your business to connect with prospective customers, communicate with existing ones, transfer tax returns to tax agencies, and download additional software tools.

A viable Internet service should either be on high-speed phone line such as DSL, or on a cable line known as broadband. Long gone are the days of using a modem on a phone line and listening to the screeching beeps as the modem connecting to a service. Broadband Internet connections are now quick, constantly connected, and capable of streaming data, video, sound, office phone communications, and more.

Most Internet service providers, known as ISPs, can set up an account either in a residential address or a business location. Residential connections for a home office will typically be combined with a TV cable system and house phone system as well. Business packages will also include the option to have the Internet service come into a network, allowing multiple machines to connect to the service simultaneously. Alternatively, you could set up your connection with a wireless router so that any device with a Wi-Fi modem can connect wirelessly to your Internet account as well within vicinity. Just make sure to use a password on the router or you could have neighbors using your account for less-than-respectable Internet activities.

## The Virtual Office

For those who really want to get into the forefront of technology with their tax practices, the idea of the virtual office with clients and co-workers is now becoming commonplace. Under this concept a tax office uses a database environment supported by a third party on the Internet. These sort of workspaces are now being referred to as "cloud computing." Via a website portal, the tax office operates and administers the entire system, but the third party provider takes care of the software, the IT maintenance, and the scaling of the system to bigger or smaller capacity, whatever the tax office needs. In return, the tax office pays a subscription fee monthly to access the system, store data, and function in a controlled, virtual environment.

The benefit of such a platform becomes apparent for tax offices and preparers that frequently travel and have to work remotely. Within such a system, entire tax client environments can be created, one for each client, where the preparer and the client can interact and transact business. Each section of the system is isolated by the tax office administrator so that different clients don't mix with each other's files. This allows the tax office to collect client information electronically, prepare tax documents, and provide them to clients within a secure environment. Meetings can be coordinated by integrated phone conferencing while examining and updating documents that both the preparer and client can see by computer and Internet connection once logged in.

The cloud approach could be a bit advanced for many tax offices and clients that still want to see each other face-to-face. However, many business and clients are adapting well to the electronic platform and find it much easier to operate electronically than to visit for a sit-down meeting at a specific brick-and-mortar address all the time. Time will tell whether the approach will stick, but four to five companies already exist, providing secure cloud environments for account and tax offices nationwide via the Internet.

## Today's Telephone

Even Alexander Graham Bell would be surprised to see how many times his invention has been reinvented. Whether you look at it as a social tool or professional tool, the telephone, in all its manifestations, is a lifeline that brings and keeps people together. More often than not, it's the way consultants and clients communicate, make appointments, and get things done.

One of your more difficult decisions will be to choose from among all the telephone options available to you, and with technology changing so rapidly devices that seemed like luxuries a short while ago may now qualify as basic necessities—both in terms of professional image and personal efficiency.

To help you decide what to do "telephone-wise," ask yourself these questions:

- How often does your work take you out of your office setting? How will you make sure you won't miss calls that come at such times?
- Do you want certain clients to be able to reach you, even while you are out of your office?
- How much time do you spend, on average, on the phone each day? How often do other calls come in while you are on the phone? How will you avoid having repeated incoming calls come up against a constant busy signal?
- Are there times during the day when you will not want to deal with phone calls? How will you handle clients that call you at such times?
- If you are working out of your home, how will you separate household phone needs from business calls?
- If you will be using a fax machine, how will you make sure that such transmissions don't interfere with your voice related calls?

If you are able to accurately answer these questions, you will be in a better position to recognize your legitimate telephone needs.

**Voice-Mail**

Like a more advanced answering machine, voice mail can answer your calls as well as take messages. It enables your callers to leave recorded messages without ever getting a busy signal. You can then access your messages at any time.

Voice-mail can also carry out many of the tasks that receptionists have carried out in the past. For example, in addition to leaving a message callers can choose from various options. They can:

- Listen to a list and description of your services;
- Find out about office hours and directions to your office;
- Be told what information to have handy in order to talk with you over the phone; or
- Be informed of most frequently requested items of information.

Having such options available on a prerecorded message can save you and your clients a great deal of time.

Voice-mail systems are changing and advancing all the time so you can select the system that suits you best. Different messages can run at different times of the day or evening; you can set up individual "mailboxes" that enable you to leave private messages for certain clients; you can pick up incoming calls while you are on the phone so callers never get a busy signal; and you can pick up your own messages from wherever you are by calling your own number.

On the one hand, there are also more advanced answering machines that offer various voice-mail features and this may be all you need. On the other hand, you can set up a voice-mail system on your computer using specialized software. Clients can call in, hear your voice and message, and leave their message on your computer's hard drive. Many of today's telephone providers offer basic voicemail service for free, so this may be something you want to look into.

### Other Telephone Options

**Two-line telephone lines:** If your office happens to be in your home, than most tax professionals report that having a two-line telephone is highly recommended: one line for business and one line for personal use. With two-line phones you will be able to properly respond to each type of call. Plus, two-line phones are available in corded and cordless models, though corded phones are becoming increasingly hard to find.

**Wireless phones:** These are convenient because you can take it with you as you move around—inside and out of your office. They also enable you to attend to other minor tasks if need be, such as accepting and signing for a delivery.

**Cellular smartphones:** These mobile phone devices have now become the office norm, especially with dropping prices along with their shrinking size and weight. Smartphones allow immediate access to office voice-mail messages and even faxes converted to digital files through a phone service. You can carry a smartphone with you just about anywhere. They're convenient due to their mobility and you can make or receive calls at any time. Coupled with texting and email services, the smartphone pretty much replaces most electronic and phone communication known today. You can therefore stay in touch with your office, and your office can be in touch with you. This may not necessarily be good thing for folks who sometimes need to disconnect and tune out.

When considering cell phone options—and what you'll pay each month—think in terms of the options you really need. Will it help your business to receive voice mail, e-mail, forward calls, or access the Internet to browse websites? If the answer is "no," then don't pay for what you don't need. Packages can be trimmed down to just the basic services desired. If you feel you need a different feature later, you can always add it on to the existing package.

**Internet phone conferencing:** We mentioned this resource earlier in conjunction with cloud computing. However, phone conferencing services don't need to be connected to a cloud system to be used. A number of services exist now that provide integrated computer presentation and conference lines as scheduled by a user. The user simply logs into his account, schedules a meeting, gets a dedicated phone line, and sends out the information to all parties involved. When the meeting starts, everyone logs into the provided link while the user operates the electronic files to be used on the conference system. Everyone sees the same document on their computer via basic Internet connection and browser software. Some of the more commonly used services are:

- Adobe Connect (www.adobeconnect.com)
- GoTo Meeting (www.gotomeeting.com)
- Webex (www.webex.com)

These conference services are easy to use, low-cost, and work remarkably well for all types of meeting sizes and scheduling. Skype (www.skype.com) is another easy to use, free way to have simply video conferences.

**Telephone headsets**: Many people who work on a computer all day but also need to answer the phone claim that a phone headset is extremely useful. It frees both hands for writing, for using the computer, or for performing other tasks while you speak and listen. It also provides you with the privacy that a speakerphone does not, as well as better sound quality than a speaker phone. The combination of a cordless phone and headset liberates both your hands and feet for other tasks—if that is to your liking. For mobile phones a number of head ear-pieces are available and can be synced to a smartphone using Bluetooth software. This program on a phone communicates directly with the ear-piece, activating it when the phone rings and connects a call. There are also simpler units that plug into your telephone.

**Answering machines:** Nearly every desk phone unit comes with answer machine technology included; these are still popular as well as economical. But the trend is shifting. It seems that while they are quite useful in the home, businesses wanting to project a more consistent and modern image are moving towards network phone systems with integrated voicemail. This allows every phone to have the same features for a caller, avoiding any unique nuances common with singular setups.

A good voicemail system also allows you to access your messages from an outside line. With a special access number you can call in and play back those messages. These machines and voicemail systems are quite inexpensive today and may include other features including recording the time and date of calls and displaying the number of messages. Most cellphones already have this feature included, but an integrated system that ties into your office desk phone as well requires a separate setup.

If all you currently do is place and receive occasional, routine calls, then a standard phone may be enough for you. As your telephone contact becomes more extensive you may want to consider these features:

- Call forwarding allows you to automatically relay incoming calls to any other pre-selected telephone number.

- Call waiting signals you when another caller is trying to reach you while you are on the phone.

- Three-way calling permits you to talk to two people simultaneously while conference calls allow you to talk to more people at the same time. Conference calling can be especially handy when managing issues with multiple parties at the same time.

- Speed dialing enables you to program frequently called numbers into the telephone.

- A "mute" button allows you to hear the person on the other line, but they cannot hear you. This is handy if you are typing as you listen and do not want to seem rude, or if you need to ask someone in your office a clarifying question as your client speaks. .

- There are also speakerphones, and phones that keep track of the date and measure the length of each call (that may be useful when charging clients for long distance calls).

**Telephone Courtesy**

Very often, the telephone is the first—and only—way a potential client has of judging you and your practice, so be sure to employ telephone courtesy at all times.

Also bear in mind that the telephone demands communication skills that differ somewhat from those used in face-to-face contact. With a telephone you must convey your attitude—your sincerity and sense of confidence—through your voice. Here are some guidelines to help you make wise use of this vital instrument:

1) During business hours, the telephone should be answered every time it rings: by you, a secretary, voice mail, or an answering machine. While on the phone, be pleasant but businesslike, relaxed and sincere.

2) A business conversation should be free of all background noise—even music.

3) When preparing for a call, try to have all pertinent information at your fingertips: client files, calendar, appointment book, etc.

4) Consider carefully how you answer the phone. Do you just say "hello," and then wait for the caller to respond. This may suffice in your home, but for business purposes it is not enough. You must identify yourself. Begin with an appropriate greeting—good morning or good afternoon—and then state your name and/or company's name.

5) Don't leave a caller "on hold" for more than half a minute, if you can help it. If necessary, arrange for the person to call back, but don't leave a caller hanging indefinitely and without a reason. It's irritating, and it may even cost you a client.

6) When giving a caller pertinent facts and figures, speak slowly and distinctly, and speak into the telephone. Many are in the habit of cradling the phone in such a way that it juts into the speaker's neck or chin. This muffles the sound and can easily frustrate the caller. With cell phones, careless cradling with the neck can cause you to hit a button and disconnect the call.

7) Be aware of the importance of language. Over the phone a client only has your words and tone to go by, so be careful of both what you say and how you say it.

8) Listen carefully and effectively. Listen to what is being said and how it's being said, and don't interrupt the caller unnecessarily.

9) Reinforce the client by acknowledging your understanding of his remarks in some way.

10) Don't hang up on your client. Wait until the other party hangs up and then proceed to do the same.

In terms of both time and money, the telephone is your most effective communication tool. It is exceptional for scheduling appointments, sharing information, answering questions, and settling matters. Learn to use it well and use it wisely.

If your life as a tax professional involves a fair amount of movement outside the office, then a smart phone can prove to be very valuable as a hand-held personal digital assistant (PDA). The various programs and features on today's smartphones organize your time and schedules, list things to do, contain memos and address book, and much more—all in one hand-held instrument. Some use small keypads, others now offer touch screens, and the latest gizmos operate on voice command. Smartphones also offer the ability to function as a recording device, both audio and video. Smartphones can be connected to your computer to transfer data as well. This feature makes it easy to back-up the data on your phone and have it all transferred regularly for saving.

**E-Mail vs. the Telephone**

When it comes to staying in touch with clients, the use of e-mail has frequently been an alternative to telephone use. There are definitely some advantages as well as serious disadvantages; you will just have to weigh how appropriate or inappropriate every communication is with regard to how it should be carried out—by phone or e-mail.

For one, e-mail is certainly convenient. You can leave brief notes, memos, or long detailed messages that can be printed out or kept by your client for further perusal or future reference, and they can be sent at any time of day or night. With email you also get a "paper trail" of what you have told someone, so you know exactly what has transpired. E-mail is also a lot cheaper than long distance calls. And, if you often find yourself spending time playing "telephone tag," then e-mail is a good way to get around that; you write and deliver your communiqué immediately. The recipient can get to it at his or her convenience.

Of course, there are those who feel e-mail is somehow too impersonal—not having a human voice to relate to—and they strongly prefer speaking directly to the other person. So this is where you will have to make a judgment call. It certainly helps to have both options available; you simply need to determine if and when to use one form over the other.

From a legal perspective, e-mail is also troublesome. Lawyers thrive on finding records of issues that can be used to contradict or embarrass a party in deposition or court. E-mail records stay in existence until they are deleted and destroyed (just deleting removes immediate access but they still exist on a hard drive where they were last saved for quite some time). If a subpoena is delivered, a party has to provide all known related records, even if they are problematic. In this regard, a tax office should use careful judgment on what issues it discusses by e-mail versus by phone with clients. Some prudent judgment avoiding the keyboard can save a lot of legal headaches later.

## The High Tech Office

The versatile telephone and your basic computer aren't the only pieces of equipment that can help you run your office more efficiently. Here are some other items worth considering:

### Fax Machines

A fax machine allows for the immediate transfer of text, drawings, or combinations thereof to any facility with a similar tool that can receive faxed material. This typically transfers via a phone line. Using a fax saves time and money, because with a fax the material sent arrives in seconds rather than having to drive to the post office and pay postage. It's quite possible that after selecting a computer and telephone system, the fax is your next most important piece of office technology to consider.

At present, fax technology is available in four basic forms:

- A machine that stands alone
- As an internal component of your personal computer
- As a phone account system
- As a computer program which sends faxes over the internet

Each format has advantages and disadvantages, its proponents and its detractors. When shopping for a fax machine, here are some points worthy of your consideration: Does it use plain paper or thermal paper? Plain paper units are more expensive, but the output is easier to read, handle, and duplicate. Are redial, memory, and copy functions available? These are handy features to have. Also, be sure it has a good warranty.

With the phone account system your business doesn't have to own a fax machine at all, but you will need an e-mail account. You will be given a dedicated phone number for your incoming faxes which people can fax to. When they do, the fax gets transmitted and converted to a print-ready document, also known as a PDF file. This file then gets sent to your e-mail account for reading, printing or archiving. This approach saves on paper costs, avoids a dedicated phone line for a fax, and provides versatility. However, you can't fax back with the account. Instead, you will have to rely on email or find a fax machine at a store or elsewhere. This approach works very well for someone who wants to be able to receive faxes but doesn't send many, if any, documents by fax.

## Copy Machines

It wasn't too long ago that copy machines were large and cumbersome devices which were simply beyond the budget of most small offices. But now you can get color copy machines that are smaller than a briefcase and cost only a few hundred dollars. It's also true that many professionals allow their fax machines to do their copying, but still, there are situations where a good copier does the job best. Too often, you will need to copy a multi-paged or odd-sized document, and a good copier is what you will need.

Quality copy machines are now affordable, easy to use and maintain, with more features being added all the time. There are many models and sizes to choose from. Again, try to determine your copy needs and purchase the one that best serves those needs. The more speed and the more features, the more potential problems you may encounter. Make sure that whatever you buy comes with a good guarantee, and that repairs will be easy when required. For very small offices, a combination machine that includes a fax, printer, scanner and copier all in one may be a very good choice. It provides all the necessary services, and it conserves on valuable space.

## Printers

Perhaps no other single piece of office equipment has come so far down in price as has the quality printer. You can get high quality printers—even color printers—for a couple hundred dollars. Since you are a trained tax professional, and you want to present yourself in the most professional manner—it makes little sense to issue documents that have anything less than a high quality, professional look, especially today, since it is so affordable to do so. A desk jet printer is not considered a high-quality document. Think laser printer.

Laser printers are top of the line. They have speed and the best quality reproduction. An ink jet printer is the next best thing but, as noted above, it gives an unprofessional impression. If the extent of your printing will be letters, statements, invoices, and related documents then you need not consider color.

Here, again, there is a lot to choose from, and the technology keeps improving. So when you shop, try to get good advice and invest in a laser or laser-quality printer that will serve you well.

### Scanners

A scanner has the ability to transfer words or images from paper into your computer in a digitized format. Once you have the words or images in your computer you can them in a variety of ways: archive, forward to others, or use it to generate documents, reports, proposals, presentations, newsletters or flyers. A scanner is most certainly not a must for every tax consultant's office, but it is worth mentioning since the price for a quality scanner keeps coming down and there are many times that they come in handy. Depending upon how enterprising you are, you may find ways of using a scanner that can help your business grow.

### Dictating or Recording Equipment

If you have a fair volume of business that involves a steady flow of correspondence then a dictating machine would enable you to delegate this task to a part- or full-time secretary/assistant who could then formally transcribe the information. For occasional work an ordinary cassette tape recorder or digital recorder will do, but once you get into heavier volume you should consider a regular office-dictating machine or computer program.

Most units today can be found in a hand-held design for low prices. The most important feature to look for in dictating equipment is sound fidelity. Your voice should reproduce clearly so that a secretary can understand what is being said. This is especially important when your work involves the careful and exact transmission of numbers, specifications, and other vital financial data. A good desktop playback machine has a variety of features to make transcribing easier including simple push button operation and earphones.

Of course, there are also software programs available that operate on voice recognition and that enable your spoken voice to be transcribed into written format on your computer. This option is certainly worthy of consideration if you find that dictating is one of your more routine business tasks.

### Postage Scale and Postage Meter

Trips to the post office are unavoidable when operating a tax practice, but there are ways to help you get your mail out more efficiently and promptly, and that can also save you money on unnecessary postage.

Since you'll be sending a lot of different-weight mail a postage scale will take the guesswork out of calculating the correct postage. It'll make sure that you don't overpay, and—even worse—underpay and run the risk of having critical mail returned for insufficient postage, or risk the embarrassment of forcing a client to make up the shortage when they take delivery. Moreover, mechanical meters are a thing of the past. Today, electronic meters are your only option. Available only through rental contracts, these postal meters are USPS approved and will officially mark your mailings with the proper postage. Plus, on the Internet, postage options are on the rise: at present, you can print proper postage directly from your office computer. These options, besides giving your mail a more business-like appearance, will also save you time in line at the post office.

For the smaller business it is also important to mention that you can often order stamps online and even print exact postage online. Check out **www.usps.com** to see what options are available to you.

## Online Business Opportunities

Experts believe that small businesses have the most to gain by offering their products and services on the Internet. The Internet is "leveling the playing field", as they put it, enabling small businesses to compete against bigger companies.

However, don't try to create an online business presence simply because it is the trend you hear about from everyone else. The key question to ask is whether there are clients and potential clients online for you, and if the answer is "Yes," then you should consider being there too. As with any other marketing device, putting yourself online—in the form of a Web site—calls for strategy, forethought, a plan and an approach. You can't just put yourself there and expect things to happen. You have to have some sense of how the Internet works, what it offers, what you have to offer online, and how to integrate an online business with your existing business.

Having said the above, you have to realize that a website, at the right time and under the right circumstances, can be a powerful tool for building a business. On a website you can advertise your services, sell your services directly to your clients, obtain essential information about clients and prospective clients, receive instant feedback from clients, and even recruit employees. Another great thing about a website is that it allows you to grow at all times of the day; your business site is open and accessible 24/7.

When a client or potential client can visit your site at any hour of the day or night, learn from your site, and respond to your site, that is a powerful way of doing business.

Of course, not every tax consultant is in a position to enter the online business world. It may not be for you at all, or it may not be for you just now, but it is important to know that it exists—if and when you choose to move in that direction.

## In Closing

Matching office technology to suit the needs of your practice is a complex undertaking. First and foremost, consider the acquisition of new technology for your practice only as you genuinely need it. Don't make the mistake of buying more equipment, accessories, and options than you actually need.

To help you determine whether you need it or not, ask yourself the following questions: Will this piece of technology help reduce my expenses? Will it help increase my income? Will it save me time and help me increase output, accuracy, and efficiency? If it doesn't contribute toward these ends then you should sincerely ask yourself whether you need it at all.

Furthermore, to evaluate the true cost of any piece of technology—high-tech or low—you will want to know more about supplies, accessories, and their availability; service and maintenance costs; the costs of special features, special furniture that might be needed, and additional expenses. For example, with a computer how will you be trained? Does the price include training? Is there a warranty, and what does it cover in terms of time, parts, and labor? All of these factors feed into the true cost of any technology you purchase.

Some experts in the field also suggest that individuals going into business for themselves should spend no more than one to five percent of their gross income toward the purchase of any new technology in any given year. Don't hold this as a standard over your own business but be prudent with initial purchases. Yes, an Apple Air notebook is a work of art, but you can get a functioning lesser-known brand notebook for one-fifth the price if you just need a decent mobile computer.

One other consideration: there is a lot of sophisticated technology available today and there is a lot of market competition—which is good for the buyer—but don't purchase without first comparing prices and features. Also, try sticking to a manufacturer with a good reputation for quality merchandise, reliability, and one who offers the best service contract and warranties.

# Chapter 6

# Successfully Marketing Your Practice

*He who has a thing to sell, and goes and whispers in a well, is not so apt to get the dollars, as he who climbs a tree and hollers!*
**Anonymous**

*The highest reward for a person's toil is not what they get for it, but what they become by it.*
**John Ruskin**

## By Way of Background

Not long ago, a chapter on marketing in a text for tax professionals might have seemed totally out of place. It was considered inappropriate for those involved in such "professional services" to go out and actively solicit clients. You could certainly develop "a practice from within"—through the traditional system of referral and recommendation—but to actively promote your own tax practice was genuinely frowned upon by the professionals in the industry.

Then, in 1977, the Supreme Court passed a landmark decision permitting professionals to advertise their services. Suddenly, those in the professional service industries found themselves in the open marketplace—able to employ all the typical marketing strategies that were previously withheld from them.

Of course, tax consultants are trained to fulfill their tax responsibilities in a technically competent and satisfying way and are not necessarily always familiar with the complex field of contemporary marketing and promotion. Nevertheless, marketing—over the years—has certainly gained in prominence as an essential component in the development of a successful tax practice. In today's technological world some sort of an Internet presence alone almost seems like a necessity.

Therefore, it is important that you become at least somewhat familiar with the field of advertising and marketing. The material gathered in this chapter will introduce you to some basic marketing ideas, while providing you with a number of practical suggestions for handling this vital aspect of your budding practice.

It has been years since the Supreme Court delivered its decision with regard to professionals advertising, but there is still some residual tension between the more traditional practitioners who favor "building up a practice from within", primarily through referral, and the "new school" whose counter argument runs: Business through referral is fine, but a new practice has no clients to begin with, so how is referral to ever take place? They also argue that the marketplace is radically different today than it was 20, 30, 40, and 50 years ago. Competition is keen, and new circumstances demand new and different strategies to attract valued clientele.

It could very well be that everyone in this debate is right. You just have to bear in mind that a developing tax practice goes through phases, or stages of growth, and each phase calls for its own type of market strategy.

To open a practice, to make the public aware of who and where you are—is a little like launching a rocket into space, and it calls for a concentrated boost of energy. At this point you may have to rely more heavily on outside advertising and marketing. But once your practice is up and running—active and ongoing—you may then rely less on outside advertising and emphasize "marketing from within," which means improving and developing client relations and working through referrals. Then again, if you should move, take on a partner, or expand into new or specialized areas, you may need to launch a new advertising campaign. It all depends on what you want to do with your practice at any given point in time.

In any case, everyone agrees that a fancy, sophisticated advertising campaign will not guarantee you success because, unlike other businesses and industries, YOU are the central ingredient to your own success. A good ad may lead to initial contacts and new clients, but only you can keep those clients coming back season after season by virtue

# Chapter 6: Successfully Marketing Your Practice

of the quality tax preparation service you provide. Then it follows that a growing and satisfied client base will gladly generate more business through referrals.

One last point: even when the Supreme Court handed down its decision allowing professional services to advertise, it was with a sense of discretion and a clear set of guidelines. In so many areas, much of what passes for advertising is downright gaudy, demeaning, and misleading You don't want any of these features to reflect upon your own professionalism and integrity. So remember, when you do advertise don't make false or misleading claims. Be tasteful and tactful rather than flamboyant; be honest and straightforward without leaning toward exaggeration and sensationalism; and emphasize your own merits rather than disparaging your competitors. In this way, your marketing efforts will be a sincere and reliable extension of the quality tax service you have to offer.

## Marketing—An Introduction

Marketing is a broad, all-encompassing term that refers to almost anything you professionally say, write, or do, and that relates to you and your tax practice. It includes all the various ways in which you, as a tax professional, communicate with and appear to the public around you: the way you look, dress, and talk; the appearance of your office; the letters you write; the ads, fliers, and brochures you print; the organizations you support and belong to. However you appear or express yourself in public can relate to the concept of marketing, in the broadest sense of the word.

As you can see above, marketing is a complex, yet fundamental part of your practice and will demand your ongoing attention. It is one thing to be an accomplished and qualified tax practitioner, but it is quite another to communicate that message to the public. That is what this chapter is all about: effectively communicating your professional image and message to the public.

Since marketing is such a multi-faceted subject, we will discuss the topic by breaking it down in the following way:

- Market Research : identifying and learning about your target market
- Market planning and strategy where we discuss the different forms of advertising
- Publicity
- Promotions
- Public relations

## Market Research

Your overall goal in marketing is to effectively communicate with prospective clients in order to elicit a positive response; market research is a vital preparatory step to help you attain this goal. It involves gathering information about prospective and current clients, so that you can make more intelligent marketing decisions. The more you know about your clients—who they are, where they are, what they do, what they read and what they need—the better you can structure your advertising message, publicity campaign, and other information sharing programs.

Market research also involves understanding who the other players are in your market. Your market can be your town, your region, or the area you do business in. Other tax practices, big and small, operate in the same arena. How these players function and which customers they bring in will influence your own business and potential client base. Knowing how these players operate can give you an advantage in your own marketing approach. For example, you may be aware that a larger firm dominates low-cost, easy tax preparation. They're not much help for clients who need expertise with complicated returns. Your marketing plan may then be to grab the niche market that needs more expertise and hands-on help with their complex tax returns.

### Your Target Market

Your first objective, then, is to identify the group(s) of clients you feel best qualified to serve. Not "everyone" out there is a potential client of yours; there is no service in the world that everyone partakes of in the exact same manner or at the same time. Some members of the purchasing public are too young, too old, too rich, or too poor and some already have a tax consultant, and so on. At the same time you cannot possibly be everything to everybody. So who are you best qualified to serve? You have to be aware of your specific skills, strengths, and limitations, and thereby recognize your potential market niche—somehow classify the public you are in a position to serve—and then tailor your marketing effort in that direction.

To help you locate prospective clients some measure of market research is necessary. But don't worry; this is not a complicated procedure.

In a previous chapter we discussed the value of demographic studies in relation to office location; this same body of information can now help you locate potential clients as well. In fact, most—if not all—the information you need is readily and locally available to you.

Remember: demographic information can identify individuals in various ways—by age, gender, education, income level, residence, or occupation. By applying demographic findings you are able to break the overall market down into subgroups based on these specific characteristics. You can address yourself exclusively to a specific geographic locale, such as young singles, young families, or senior citizens. You might want to focus on a particular age, or certain professions, or owners of small businesses—or combinations of the above. Over a period of time, you might test various messages on different populations and see where you strike the most responsive chord.

You can find all the demographic information you need at the following facilities:

- Your local library,
- University business departments,
- The local Department of Commerce,
- The Chamber of Commerce,
- The Census Bureau,
- Small Business Institutes,
- Utility Companies, and
- Regional or local planning commissions
- And online.

Also check into marketing periodicals. You can also discuss these matters with local public officials and people in the business world.

Once you have gathered some information and have identified your target market(s), you are ready to create and design a message for that segment of the population.

**Your Marketing Message: A Good Place to Begin**

At first glance the following exercise may seem simplistic, but it is well worth your time:

As best you can, in writing, clearly describe exactly what you do professionally. Briefly state the services you render: you can list them, mention specialties, even elaborate on each point if you want. You might even draw up several versions of this exercise: a concise statement as well as a more drawn out explanation. However you formulate the sheet, when you finish you should have a precise description of the services you provide as a tax professional.

Now on another sheet, list and describe all the benefits and advantages you offer your clients. Formulate all that you can do for them:

- Do you save them time, money, energy, bother, confusion, worry or anxiety?
- Do you provide them with a sense of confidence, relief, security, clarity, peace of mind?

After drawing up these sheets you will have the two essential components of your marketing message: One sheet addressing "what I can do" and the other sheet addressing "what I can do for you". The result is basically the heart of your message.

In one form or another, what your office can provide is the message you want to communicate to the public. You can always modify it, shorten it, lengthen it, highlight certain features over others—all depending on the purpose and context in which it appears—but the message remains basically the same for you to draw upon and work with as the need arises.

In a greatly reduced form these ideas may appear on a business card or flier. In a more elaborate form it may fit into an article or brochure. But once you have taken the initial time to express and formulate this information you will always have it to turn to. The tone and content as it reappears in various formats will also lend a consistency and professionalism to your practice, to the literature you produce, and will provide clients and prospective clients with clarity and confidence about your practice as well.

Targeting your market and formulating your message are two fundamental and important considerations in launching a successful marketing campaign.

## Learn From the Experience of Others

Another worthwhile way of finding information to help you in market research is to read the results of articles and studies that relate to your field. From time to time articles appear that bear directly upon tax professionals and the public they serve: some inform readers of what to look for in a tax professional; others report the experiences of practitioners in such areas as marketing or public relations. By reviewing such articles you are in a position to benefit from the research, findings, and experiences of others by applying the knowledge gained to your own practice.

For example, one financial journal recently instructed readers in how to shop for a tax professional. Briefly, the article stressed the points that prospective clients should look for:

1) Straight talk about fees... spell out clearly and directly how fees are calculated.

2) Easy access... calls should be answered promptly, in or out of tax season.

3) Clear explanations... of all services rendered and of everything the tax professional is doing on the return, including deductions and other items.

4) Education... time spent with a tax professional should give the client a better understanding of personal finances and of how various tax laws affect him. The client should then be more aware of what records to keep and procedures to follow to stay in compliance.

5) Year round tax tips... by November a tax professional should contact clients and alert them to last minute ways of cutting tax bills.

6) Long-range tax planning advice... a good tax professional should provide clients with financial tips that go beyond the current tax return.

7) Audit-aid... a tax professional should be willing to advise and accompany clients on an IRS audit.

In yet another report, readers were told to apply the following criteria when hiring a tax consultant:

1) Does the professional answer your questions with ease and with apparent technical competence?

2) Is the professional up to date on recent changes in tax laws, recent IRS regulatory changes, and current court decisions?

3) Does the professional provide you with a comprehensive analysis of your tax situation in clear and understandable language?

4) Does the professional spend time discussing legitimate methods to reduce tax liabilities?

5) Does the professional provide you with practical audit planning suggestions?

6) Does the professional keep appointments on time? Is he/she accessible and prompt in returning telephone calls?

7) Does the professional provide you with a clear understanding of fees and costs, up front? Is the price reasonable?

8) Will he/she represent you at any audits, and if so, at what cost?

9) Are the two of you compatible? Do you feel that this is someone you can confide in and be up front with?

One firm of tax professionals wanted to know specifically how they could improve the firm's services, so they hired an agency to objectively survey their clients in person, through interviews and written reports. In such an undertaking, not only the agency, but the clients too, were compensated for their time and services. Among the lessons learned from this particular survey were the following:

1) It was discovered that in this firm the personality of the principal partner was the most important reason for clients choosing this firm over others—all other features of a firm's competency being equal.

2) Many clients felt it detrimental that the firm was losing its "personal touch" since the tax preparation procedure had become increasingly computerized.

In fact, on account of this, some clients were seriously contemplating a switch from one firm to another.

3) The firm also learned how important it is for each client to clearly understand the basis and breakdown of the practitioner's fees.

Guidelines such as the ones listed in the three examples above can be helpful in several ways:

- They can serve as a standard by which to examine and assess your own performance level in your practice. Just ask yourself: To what extent do you fulfill these expectations?

- By being aware of such concerns you can improve the quality of your interactions with clients. By being sensitive to and openly discussing these matters you create a climate of confidence and trustworthiness in the practitioner/client relationship.

- You can also emphasize these concerns in your marketing efforts. Knowing that these are important issues to your public, you can address them in your advertising campaigns.

- As a rule: to know what your prospective clients are interested in and concerned about is an essential part of market research and planning. If you can satisfy these needs and allay these concerns, then you are just who the prospective client is looking for.

## How Feedback from Your Clients Can Strengthen Your Practice

Until now our discussion of market research has centered on how to effectively utilize "outside" data, findings you can gather from beyond your office walls. But you can also gather helpful information from your own clients. It would indeed be advantageous for you to know what perceptions your clients have of your practice: what are your clients' needs, expectations, and concerns; in what ways might you improve the services you offer them; or what additional services could you provide. Getting a handle on such information is certainly worth your while, and there are several ways in which you can go about gathering it. Of course, bear in mind that you must always be tactful and considerate. You are dealing with your own clients and you must be sensitive to the manner in which you elicit such information from them.

1) Depending upon your rapport with any particular client—if it's an open, established relationship based on shared confidences—you may find that you can get the answers you need by speaking to the client directly. By asking brief, relevant questions, the client will share with you the feedback you are looking for.

# Chapter 6: Successfully Marketing Your Practice

2) If you think you would get a better, more objective response if the client answered in writing—and even answered anonymously—then you could send out a brief cover letter and questionnaire. The letter could open with the following remark.

> *Dear Mr. Smith,*
>
> *Client satisfaction is one of the most important services I can offer you. I am always interested in improving the quality of my practice, and would like you to help me by answering the following brief questions.*
>
> *Thank you for your time and information, and I hope to continue being of service to you in the future.*
>
> *Respectfully,*

Then construct a list of important, specific questions highlighting key features of your tax practice procedure. To make things easier on your client you might follow each question with a rating scheme of 1…2…3¼4¼5—moving from poor, fair, good, to very good, and then excellent. After each question you could still leave space for the client to enter any personal remarks and suggestions if she wishes to.

The following is a list of possible starter questions: you can add, subtract, or modify—tailoring the questions to meet the needs of your own practice.

- Do we respond quickly to your inquiries?
- Are we sufficiently accessible to you?
- Are we sufficiently courteous and helpful to you?
- How would you rate the quality of our service?
- Would you recommend us to others? If yes, why? And if no, why not?

The more specific the question is, the more applicable it is to various aspects of your tax practice, the more valuable the answers will be to you. The point is to try and get an accurate reading on pertinent and specific aspects of your practice and quality of service. Note that if your clientele is young or highly technical, there are many excellent online survey tools that you can use.

3) You can also gather client information without asking your clients anything.

Simply write down your own personal observations, and study the data you have regarding your clients in order to get a better profile and understanding of the types of clients you service best. Then based on your own findings, you can do the following:

- Devise methods to better service the clients you have.
- Devise marketing strategies that appeal to potential clients who are similar—in significant ways—to those you presently serve.

A successful tax practice is not a static affair. It is a dynamic, evolving enterprise, and some measure of market research is always called for just to stay in touch with the needs of an ever-changing marketplace.

The more inquisitive and methodical you are to gather pertinent client data for the sake of your practice the better prepared and informed you will be to handle both your clients' needs, and those of your growing practice.

## The Market Media: Planning & Strategy

Before discussing the various advertising media, we will first briefly describe the following essential marketing tools:

- Your professional name
- Your logo
- Business cards
- Your e-mail signature
- Stationery
- Brochures
- Website

These are important marketing items: they describe, represent, and transmit to the public the overall image of your practice. When you e-mail, regular mail, post, or distribute any of these items, it is like leaving a bit of your professional self behind. They serve to identify you as a tax professional, and though they are an essential part of your "marketing plan," they are not really examples of advertising—in the strict sense of the word.

### What's In a Name? Selecting an Appropriate Name for Your Practice

Choosing an appropriate name for your practice is an important, but pleasant task. You want to select a name that you like, one that is easy to say and remember, relates to your practice, and has a professional ring to it. So before you decide upon a name, consider the following:

# Chapter 6: Successfully Marketing Your Practice

- Try to keep the name straightforward and descriptive. If possible, the name should somehow indicate what you do rather than raise questions or doubts about your services. For example: *Adams Tax Consultants rather than Adams & Associates.*

- Try to keep the name short, specific, and pronounceable. Long, cumbersome names are difficult to deal with and easily forgettable. If your own name fits the formula, use it. But if your own name is too long and difficult to pronounce, then think of something else.

- Try to think of a name that is distinctive and memorable. Also, be sure to check if the same name is currently in use, to avoid later business and legal complications.

- Try to avoid clever and humorous names. For example: *"Give Me A Break Tax Consultants"* may seem cute at first but you have to remember... some may not think it's funny, and others may simply write you off as unprofessional. In any case, when it comes to naming a professional practice, humor is a questionable marketing tool and may not serve you well. Also, try to stay away from trite, overused terms, or superlative, grandiose sounding words like "Ace Tax Consultants" or "Universal Tax Service." These are overused terms and tend to have a hollow ring to them.

- Finally, before settling on a professional name, try to get some reliable feedback from people you trust. You want to be comfortable with the name you choose, and you want it to project a professional image to the public.

In addition to a name, a short, effective slogan can enhance your image and make your name and practice more memorable and appealing to the public. If you do use a slogan, just be sure it suits your image: keep it short and to the point, and stay away from silly, exaggerated remarks.

## Logos

To further complement your business identity you may want to select a logo to enhance or accompany your name. Choosing a distinctive typeface or some sort of type configuration may suffice for a logo, or you can have someone design an appropriate graphic symbol to accompany your name. A good logo can be eye-catching, prompting people to notice and remember your practice.

If you do select a logo, be sure to use it extensively: on signs, business cards, ads, stationery, bills, letterheads, brochures, website, press releases—anything that comes out of your office. It will help you achieve quick, easy, and extensive recognition.

## Letterheads and Envelopes

Your letterhead refers to your business stationery, and it should be used for all your business correspondence. Having such stationery lends credibility and professionalism to your practice. If possible, it should contain your logo, and certainly your business address, email address, phone and fax numbers. A well-designed letterhead should also serve as the basis for all your press releases and other promotional literature.

## Business Cards and E-mail Signatures

Do not underestimate the value of a good business card. While the business card today may seem archaic in the modern, technology world, it can still be a very effective, creative, and versatile marketing tool, so be sure to have cards printed as soon as possible. Then, distribute them freely: attach them to your mailings, press releases, letters, and direct mail campaigns. Leave them at appropriate public places, with CPAs and bookkeeping services, or attached to bulletin boards, and whenever you deal with another business or individual, be sure to politely give him your card. If you can afford it, magnetic business cards are a great way to advertise as they often end up front and center on people's refrigerators.

Another consideration for this high-tech day and age: You can create a "virtual" business card by using a "signature file" to add an automatic footer to all your e-mail messages. This can include your name, slogan, logo, what you do, the type of clients you serve, and how you may be reached—by phone, fax, or electronically. Every communication that leaves your office, including electronic messages, should have your basic contact information on it. It never fails that a connection can be made by someone who remembers an e-mail signature or a business card that they received months before.

Here are two brief business card tips:

- Before you print your own, examine other cards and see what attracts you to some and not to others: Is the primary information legible? Does it stand out? Is the logo or name a memorable one? Is it clear from the card what service is being offered?

- It may be worth your while to print on both sides of the card and embellish the second side with added information, giving a recipient more reason to hold on to the card. This second side could be used for anything from a chart of weights and measures, a conversion scale, a tipping chart, to a short inspirational message, tax tips, or even a brief rundown of the services you render.

## Brochures

Even though paper brochures are a bit archaic in the Internet age, in practice they are still an effective and relatively inexpensive marketing tool commonly used to inform the public of your services. It can deliver more detailed information about your qualifications, expertise, and the services than usually appears in an ad flier. It can be an effective mailer in its own right, it can accompany a press release, it can be made available or distributed at public gatherings, presentations, or simply left at offices, schools, and other public facilities.

A good brochure should clearly identify you and your tax practice, list your areas of expertise, describe the extent of your services, and tell what benefits you provide for your clients. If there's room, it may include a brief biography, listing qualifications, awards, honors, and interests.

A good brochure need not be expensive or thought of as a complicated, extravagant project. The point is to explain who you are, what you do, and what you have to offer—attractively, but with an economy of space and words. For this, a single sheet of standard sized paper—8-1/2" x 11" folded in thirds, or 8-1/2" x 14" folded in thirds or fourths—will suffice. You can print on both sides and even leave one panel free for mailing purposes. Of course, brochures can get lengthier and fancier, but if you select an appealing typeface along with complimentary graphic material, you can certainly come up with a well- designed—inexpensive, yet impressive—piece of work. You might even incorporate some tax tips or other worthwhile information into your brochure. This will give the public added reason to hold on to the brochure for future reference.

**Bulletins and Newsletters**

It may not be an immediate consideration, but when the time is right, a periodic client bulletin or newsletter can be a most effective way of maintaining contact with clients, or establishing contact with prospective clients. It can serve the dual purpose of informing the public of vital tax related news, while promoting your practice in a meaningful, constructive way.

Whether you call it a bulletin, a news brief, or a newsletter—it doesn't really matter—the terms are basically interchangeable, and the format is primarily the same. To begin with, keep your style and content simple: one page, 8 1/2 x 11, or 8 1/2 x 14, printed on two sides. Use your logo and put a masthead across the top to give your publication a professional look. Be sure to incorporate information that your public will find useful.

Material for such a bulletin can include news briefs, excerpts from pertinent articles, tax planning ideas, new regulations and requirements, or other informative features. For ideas you can draw upon any number of resources: weekly tax services, IRS bulletins, accounting publications, business journals, questions raised by your clients, online blogs and newsletters, and your own ongoing office experience. You can always put in short fillers: personal anecdotes, interoffice news and changes, tidbits, sayings, and humorous asides. You can start by coming sending this out 4 to 6 times a year, If you do use material from other periodicals be sure to cite the sources in your publication.

If anything, newsletters are usually lengthier, and more elaborate than bulletins, yet they draw upon a similar pool of material. At a certain point of professional development newsletters are an excellent way of broadening and developing client relations and services.

Newsletters tend to be an expensive and time-consuming venture, but you can also purchase one of the commercial newsletters that are available, affix your own logo or letterhead to the top, and send it out to clients and other contacts. A quick way to generate regular newsletters is to simply repeat the major news in your industry that your clients may want to pay attention to. For example, the IRS puts out a weekly email on tax tips and tax rule changes affecting regular taxpayers. After signing up on the IRS website to receive these emails, you can practically cut-and-paste these blasts to your own newsletter and send it out under your own name summarizing the same tips. Clients will quickly appreciate the regular reminder of your help, especially near tax time. This approach takes very little effort and generates regular, useful material.

Whether you decide to work with a brief bulletin or a lengthier newsletter, both are excellent marketing tools: they show concern on your part, they are informative, they serve as a communication link to regular and even occasional clients, and they give the public awareness of what you are capable of doing. Finally, such communiqués can generate a lot of response—with people calling, commenting, and asking questions. You may even want to have a reader response column where you answer interesting inquiries from those who contact you.

## Advertising

At this point, assuming you have some idea of a target market and a message in mind, we will deal with the subject of advertising.

Advertising is basically any paid communication you create and transmit via any of the media available to you. We often think of the "media" as referring exclusively to such mass media as radio and TV, but it encompasses all of the print media as well: newspapers, magazines, posters, billboards, mass transit ads, hanging signs—and in the computer age, as we shall see—it encompasses advertising on the world wide web.

Each of the media has its own distinct advantages and disadvantages, and you will have to weigh your options to decide which medium or "media mix" (where you make use of more than one at a time) you wish to employ.

We will now briefly discuss them individually.

## Electronic Media—Radio and TV Advertising

From a financial perspective radio ads may be an affordable type of advertising if you use local stations, but there are other factors to consider. You have to remember that people usually listen to the radio when they are doing something else: dressing, driving, washing dishes, and so on. Therefore, the all-important specifics of your message may get lost. Those listening may not be able to write down or remember your number; they might be driving at the time, making it near impossible. Also, a lot of listeners tune out ads when they come on or switch stations. However, if you do use radio, remember that the key is repetition, though timing is very important as well.

Focus on the weekday morning time and evening when people who work are commuting on the highways or roads. They are more likely to listen and pay attention at those times than any other time of the day. Also, place your radio ads at the appropriate time of year for tax considerations, i.e. prior to the peak of the season. Another point to consider if you use radio is that, to a certain extent, you can select your audience—insofar as certain types of people listen to certain types of programming on specific stations. If you do decide to run an ad on the weekend, do so consistent with weekend programs that focus on finance and money, again targeting consumers who are prone to listening to tax topics.

Using television is probably the most expensive form of advertising. It reaches out to the largest number of people at any time and is visually impressive, but remember too that the message is fleeting; it may be wasted on many who are not really part of your target market, and yours may not be the type of message that needs TV visual accompaniment to begin with. Also, the point made above regarding radio applies here as well: people either tune out or switch channels when ads come on.

Considering the pros and cons of the electronic media, and judging by the experience of most tax practitioners in the past, it would seem that your advertising dollar may be better spent in the print media.

## Print Media—Newspapers

Newspapers primarily serve local markets and concentrated populations. Of course, "local markets" can mean a small town or a large metropolitan area, but whichever the case may be, your newspaper ad will basically reach out to the local population serviced by the particular paper.

Newspapers are immediate and practical sources of information, and most Americans consult with them daily, even in an electronic format today, so advertising in newspapers at least assures you a lot of exposure. However, studies indicate, and most advertising managers agree, that newspaper ads require repetition to be genuinely effective. So choose smaller ads that appear more regularly than a large ad that appears less frequently. Remember too, newspaper ads have a short life span—about one day—after which they are usually discarded. There are also a lot of other ads or features that your ad must compete with on any given page, so your ad may be overlooked or lost in the confusion.

One option that will increase attention is to purchase newspaper ad space with some sort of a coupon feature. While doing so means you will give up whatever revenue the coupon is worth, it creates immediate value for whoever reads the ad and decides to use the offer of discounted services. Businesses use coupons all the time, and when economic times are hard people are more likely to favor businesses offering savings than those that don't.

To a certain extent, when you advertise in newspapers, you can select your audience by placing your ad in a specific section of the paper or in a section that appears on a specific day of the week (sports page, business section, a "home" or "family" page, and so forth). You thereby increase your chances of being noticed by the market you aim to address. Nevertheless, to a great extent, much of a newspaper's circulation is "wasted," as far as your ad is concerned simply because a substantial number of readers will not pick up on it. They may overlook it or disregard it either because they don't need the service, they live too far away, or for some other reason. Therefore, advertising in smaller papers—neighborhood papers, suburban papers, special interest papers, even weeklies or monthlies—may prove more rewarding than advertising in large, daily, metropolitan papers.

Display ads—the larger ads that appear on pages that carry other features or news articles—can be quite costly, whereas classified ads are much cheaper and therefore easier to repeat. Even though classified ads are not seen by as many readers as display ads, those who do read the classifieds are more likely to be in the market for something specific, especially if they are already looking for tax services.

## Print Media—Direct Mail

Direct mail is advertising literature that is sent through the postal system. For the tax professional it has several distinct advantages over other print media advertising channels. If carefully planned, constructed and properly executed direct mail can be a very effective way of reaching new clients.

People oftentimes—and erroneously—refer to direct mail advertising as "junk mail," but it is never junk mail unless it is the wrong message sent to the wrong person, or unless the piece is so poorly conceived and assembled that it is not worth paying attention to. Otherwise, if the message is clear and creatively executed, if the message speaks to or answers a definite need, and if it comes to the right person at the right time then it is most definitely not junk mail, but an effective and welcome promotional tool.

However, direct mail needs to be targeted. Just blanketing an area will waste a lot of advertising dollars and paper. Instead, try getting a mailing list of names and addresses that have already ordered some sort of financial service. These folks will likely be more prone to read a direct mailer before throwing it away than the person looking for his latest edition of a sports magazine in the mailbox.

**Direct Mail has the Following Advantages:**

1) In a broadcast or print ad, you have to be very selective and mention only brief highlights relating to your tax service. But with direct mail you can elaborate and tell as much or as little of your story as you wish. You can modify your message and speak more directly to specific needs, and you can describe various problems and solutions. You also have greater flexibility as to the nature of the material you discuss—both in format and content. Your mailing piece may be little more than a postcard, or a foldout sheet of paper; it can even serve as a brochure. In fact, you can design something to function as a brochure as well as a direct mail piece.

2) You can also target your direct mail advertising with great precision, because you are in control of where your direct mail piece is sent.

3) You can develop your own mailing list from current clientele, referrals, family and friends, or you can purchase or rent ready-made lists that virtually pinpoint almost any segment of the consumer market you wish to address.

4) You can use the option of "occupant" or "resident" mail if you simply want to blanket a certain geographic area. Your local post office can supply you with the necessary details.

5) With direct mail you can repeat or follow up on your message whenever you want to, and time your mailings to more precisely meet your needs. You can also be more exacting in how you measure the responses to your mailings in order to calculate their effectiveness.

With direct mail you have more freedom, flexibility, and control over all aspects of your advertising campaign. Direct mail is flexible yet selective at the same time.

Another advantage of direct mail is that it can be quite effective when used in conjunction with another medium, such as the telephone. When one medium serves to complement or reinforce another it is commonly referred to as a "media mix." Toward this end, a direct mail piece fits in with a telemarketing campaign as part of a single marketing strategy. The promotional piece received in the mail can pave the way for a follow up call within a week.

One final thought: experts in the area of direct mail caution those who are just beginning to make small mailings at first and expand from there. You may even want to sample certain areas, gauge your response, and then move to another area, until you find those areas or populations where the response is best.

Remember too, that major mailers consider a 1 percent response to be quite good. They would be ecstatic about a response of 3 percent to 4 percent. So be realistic in your direct mail expectations and be persistent!

### Direct Mail—Lists

As noted earlier, since direct mail is the most personalized and targeted of all the print media, a well-planned mailing list lays at the heart of every successful direct mail campaign. Every mailing list is distinguished by its own unique combination of features, and you will have to determine what type of characteristics you will want to use:

- You can develop your own list beginning with friends, neighbors, relatives and acquaintances.
- You can compile a list of potential clients on your own. For example, if you want to mail to certain businesses or professions you can gather names from the local yellow pages.
- If you think certain neighborhoods are good prospects you can get voter registration lists for a specific area.
- Otherwise, you can buy lists or rent them from list rental firms.

### Direct Mail—Timing

Many products and services are closely related to a specific season of the year. Therefore you will find that soft drinks and air conditioners get a lot of media attention in the summer, while hot chocolate and snow plows get much more in the winter.

Similarly, as a tax professional you should concentrate most of your advertising efforts into those months leading up to and including the tax season (don't forget the tax extension time as well leading up to October!). It's just common sense that most people are more receptive to what you have to offer at the appropriate time of year. This holds true for all your media exposure, and is most certainly the case when it comes to such a concerted effort as an extensive direct mail campaign.

### Print Media—Directories

A directory is not usually an active, persuasive advertising medium, but rather a reference medium. People usually turn to a directory when they are looking for a particular product or service. Among the advantages of placing an ad in a directory is that it tends to have a long reader life, and if it is a practical, popular directory (such as the Yellow Pages) then usage can be quite high and consistent.

You may want to settle for a regular directory listing or a bold print listing. You may also want to consider a display ad—business card size or larger—because if you place a distinctive, attractive, practical ad in the Yellow Pages, or some other directory, then those individuals actively looking for a tax professional may just decide to call you first. It is also important to be listed in as many directories as possible—Yellow Pages, community business listings, neighborhood directories—or any place where potential clients may come across your services.

## Tips for Writing an Effective Ad

The following tips will help you write effective ad copy:

1) Select a brief headline or lead-in that captures the reader's attention: offer a benefit or ask a potent question. Many readers don't get past a headline, so this part of the ad must have direct and immediate appeal.

2) In the body of your ad you can elaborate and be more specific: describe your services and what you can do for the reader.

3) Speak in positive terms, use everyday language, short sentences, and write sincerely. Be personable and direct: speak to the reader using the singular "you" or "yours." For example: "We can help you reduce your taxes!" Or: "Are your taxes too high?"

4) Be credible. Don't make outrageous, sensational claims. Don't use subjective phrases or opinions like, "we are the best" or "we are the only." Instead, be straightforward and point out the very real advantages and benefits of your practice.

5) Use an attractive layout and design. If there is room for graphics to accompany your text they can be helpful.

6) Be sure to always include the name of your tax practice, address, directions if necessary, telephone number, e-mail address or fax number, website, available hours, and your logo if you have one.

7) Try to have someone else proofread your copy. Whether it's for an ad, a brochure, or an article, very often you are so close to the project that you fail to notice even the most obvious mistakes. Someone whose standpoint is more removed—and therefore more objective—is in a better position to catch these errors.

A related point: as you get involved with writing ads, you will very likely get involved with typesetters (unless you do your own typesetting and graphics), and printers as well. Typesetting involves the art and science of choosing lettering and font for a document or poster. Good typesetters and printers will take the time to work with you and answer your questions, so try to find those who will be helpful companions in your growing enterprise. It's a good idea to get quotes from more than one typesetter and printer. Get personal recommendations, and in every office you visit, be sure to look at a sampling of the work they produce.

Also bear in mind that you are selling a service rather than a product. Oftentimes, service benefits are more intangible than product benefits, and it's harder for the public to "picture what they are getting" for their money. Therefore, when you formulate and structure any of your print information, try to be specific, and make what you have to offer as clear, concrete, and graphic as you can.

**Keeping Track**

Another important, ongoing part of market research is **to track the results of your advertising.** You need to know which media, which messages, which times of the week, month, and year are working best for you, and which marketing efforts are just a waste of time and money. For example, you might test various ideas on different segments of the population and discover that a certain message does not work well with one group but does with another. So you have to evaluate your results and refine your strategies in order to get an ever better return on your advertising investment.

By simply asking clients, one successful practitioner was surprised to learn that the key selling point in her own advertising was this statement: "the return will be prepared with you in the privacy of your own home or office." Needless to say, she continued to utilize this strategy in her advertising campaigns.

Over a period of time—by keeping track—you will get an ever-clearer indication of which marketing messages and techniques are working best and who is responding to them.

Another interesting result of your research may be that you will uncover a market gap: You may come upon a segment of the population in need of your service that you never even considered before. It sometimes happens that the needs of the larger market will help determine the shape and direction of your own practice, and it may mean moving in unexpected directions, rather than according to your personal plan. But as an up-and-coming tax professional, you will always have to be on the lookout for such marketing opportunities and new ways of reaching clients.

What follows is the personal account of one practitioner's experience with advertising a new tax practice. The article appeared in a leading national accounting periodical, and the results of the author's findings appear here in abbreviated form. And even though this is far from being "the last word" on the subject, the author's insights may be helpful to you.

# Chapter 6: Successfully Marketing Your Practice

## Phase 1

1) The author relates that he first clearly defined for himself the "services" he was selling and the market he was targeting. He chose to emphasize tax service, financial planning, and write-up work.

2) The initial goal of his ad campaign was to gain exposure and name recognition. He placed ads in several local newspapers (in late November to get pre-tax seasson exposure) to announce the opening of his practice (listing available services, hours, evening availability, phone number, and office location).

3) The "new office" ads led to many calls and several clients.

## Phase 2

1) From late December to April, the author aimed at obtaining a large number of tax preparation clients. When he spoke to prospects he learned that his best results came from ads in local suburban papers. Ads in a local, specialty business paper brought in average results, and spot ads on the radio brought in the poorest response.

2) The author has an enthusiasm for horses and raising horses, so he put an ad in a paper that caters to fellow enthusiasts. This ad generated an excellent response: Out of 20 calls, 19 resulted in new clients.

3) Ads in weekly suburban papers paid off well and new clients responded especially well to the availability of Saturday and evening appointments.

## Phase 3

1) The author's third goal in advertising was to obtain year-round business from clients, and toward this end he found that display ads in the yellow pages were very helpful.

2) The author continues to monitor new clients to determine which ads work best, and he seeks further exposure by teaching about tax-related matters, money-management, investment, and other topics related to finance. By public speaking and by attending functions that reflect areas of personal interest, he has managed to bring in more clients.

3) The author concludes that his ad campaign was successful: He developed a substantial client base in his first year of practice, he learned where to spend his advertising dollar, and he proved to himself that a successful new practice can be established without an existing client base—with the help of an appropriate advertising campaign.

## Educating the Public—A Type of Market Strategy

It's amazing how little most Americans know about the content and structure of federal tax law. State law doesn't even register on the radar of 99 percent of people. Then again, it's understandable too: tax law is complex, undergoing constant revision, and given society's hectic pace, most people just don't have the time or patience to keep up with it. Consequently, many of your potential clients may not even be aware of how a tax professional can be of help to them. They may have misconceived notions of what a tax professional does, who she services, or they may not even have any notion at all. Being unaware of the benefits, they may never avail themselves of your services.

Therefore, you may find it advantageous to make "educating your public" an integral part of your advertising campaign. Make it a point to inform prospective clients of precisely what way you can help them save time, worry and money. You can incorporate such information almost anywhere: in a brochure, in a brief message on the back of a business card, on a flier, in an ad, as an article, in a column of tax tips in an office bulletin, or as part of a direct mail campaign.

Perhaps most important of all, educate clients in the course of your daily interactions with them. Coach them in how they can help their own financial situation along; show them how they can prepare themselves to meet with you; make them aware of up and coming tax law changes in tax policies that may affect them in one way or another. You will find that the more informative you are the more trusted you become. Your extended, highly personalized service will be greatly appreciated, and you will have acquired a client for life.

Therefore, educating the public can be a worthwhile part of your overall marketing plan. Not only are you a source of convenience and professionalism in service, but a source of reliable information as well.

## Neighborhood Networking

Advertising studies bear out that those who live and work in a specific area respond to neighborhood marketing conducted by local neighborhood businesses. This is another good reason to initially plant yourself in a carefully selected location.

With this in mind, think in terms of effectively reaching out—by phone, card, brochure, e-mail, or personal visit—to facilities that operate in your neighborhood:

- Neighborhood offices and businesses, and their customers and clients
- Neighborhood employers and their employees (restaurants, gas stations, dry cleaners, etc.)
- Neighborhood associations and organizations along with their members

- Neighborhood educational institutions, their staff and students
- Neighborhood non-profit groups and their supporters

Some of these groups may publish their own newsletters or bulletins. So put an ad into these publications or offer them an article or column of tax tips.

Finally, don't forget the importance of your daily interaction with people on the street. Your conduct in such a setting can go a long way towards promoting your professional image. Be courteous, patient, of good cheer and the neighborhood's opinion of you will grow in a positive way. Furthermore, if you have bulletin boards or window space open to public view, allow community groups and organizations to post their notices and events there. This too will enhance your neighborhood image, as it attracts added business to your office.

**Pro-Bono Work**

Pro-bono work is a term typically used by attorneys who provide free legal services to the needy. However, the concept is not restricted to lawyers. Any professional can take part of his time and help out those who otherwise could not afford to hire such expertise and services. In the tax service business, there are a number of people in any region, big or small, who need help at tax filing time. Often, these are seniors on fixed incomes.

Professionals who provide such free services can leverage them into goodwill marketing. There's nothing wrong or unethical about this. It also shows that your business is giving back to the community and helping even the neediest get their taxes done and stay in compliance with federal or state tax law. This helps everyone, and it gets noticed. People are more apt to work with a business that helps their neighborhood than one that just takes from it.

# Publicity

Technically, any mention of your practice in the media—that you pay for—can be classified as advertising, while any mention of your practice that you do not pay for can be termed publicity. The information may be solicited or unsolicited, but when the media makes use of it you get the publicity, which amounts to free advertising. Although publicity can take place in any of the mass media, the most common form, and the one we will elaborate upon, is the written press release.

A press release is a primary means of relaying newsworthy information about you and your practice to the print media at large. A publicity press release can inform, explain, or educate. You just have to pick out a noteworthy point to expound upon. Journalists and editors, their bosses, jump on interesting information, so it helps to provide tidbits in a press release that they can actually use. Just telling them about your business will not suffice.

Here are a few suggestions that can form the basis of a more elaborate feature, story, or article that can highlight your practice: grand opening events, expansion of services, new partnerships, change of location, outstanding achievements or honors earned, human interest stories or public service activities. You can write about a unique aspect of your practice, and if you can't think of one then create one! For example, provide a free consultation day or learning seminar, and then write up the event—before and after—as a press release. You could also provide a comment or interpretation of tax law that affects a lot of people, or propose a solution to a common tax problem and submit the article as a press release.

Remember too: don't overlook or underestimate neighborhood or local press coverage just because it isn't the *International Herald Tribune*. Be realistic and practical. The smaller, more community-oriented resources of publicity—such as weekly and suburban newspapers, shopping bulletins, church bulletins, public bulletin boards, newsletters, periodicals from special interest groups, clubs and service organizations—are channels that are usually more willing to use your material. These resources are generally more in touch with your potential target market as well.

Of course, if the opportunity arises whereby you can appear on TV or be interviewed on the radio, don't pass up the chance. But at the same time, don't overlook the potent and practical opportunities that are close at hand.

**Here are some suggestions to help you write your own press release:**

1) First, identify a newsworthy event or piece of information (use suggestions above), and then be sure to write your article from an objective point of view, in the third person—as if you are reporting or commenting on the event or information. Don't write in a way that appears as though you are merely "patting yourself on the back," or simply presenting a "self-promotional" piece. If written well a periodical may actually use the entire press statement word-for-word.

2) Select appropriate publications for your press release. Consider the various publications available to you, and then select the ones you think are most suitable and likely to print your pieces. In fact, study the releases that appear in those periodicals and become familiar with their style and content. You might clip and keep a file of releases for future reference. This way you will be better able to tailor your own writing for publication.

3) When you write your article, keep the following in mind:

   a) Write a short, attention grabbing headline, and a first sentence that sparks further interest to hook the reader.

   b) Write the more essential and more interesting information at the beginning of your article, and put the less important information at the end of the piece.

   c) Do not write long sentences. Keep the language simple and straightforward, and limit your article to somewhere between one and two, double-spaced, typed pages.

   d) Your press release should have a neat, crisp, businesslike look: typed or computer printed, easy to read, with even margins all around the page, and submitted on your own letterhead stationery.

4) In addition to your name, firm name, telephone number, fax number, e-mail address, and person to contact for further information, your release should include:

   a) A release date. Most press releases carry the line FOR IMMEDIATE RELEASE to inform the media that the article can be used right away or at the editor's earliest convenience.

   b) Suggest a headline that briefly summarizes the content of your press release in an exciting way.

   c) Include a copy of your brochure or business card as part of your mailing.

5) Be sure to send a gracious thank you letter to anyone who uses or prints your release. It's common courtesy to do so, and such acknowledgment may pave the way for the publication of other articles and letters.

6) Most of all, be persistent in your efforts and they will finally pay off. In your contact with editors and program directors, remember that they are not looking to give you free publicity; they are looking to inform and entertain their readers, listeners, and viewers. Shape your release with that perspective in mind. If you write in an obviously self-serving way, you will not get the publicity you're after. But if you simply persist—bearing in mind that not everyone will print your releases—you will see that your efforts will eventually serve you well.

7) Remember, also, to be resourceful: If you wrote a press release or an article, and it found its way into print, then turn it into reprints that can serve as handouts or mailers. The reprint can be attractively assembled with your logo or letterhead across the top. You can then send it to clients or prospective clients signed at the bottom, "With compliments from...", followed by your name; or you can make them available at meetings, conventions, or public speaking engagements. Similarly, try turning your press release into a more full-bodied

article, develop your article into a speech, or turn a speech back into an article or press release. In other words, use your imagination and try to get as much mileage or publicity out of your efforts as you possibly can. Also, keep a running record, or scrapbook, of all your press releases. You'll find that it's a rewarding experience and will impress your clients favorably as well. Many companies frame publications that mention them and hang them on the office or waiting room walls.

**Aside from press releases, here are some other opportunities for publicity:**

1) Write small, filler articles for newspapers. These can be anecdotes or tax-tips about 50 to 80 words in length and you can send several at one time.

2) Write letters to the editor. Provide a timely reply to a subject you read about in the newspaper or respond to some current, topical issue. It may not even be related to your tax practice, though it helps if it is. Such editorial replies usually run between 200 to 250 words. When you write such letters remain focused on the subject at hand. Rely on logical, straightforward arguments, and well-documented facts and figures, and be sure to sign off with your name, firm name, address, title, telephone number, or e-mail address. If you have any further questions about such letters, study some samples from the periodicals you wish to address and model your own replies after those.

3) If you are appearing somewhere—to speak, give a seminar, or to offer advice and answer questions—be sure to notify the media beforehand; they usually allot some measure of time and space for public service messages. Contact local newspapers and radio stations and ask what their procedure is for printing or airing such information. It's a valuable source of publicity for you.

4) The most effective form of publicity, after all is said and done, is word of mouth recommendations from your own clients. Satisfied clients who tell their relatives, friends, and work associates about your practice can establish and develop your credibility in a way that no other planned strategy can. Especially in the area of personal services, people simply recommend to others those professionals they have come to know and trust. Therefore, the ultimate focus in a successful tax practice is simply you. To generate a loyal clientele, you have to make sure you provide the kind of quality service clients will want to tell others about. That's the best publicity of all.

## Promotional Events

Promotional events are special occasions designed to increase contacts, exposure, and general awareness of the services you provide. Such occasions may include the opening of a new office or a change of address; they can promote a unique and timely service; they can serve as an educational device; or they can tie in with a specific occasion (office anniversary), or special time of year (a pre-tax season counseling day).

Ever heard of the term, "swag?" This refers to those items that have business logos, names, and addresses on them. It's common and helpful to have certain promotional items or "giveaways" on hand at any promotional event, something useful that can serve prospective clients as a reminder of who you are, where you are, and what you do. People love free items, especially if they are useful like a pen or a notepad. Such giveaways should always have your logo, name, or other form of identity printed on it so that prospects can get in touch with you.

Aside from business cards and brochures such items might include custom printed calendars, pocket calendars, bookmarks, ball point pens, key rings, rulers, plastic clipboards for notepads, refrigerator magnets, and so forth. But before you order such items, think of something that is useful, relates to your practice, and does not call for any great investment of money.

**Here is a sampling of some promotional endeavors worthy of your attention. Depending upon your talents, skills, and inclinations, you might consider trying one, some, or even all of the following measures at one time or another.**

1) Announcing the opening of a new office, a change of address, a new partnership, or expansion of facilities. Any of these can rightfully lead to a promotional event where you send out announcements or invitations, have an open-house, provide refreshments, offer advice and information. Afterwards, you can write up the event as a press release.

2) There are all kinds of fairs and exhibits where you, as a tax professional, may participate: community fairs, neighborhood fairs, business fairs, career days at a college, or educational fairs—where the public comes to learn about various professions and professional services. If you become involved in such appearances, even occasionally, it may be worth your while to design an interesting booth or display to appear on portable panels that can easily be assembled and taken away. Use your imagination, but an innovative display can be a great conversation piece, and can attract a lot of attention from prospective clients. For example, you might devise a board that provides a brief historical overview of taxation in this country—with words and plenty of pictures. Or with the use of charts, diagrams, and photographs, you might show how the system of

taxation operates. Or you could post various tax tips, regulations, and other informative and practical features. With time and practice, such presentations could easily evolve into a lecture you could give. In any event, whether you attend a fair or convention as an exhibitor or as a visitor, you are sure to make a number of worthwhile contacts there.

3) Teach a class or give a seminar. This could be done in your home or office, in a school or other community center. In this way you can inform the public about a variety of tax related matters: what a tax practitioner does, what clients can do to help themselves, tax tips, financial planning, new regulations, and so forth. There may be certain public places—such as libraries, colleges, or shopping centers—where you could situate yourself on certain days of the year in order to answer questions and offer tax related advice, and thereby make the public more aware of your services and range of expertise.

4) Be a public speaker: contact libraries, community centers, religious organizations, and offer a public service lecture relating to tax tips, the effects of changing regulations on the taxpayer, and other aspects of financial planning. If you are inclined to public speaking then this is a skill you can gainfully employ in promoting your practice. Just make sure you prepare for your speech accordingly:

   - Prepare for your talk by familiarizing yourself well with all the pertinent material. Do the necessary research and be certain of your facts.
   - Thoroughly practice your speech and its delivery. Some do this into a tape recorder and then listen back in order to make corrections and adjustments.
   - When you deliver your talk, be aware of your posture, your voice and range. Be sure to project your voice properly and make eye contact with your audience.
   - Keep your presentation on the short side, and be sure to leave over enough time for questions, discussions, and audience participation.
   - If someone asks you a question to which you do not know an answer don't fake a response. Simply reply that the question requires some research, take down the person's name and number and tell him you will contact him when you find out the answer.

If you lack confidence in public speaking but would like to give it a try, you might take a public speaking course. Or, gain experience and confidence by experimenting in smaller settings, starting with a high school classroom or a mini-seminar and slowly advancing to larger gatherings. Then again, if public speaking is simply not for you simply overlook this particular form of promotion and focus on the others.

In connection with business fairs and conventions, we mentioned the advantages of setting up a booth or panel display. Very often, such displays can stand on their own—open to public view—without your having to be there. Libraries, schools, recreation and community centers often have wall space or cases available for displays. If your display is interesting and informative you could get a lot of free exposure in such settings. Just be sure to pin your own brochure to the display as well and leave plenty of business cards around.

## Public Relations

"Public relations" is a difficult term to pin down. On the one hand, it does relate to your tax practice; on the other hand, it goes far beyond the scope of your professional endeavors.

In a way, public relations concerns the greater you, the community-minded you, or the YOU that extends and interacts with different facets of the community around you. It may involve coaching a little league team, or volunteering time to an Ambulance Corps. Such further extensions of self may or may not relate to or involve your tax work, but these activities somehow reflect upon your career as well—as if to say your professional and personal life are in some ways inseparable.

The suggestions that follow fall more easily into the category of "public relations" than they do into the other headings listed above, so we discuss them at this point.

It is a long-standing and proven rule that one of the best ways for a tax professional to build his practice is to get involved with his community (remember our discussion about pro-bono work earlier?). Many professionals claim that there is no better way for a tax specialist to make a significant contribution to his community than by way of his particular expertise. At the same time, he is establishing a network of friendships and professional associations that will result in the development of a lasting practice. This sort of community interaction is usually classified as public relations. Consider the following:

1) Join organizations. For example, get involved with various non-profit organizations, the local Chamber of Commerce, the YMCA, religious groups or clubs, libraries, hospitals, and so forth. Of course, you don't have the time to join all of these, but try to connect with the groups toward which you feel an affinity—where your heart is—and then make sure you can manage it in keeping with your professional obligations.

2) Become a sponsor or donor in various charity or fundraising groups. Many such organizations can use your help and your expertise, and will give you free publicity in exchange for your contribution, either in a printed program

or journal, or in a newsletter, or publicly at meetings or celebrations. Such involvement on your part can also be the topic of a unique press release.

3) Participation in various community projects can put you in contact with individuals in other significant positions.

4) Try to attend various public functions and gatherings. The friends and acquaintances you make there can have a positive impact on your practice.

5) Also be sure to attend functions that relate to your own special interests: sports, hobbies, and youth clubs. These, too, can be excellent channels for meeting new clients.

6) Welcome Wagons: Some neighborhoods, towns, and communities provide a greeting service that distributes community information to newcomers in the area. Being a part of this service can also be a valuable resource for new clients.

## Advertising on the Internet

Advertising on the Internet is certainly not for everyone, nor should it be. Indeed, it calls for a significant investment of time, money, attention, and other resources. While setting up a website may sound easy, it takes a lot of ongoing work to actively maintain one and keep it lively for people to keep coming back to it. However, depending on your circumstances, and the manner in which your practice is developing, it may, at some point, become an option to consider.

But first, ask yourself: Are you sure there are clients for you—that you want and are able to reach—online? Are you able to create your own website, or hire someone to design a site for you? Are you able to update information on your site, or hire someone who can do so, on a regular basis? Keep in mind that creating a website can add to your practice's growth, but it can also add new levels of complexity and challenge to your practice as well. It's a sizeable step to take, and the best time to weigh your options is before you actually get involved.

On the other hand, a website is a marketing tool that can bring in many clients. You can describe your business to thousands of potential clients. You can offer information of general interest about taxes and tax news, and you can be very specific about your own business and expertise. In a way, your website can function as a fluid brochure—ever available, ever changing—and of course, it always posts your e-mail address, telephone and fax numbers, or other ways of reaching you.

Here are some of the considerations involved in setting up a website:

- A site has to be designed. It can be very simple, even a page; or it can be more complex. You can do it yourself or hire someone. It can be done for under $100

- or it can run into the thousands. You can even design a simple page at no cost if you subscribe to an online service, but someone has to construct the site for it to actually exist on the Internet.

- You will need your own domain name like a .com name, and you'll have to pay a one-time fee to register the name. If not, then you will need to rent space on someone else's domain. This makes Internet addresses more complicated to remember, so it's best to have your own domain.

- You will need to be able to take credit cards if you want to transact business online which means establishing a merchant account (there are many options).

- You will need to enter your site into search engines, create cross-links with sites of a similar nature, and devise ways of drawing people to your site, such as banner ads.

- You have to realize that there are ongoing costs involved in maintaining a website as well, so check out the requirements fully before you commit to anything.

**If you do follow through with your own website, there are certain points to keep in mind that can contribute to making your site a more successful one:**

- Create a site that is interesting, useful, and unique.

- Put in value-added information—news, tidbits, helpful hints—consisting of information people may not be aware of, but would be interested in learning more about by contacting you.

- Give clear contact information. Make it easy for potential clients to get back to you if they want to know more. Include your name, logo, e-mail, phone number, and address.

- Add special discount offers if viewers respond by a certain time.

- If you can offer something unique in the way of services, or appeal to a particular market, then explain it on your site in order to attract more viewers.

## In Conclusion

As you can see from this chapter, our concern here has been to present you with numerous ways of providing reliable information to potential clients in order that they recognize and become familiar with the benefits of your tax practice.

In truth, however, we have only scratched the surface of a subject to which entire textbooks are devoted. Nevertheless, you do have sufficient material here with which to make productive headway in effectively marketing your practice. Just remember that successful marketing—by presenting an honest picture of you and your service—can help you build a practice, but only you, by providing an overall quality service, can maintain the practice and keep it growing.

# Chapter 7

# Purchasing a Client or a Practice

*Time is money.*
**Benjamin Franklin**

## Purchasing Clients or an Entire Practice

The majority of tax specialists are content to establish and build their practice by starting with a small nucleus of clients and gradually widening that circle through effective marketing and superior service. But there is a quicker, though more expensive, way of establishing or expanding a tax practice, and that is the direct purchase of tax clients from other practitioners. This method of obtaining clients is employed by all professions and generally works to everyone's satisfaction, assuming the buyer will provide service that is equal or superior to that given by the previous practitioner.

You may establish or expand your practice either by purchasing an entire practice or just a group of clients from an established practitioner. Although individual clients may also transfer from one practitioner to another for various reasons (which we will soon discuss), you must nevertheless be willing to pay a fair purchase price to obtain a group of clients or a complete practice all at once.

The most obvious reasons for selling an entire practice are the death, illness, or retirement of the present practitioner. But occasionally, a tax specialist will give up a practice either because he has taken on a fulltime position, is moving out of the area, or is going into another field of endeavor.

Though it is more expensive, this approach may have certain advantages over launching your own tax practice: You have a fixed clientele, an established location, and very often a full inventory of supplies and equipment—perhaps even an experienced employee. If the owner is anxious to sell, you may get a very good price as well. Buying an ongoing practice can also save you time, energy, and money you would otherwise spend establishing a practice. Nevertheless, you have to be wary of such encounters, and there is a fair amount of research you will necessarily have to do.

Here is what you need to know:

- What condition is the practice in? Is it in a healthy state or one of deterioration? What has been the business trend for this particular practice over the past five years?

- The practitioner who is selling may praise his own operation up to the skies in order to get the highest selling price, but what are his real reasons for selling the practice?

- What about the general neighborhood—is the area growing or declining?

- What kind of reputation or public image does the practice have—favorable or unfavorable? If it's positive, then you can capitalize upon it, but if it's a negative one, then you will have a lot of overhauling to do.

Also, be sure to get good advice from reliable friends or qualified professionals, i.e. lawyers and neighborhood bankers. This is not the sort of decision you want to make on your own. The cost and ramifications are simply too far-reaching. Then, after a thorough investigation and if major considerations check out favorably, go for it. But if you unearth concerns it would be strongly advisable for you to look elsewhere.

## Should you Purchase an Entire Practice?

If you are relatively new to the tax field you ought to think carefully before taking on a full practice all at once. For one thing, it calls for a rather substantial investment of money. Suggested purchase prices will soon be discussed. Consider, too, that at first, you may not be able to handle some of the more complicated returns, or your clients may sense that you are unsure of yourself, and coming from a seasoned practitioner, they may look for someone more capable. On the other hand, an established, experienced practitioner incurs less risk when taking on a full practice if she can handle the additional workload.

Our suggestion, if you are just starting out, is to look for a practitioner willing to sell a group of clients, preferably small or middle-income returns; or look for a part-timer with just a small number of clients. Even when a larger practice is up for sale, the practitioner may be willing to break his clientele into segments, transferring the larger share to one buyer, and all or part of the smaller share to someone else.

If you are interested in pursuing this method of establishing or increasing your practice, then you will need to do the following:

- Locate a prospective seller.
- Establish contact with the seller.
- Negotiate a mutually satisfactory purchase price.
- Effectuate a smooth transfer of clients.

We will now discuss each of these steps in detail.

## Finding a Seller of Individual Clients

Experience has shown that the following are likely to be prospective sellers of individual clients or groups of clients:

### 1. Semi-retired tax practitioners

Very often, as a tax professional approaches retirement, he will gradually cut back on his practice by eliminating smaller, less lucrative clients. Yet these clients can be a very welcome addition to your developing practice. Bear in mind, however, that before seriously discussing the transfer of these clients, the practitioner will want to be sure that you are professionally capable of handling them. So it is important that you are able to assure the current practitioner of your professional skills.

### 2. CPAs cutting down on individual tax clients

Many CPAs or even large, non-CPA accounting firms, become so busy—with management consulting work, electronic data processing, pension and profit sharing plans, and other specialties—that they simply lack the time and personnel to handle individual, or even small business clients. While many of these firms are reluctant to accept any such new clients, they are somewhat committed to a number of these "return" clients from previous years. They would be only too glad to transfer such clients to another practitioner, one who is able to provide quality service. Here too, before transferring clients, firms will want to be certain that they are being moved into capable hands.

### 3. Attorneys

Although most lawyers are not expert in tax law or procedure, many of them—in the early years of their practice—do tax work to creatively occupy their time and bring in needed income. As their law practices develop, they generally reach a point where they prefer to divest themselves of all tax-related work. If you happen to contact them at the right time with the right offer you may be welcomed with open arms.

### 4. Real estate brokers and other non-professional tax practitioners

Almost every community has real estate, insurance agents or other individuals who do some tax work but who have never really developed a sizable practice. Oftentimes, these individuals decide, or can be persuaded, to part with a portion or even all of their clients, so they can fully devote themselves to their primary occupation. Even those who are not quite ready to give up their practice find that some clients have simply outgrown their ability to accommodate them, and they would be glad to transfer these clients to someone more expert than they are.

Your next question may be, how do I find out if and when these individuals or businesses have clients for sale?

If you are in touch with other tax specialists, chances are you will hear through "the professional grapevine" about practitioners planning to prune their clientele. Even if you are not in direct contact with tax practitioners as a group, you may have an accountant friend or relative who you can confidentially ask to "keep his eyes and ears open." But there are other resources that can lead you to the acquisition of new clients as well.

- **Tax service and office supply personnel**

    These sales representatives are constantly in touch with tax professionals. They may even be among the first to know if someone is over-burdened, ill, or otherwise wants to divest himself of clients. Let these individuals know that you are in the market for clients, and they will be happy to make the initial contact for you—especially if you let them know there is some compensation in store for them as well.

- **Your own new clients**

    A good indication that a certain practitioner or tax firm is giving up business may be the sudden appearance of new clients. You may at some point experience a flow of new clients, all coming from the same firm. This should alert you to begin making discreet inquiries as to the reason behind the sudden switch: Is their current practitioner ill or too busy? Is he changing his specialty, or moving into another field?

Finally, you may just try the direct approach of randomly contacting a number of tax firms and other professionals and respectfully inquire if they are in a position to transfer any clients.

## Approaching a Prospective Seller

Once you locate a likely resource for new clients, your next step is to approach him—directly or indirectly. Bear in mind that professional clients are not to be treated or traded like so many head of cattle, so your approach must be discreet and dignified.

One method is to send a friendly letter expressing your interest and asking the recipient to respond by mail, or phone, to set up a conference if he wishes to discuss the matter further. The following is a sample introductory letter to this effect:

> *Dear _____,*
>
> *I am engaged in tax practice. at the following address, and I am currently interested in purchasing additional clients.*
>
> *It has occurred to me that due to the growth of your practice, staff shortages, specialization on your part, or other developments, you may wish to consider the sale of some of your individual clients.*
>
> *If this is in fact so, please phone or write me so that we can set up an appointment at your convenience to discuss the matter further.*
>
> *I can assure you that in serving your clients I would try to maintain the high standards of service that they have come to expect from you.*
>
> *Needless to say, your response and all negotiations would be held in strict confidence.*
>
> *Sincerely,*
> *John Doe*

If you know the prospective seller personally (or if he knows you), and you are fairly certain that he is planning to drop some clients, then a phone call from you might be more efficient and effective. However, be prepared to beat a hasty retreat if it turns out that you are mistaken. At that point you can politely close the conversation by letting him know that you would be interested in speaking further if he changes his mind, or if the situation changes in the future.

### How to Locate Entire Practices Available for Purchase

As we mentioned above, the most common reasons for selling a practice are death, illness, retirement, or a move to a new location. When a practitioner dies, you will probably find out about it soon enough.

We suggest that after a decent lapse of time, you ascertain the name of the attorney handling the estate and advise him that you are interested in purchasing all or part of the deceased's practice. It is best not to approach the widow or children unless you have a mutual friend who can delicately broach the subject with them.

When you hear that a practitioner is about to retire, your best approach would again be through a mutual acquaintance, or other mediator, such as a lawyer or banker.

Another resource for finding a practice up for sale is the classified column in city newspapers; the hefty Sunday edition is usually the best source for such information. Professional accounting publications, tax journals and related periodicals also carry classified announcements of entire practices for sale.

### Negotiating the Purchase Price

To arrive at a satisfactory purchase price, the question uppermost in your mind should be: How much are these clients worth to me? Regardless of how valuable or lucrative any client is to the seller, he will be of little value to you if:

**a)** He won't stay with you, or

**b)** For one reason or another, you won't be able to service him properly.

Assuming you have a list of clients who, as a group, you can expect will stay with you, you nevertheless have to anticipate some degree of drop-off in the first year or two.

For one thing, some clients may have had intentions of switching to another practitioner for some time and were just waiting for the right opportunity to do so. Others may have developed a strong bond with their previous tax consultant and are not willing to adjust to your style. For other clients you may be too young, too old, too new, too busy, or what-have-you. The point is that a certain amount of drop-off is inevitable. It should not be cause for concern, but it must be taken into account when establishing a purchase price.

The most common and accepted method for arriving at a purchase price is on the basis of gross volume. You will generally find that the going rate is between 100 and 150 percent (on rare occasions even higher) of annual gross fees collected from the particular clients. However, you should insist, if possible, on a contingency agreement whereby you pay the full purchase price only for those clients that remain with you at least two or three years. Clients who drop out earlier are then paid for on a sliding scale. For example, if the agreed upon price is 100 percent of one year's gross, we suggest that the purchase price be paid over a period of two years at the rate of 50 percent of gross billing per year. So for those clients who drop out after one year you will have paid only 50 percent, while the full price is paid for clients who stay with you two years or more.

If the agreed upon price is 150 percent of the gross, try to stretch payment of the purchase price out over three years on a similar basis. However, the seller may insist on a two-year maximum on the theory that if a client leaves you after two years, it is your fault, not his. Indeed, it's difficult to argue with that position.

A variation of the above method is to set a price equal to between 100 and 150 percent of one year's gross fees, less allowance for estimated drop-off. Then, if the total gross fee earned last year from clients transferred is $10,000, you might propose a purchase price of $10,000 to $15,000, less 20 to 25 percent drop-off allowance.

Even if you negotiate a flat purchase price, try to avoid a one-year all cash deal. Payments spanning two years, or even over one season will give the seller considerable incentive to "deliver the goods," i.e. do what he can to ensure a smooth transition and urge his clients to stay on with you.

## Implementing a Smooth Transfer

Your final step is to make sure your new clients are transferred to you with maximum efficiency and a minimum of inconvenience to them. This, of course, will require full cooperation from the seller. This is one of the most sensitive moments of transition for customers. Many will be apprehensive when suddenly hearing that their professional help, as well as their files, just got handed like a box of goods to some unknown name. To turn this concern around you have to get yourself "known" quickly. Otherwise, skittish clients will walk.

First, the original owner should write a letter to each client advising that since she is no longer able to be of service, she has made arrangements with you—another practitioner—to handle the account, and has therefore transferred all necessary files and records to you. Although some send this notification letter as soon as the deal is closed, we suggest that you wait until the beginning of the tax season. This will minimize the chances of a client's looking for someone else.

A short while later, contact the client by phone or letter expressing your desire to continue the professional relationship he has enjoyed with the previous practitioner and suggest an early appointment. Prior to the appointment, carefully look over the client's files and familiarize yourself with his particular circumstances and tax situation. It will also help the transition immensely if you can get the seller (if he is available) to give you a briefing—in writing—on those clients with special tax problems, personal concerns, or idiosyncrasies that call for special attention. With this sort of pre-planning you can avoid a lot of aggravation later. Moreover, many clients will appreciate the fact that you took the time and trouble to acquaint yourself with their particular situation before meeting with them.

As noted earlier, it's natural, too, that a number of clients coming to you from another practitioner will be somewhat uneasy at first. This is especially true if the previous relationship was a close and long lasting one. They will wonder whether you "have what it takes" to service them properly, or whether they can really trust and confide in you. In short, they want to be sure you measure up.

It follows then, that you will have to exercise extra care with these clients.

Make sure that all your work is meticulous, double-check your figures, and allow extra time to become acquainted with their situation and tax concerns. If possible, do not charge at first, more than the previous practitioner—unless there has been some material change in the client's circumstances or type of return. But once he has stayed with you a year or two, you will of course want to treat him like any of your other clients. At the same time, if the previous practitioner's fees were above your level you have no moral obligation to charge the client less. However, if and when you raise your fees we suggest that you only increase these clients' fees proportionately.

## Individual Clients

When you purchase individual clients pay only on the basis of regular recurring fees, such as tax return preparation, payroll tax returns, etc. Fees collected for representing clients at audits should not be taken into consideration because these tend to be non-recurring. However, when buying an entire practice, you will—by the law of averages—earn a certain annual amount in audit fees, even though not from the same clients. So don't haggle too much over the purchase price on that account.

When you buy an entire practice, the seller may also want to dispose of his office equipment, fixtures, perhaps even the office itself. Tax-wise, it would be to your advantage to allocate as much as possible of the purchase price to the physical equipment and furnishings, and to minimize the "goodwill," or price paid for the acquisition of clients. The reason is that, of course, the former is depreciable for tax purposes, while the latter is not. So try to arrive at a fair compromise, but don't let this consideration ruin the transaction, if it appeals otherwise.

Finally, if office equipment does become part of the sale, be sure to check it out carefully before the purchase: it may be of inferior quality, in poor working condition, outmoded, or otherwise unsuitable to your needs.

## A Few Additional Thoughts Before You Buy

Regardless of how eager you are to take on a full-fledged practice, and in spite of how attractive the "entire package" may seem—make sure you approach the transaction objectively and cautiously. Emotions have a bad habit of getting people into trouble at the last second.

- Thoroughly check out the condition of the business' neighborhood, as well as the office facility. Speak to bankers and managers of other business establishments in the area.

- Since the practice has a history, files and records should be available to you for closer scrutiny. Get professional help to go over the records with you to get a more accurate picture of the condition of the practice. A third party perspective can be very helpful once you become personally engaged in the deal itself.

- Determining a fair price is usually a problem: the seller tries to get as much as he can and the buyer tries to get away with as little as possible. A fair price—agreeable to both parties—lies somewhere in between, and the way to arrive at that fair price is through effective negotiation.

    Negotiation tends to be a stressful encounter, but it need not be if you prepare yourself accordingly—both in attitude and technique. Here are some helpful suggestions:

- Approach negotiation as if it were a mutual problem-solving venture, where you are seeking a solution that will be beneficial to all parties concerned.

- Plan and prepare for your meetings with the seller by becoming as familiar as you can be with the issues at stake. This is one instance where ignorance is not bliss. On the contrary: be as knowledgeable as you can be about the condition and the facts relating to the seller's practice, and be as clear as you can be about what you wish to accomplish.

- Begin by discussing issues you are both agreeable to, and as you move along, seek solutions to where you differ. Keep summarizing whatever progress you make as a form of further encouragement.

- If possible, try to have a neutral intermediary present to serve as a sounding board to facilitate the discussion.

- No matter what happens in the course of the meeting, try to end on a positive, friendly note: leave options open so that you can meet again, if necessary.

# Chapter 8

# Expanding Your Practice

*A professional is defined, not by the business he is in, but by the way he is in business.*
**Anonymous**

*When you get right down to the root of the meaning of the word "succeed," you find that it simply means to follow through.*
**F.W. Nichol**

## What is a Client?

A classic poster is on display at the headquarters of L.L. Bean in Freeport, Maine. In the text of that poster you'll find the word "customer" and we have replaced it with the word "client." The meaning and intent, however, retain their value and importance.

*A client is the most important person, ever, in this office... in person or by mail.*

*A client is not dependent on us...we are dependent on him.*

*A client is not an interruption of our work...he is the purpose of it.*

*We are not doing a favor by serving him...he is doing us a favor by giving us the opportunity to be of service to him.*

*A client is not someone to argue or match wits with.*

*A client is a person who brings us his wants and needs.*

*It is our job to handle clients profitably...for their sake and ourselves.*

Once you have overcome the first hurdle—of developing a nucleus of clients—chances are you will want to raise your sights and look for ways to expand your practice. Depending on your goal, you will want to attract sufficient clientele to provide you with either a comfortable second income or a viable, full-time tax practice. Of course, if your aspirations are more modest, and all you wish to handle is a small number of clients, then you may have reached that point already and will not be interested in further expansion at this time. But if your sights are set on a larger practice, you will find that growth will come from three primary sources:

1) Recommendations and referrals from current clients.

2) Through the normal influx of additional new clients, for example, by advertising.

3) By upgrading your level of service to current clients, generating up-selling revenue.

## Your Present Clients as a Source of New Business

As we mentioned above, your most effective and prolific source for new business is your current pool of clients. Personal recommendations and referrals from satisfied clients are vitally important for tax specialists striving to develop a quality practice.

Needless to say, you can't expect them to recommend you to others unless they are fully satisfied with your service, integrity, and technical know-how. To the point that they will come back to you year after year, but they will recommend you to others as well. We will therefore discuss various ways to satisfy clients and impress them with your knowledge, competence, and professional skills.

### Retaining Your Present Clients

In planning for the growth of your practice, direct your initial efforts at retaining the clients you now have. Some practitioners go to great lengths to acquire new clients, while putting little effort into keeping their client base. Not only is it easier, but wiser, to do all you can to keep current clients satisfied, rather than spend time chasing after new ones. The reasons for this are simple:

1) The law of inertia teaches that it is easier to retain a current client than to acquire a new one.

2) The cost of attracting a new customer is far more than the cost of keeping a current customer happy.

3) An established client is more likely to promote your services than one who flits about from one tax consultant to another.

4) Most new clients tend to be relatively small, lower-fee taxpayers, while those who have been with you for some time stand a good chance of developing into larger, more lucrative clients.

Moreover, a client who has been with you for a while and with whose financial affairs you are familiar with requires less time and effort (all things being equal) than a new client with whom you must first get acquainted. In other words, you will spend less time on his return and earn a higher fee per hour—than with a new client.

## How to Keep Clients Satisfied

Fortunately, it is not hard to keep a client satisfied. If you can display technical competence along with the right interpersonal skills, then you have a combination of talents that would be hard to beat in any field of endeavor. What follows is a summary of some of the more important features to keep in mind in your dealings with tax clients. A few of these points are discussed in greater detail in other sections of the text.

1) Always be friendly and avoid being arrogant. In fact, there may be no quicker way to lose a client than to exhibit this fatal characteristic.

2) Express a personal interest in your clients and listen attentively to what they have to say. The focus of any meeting should be the client and not you.

3) Be patient, don't hurry. Impress each client with the fact that regardless of the size of his or her income, and no matter how busy you are, this case will be receiving the utmost in personal attention, and that you will try to find all possible legal deductions and tax savings to benefit the client.

4) Be reasonable in your fees. In your initial interview spell out clearly what all your potential charges are and how they are calculated. This avoids problems later when a client feels he wasn't told the details before getting into a complex project.

5) If possible, surprise your client by doing something extra or unexpected. For example, your examination of his financial transactions may bring to light certain deductions that were lost because the payment wasn't handled properly. If you point this out to the client and explain how he could handle such matters in the future to get the greatest tax benefit, you will have taken an important step towards winning his confidence and gratitude.

6) Don't be a "know it all." Do not hesitate to check your reference material or indicate the need for further research when you are in doubt. Most clients realize that tax law is too complex to be stored in one person's mind. They will

appreciate the fact that you are taking the time and trouble—in spite of your busy schedule—to make sure their return is being prepared correctly.

7) Impress your clients with the importance of keeping adequate financial records.

8) The taxpayer who is in the habit of recording all of his expenditures can be reasonably certain that no important deductions will be overlooked when the tax season comes around.

9) Make sure your clients retain all checks, bills, and other proof of deductible expenditures. Stress the importance of having all this information readily available in case of an audit on the return. It's also important that clients try to keep their paperwork in order too. The more organizing that is necessary, the longer it will take you to organize their "shoebox" of receipts, and the more expensive their return may be.

10) Always search for new ways to serve your clients. Some services will result in additional income for you, while others will serve to keep your clients pleased and will pay off financially in the long run. If your client is fairly intelligent and knowledgeable in tax matters make it a point to explain what you are doing and why. If it entails extra work or some risk of an IRS audit or disallowance make sure to spell it out clearly to him. On the other hand, if the client does not know a thing about taxes—and cares even less—then there isn't any point in being overly explicit, except to point out the extra work or risks involved.

11) Strict confidentiality (as we will soon discuss) is of paramount importance. However, there is nothing wrong with passing on information of a general nature (without any form of identification) of something you learned while preparing another return, and that may be helpful to this particular client. For example, you may have learned from other taxpayers that IRS auditors are zeroing in on particular deductions or income items, or you may have picked up some business ideas that would be helpful to your client. Passing on such information can only enhance your reputation and the value of your client relationship. Be careful not to pass along any proprietary information disclosed to your practice in the course of business, especially if it has been covered by any kind of a non-disclosure agreement. In some cases, discretion is the better course of action.

12) When setting up an appointment with a client, especially a new one—regardless of how much free time you have—it's generally a good idea to suggest a convenient hour a day or two ahead, and not immediately, unless the matter is urgent. It's a well-proven axiom that "success breeds success." You want to appear "busy" rather than "unoccupied." Nevertheless, don't give a client or prospective client a hard time getting an appointment, or he may take his business

elsewhere. Also, pay special heed if the client describes the matter as urgent. Remember: the problem may seem basic to you, but it may be giving your client restless nights.

13) Try to impress upon your clients that they should consult with you before venturing into any sizable acquisition, business deal, or other financial arrangement in order to consider the tax aspects and to minimize any unfavorable tax results. Very often the tax consultant finds out "after the fact" when it's too late to be of any practical help. You should actually try to educate your clients to think "tax-wise" all year round, and not only during the tax season.

14) To keep clients genuinely happy requires some insight—on your part—into their personalities. For example, some clients have a primary concern of keeping out of trouble with the IRS. They would much rather pay a larger tax bill and forego some deductions so that the return will not be questioned. Others are ever ready to don their armor to do battle with the IRS, if they have some chance of winning. So when you come across "gray area" deductions, tax-saving maneuvers or other techniques guide yourself accordingly. There is no point in saving a client a few hundred dollars if it will give him sleepless nights throughout the year.

15) Be tactful in dealing with clients. Never joke about a client's income, his means of income, or about his losses. All of these are serious matters to him, and they should be to you as well.

16) Finally, pay particular attention and be especially sensitive to new clients who have never before employed a tax professional. They may be hesitant or embarrassed about disclosing their financial affairs, so be pleasant and understanding as you guide new clients through the tax procedure.

**Personal Relations Along With Quality Service**

Until now we have discussed practical ways of projecting your image as a competent, skillful, and dedicated professional. But clients are not machines; they are human beings who want a practitioner who is not only knowledgeable in his field, but also exhibits a sincere personal interest in his clients and does not relate to them as mere cases or numbers. In fact, when clients make overall judgments about a practice they take a variety of features into consideration including the appearance of the office and staff, as well as how they are treated—it isn't just a matter of a practitioner's technical skills.

There is also another good reason to establish a healthy personal relationship with your clients. You will find that your stiffest competition is not from CPAs; their fees are too steep and they are usually too busy to aggressively seek new clients. The same applies, to a lesser degree, to non-CPA public accountants. Nor do you have much to fear from the small, independent, part-time tax preparer. As we mention elsewhere, many of these are inept, poorly trained, and hopelessly outdated in their work. Your up-to-date technical training and knowledge gives you a decided edge over them.

The heaviest competition that most practitioners encounter is from other tax preparation entities, particularly the large tax services that are always hungry for more business. Their main weakness, however, is their impersonal, hasty, assembly-line approach to tax service. This fatal flaw, perhaps more than any other, prevents them from taking over an even greater share of the tax market. No doubt, this is primarily what keeps them from forcing out the capable, independent specialist.

Therefore, friendly, personal service, and attention to client detail is perhaps the most powerful weapon you have in your battle with the super-giants. Use it well, to your own and to your client's advantage!

Use every possible opportunity to add a personal touch to your dealings with clients. There are many ways to show your personal concern; if you make it a habit to seek out such opportunities, you will build a strong personal relationship with many clients. This will lead to the development of a successful and gratifying practice.

Here are just a few ways whereby you can add that personal touch in your dealings with clients. It is by no means an exhaustive list, and you can certainly add to it with innovations of your own.

1) Be a courteous host in your office. Greet clients at the door and hold the door open for them. Offer to hang up a client's coat. Seat your client before you seat yourself. At the end of the appointment escort your client to the door.

2) Take note of pertinent, personal information regarding a client: names of family members, a vacation she plans to take, a class he attends, or a hobby she enjoys, etc. Keep a written client file to help you record such information and to use for reference prior to any appointment or call you make. That way, you can ask about his family, a vacation taken, a graduation, or other events that transpired.

3) Make sure you refer to and pronounce your client's name correctly. If you're not sure, at least ask politely how to pronounce it correctly. Slaughtering a name is a fast way to turn off a new client.

4) In your client file, keep a record of special dates and events, and on such occasions—birthdays, anniversaries, graduations, weddings, births, etc.—be sure to send a personal card or note.
    - Send seasonal greeting cards.
    - Send letters of appreciation after a service is rendered.

# Chapter 8: Expanding Your Practice

- When you hear that a client or some member of his family is not well, be sure to send a get-well card along with a personal note. If it seems appropriate, try to pay a personal visit.

- If you come across a news item or other information of special interest to a client, pass it along to him.

- At any other momentous occasion—buying a new home, opening a new business or having won an award—be sure to send along a congratulatory message.

5) Have light beverages or snacks available for clients, and offer it to them. For children, have candy on hand or other little items to either give away (some parents don't want their kids hopped up on sugar but toys are fine) or to occupy their attention while you meet with the parents. Always make sure to ask permission before giving a child food. If you happen to remember a client's preference in beverage or refreshment try to have it available when you meet.

6) Be informative as you discuss professional matters with clients. Take the mystery out of what you do by providing clients with a better understanding of certain terms and procedures. This will make them feel more at ease, more comfortable with you, and more confident with you as their tax consultant.

7) Make your clients feel special and important however and whenever you can.

    - Compliment clients sincerely. Develop a genuine interest in what they do.

    - An appointment with you should be a boost in their day, a lift to a client's spirits and self-esteem. Clients should leave their meetings with you feeling optimistic and good.

    - Let clients know that you are thinking about them. Make out of season calls just to see how a client is doing.

    - Also encourage clients to keep in touch with everything from questions to criticisms.

    - Try to respond to a client's call or written correspondence promptly.

8) If dealing with a new client, do something extra. For example, ask if he or she needs directions to your office, and explain precisely where parking is available. If it's possible, you might even fax over a map with such directions clearly laid out.

9) If you cannot be present for an appointment, excuse yourself beforehand and offer some sort of explanation. But don't just fail to show up with no prior explanation.

10) Many clients may be neighbors of yours, or fellow members in a community club or organization—people you have occasion to meet throughout the year. Undoubtedly, opportunities will arise to render small favors to these individuals, especially if you keep your eyes and ears open... a lift in your car, the loan of a book or tool, or an offer to help with some small chore. Such gestures can easily turn an acquaintance into a loyal friend, and even into a promoter of your professional services.

11) Office hours: Being available at times when clients need you most is an excellent way to satisfy clients and generate new business. It could be that many of your clients (and prospective clients) are occupied during conventional business hours, and would find it both helpful and convenient if you could meet with them evenings, week-ends, (even mornings)—or even in their own homes or offices. If you can accommodate them—in terms of time and place—you may find this to be a key selling point in developing your practice.

## The Benefits of a Follow-up System

Not all notes in a client's file are about engaging the client; some are just to make your work easier the next year. Thus, another important step when preparing a tax return is to immediately make a list of items to consider for next year's return. This includes carryovers (such as capital losses), contributions, investment credit, special notations, and memos regarding items to be aware of: i.e., loose items such as the sale and expected purchase of a replacement residence, copies of estimated tax paid, and items affecting the basis of property to be depreciated. Also, in this file, make note of any special problems you had with the client, or special items, or peculiar deductions that were questioned by the IRS in previous years and that are likely to recur. There is another item often overlooked: when a client or their spouse turn 65, he or she will be entitled to an extra exemption. Put a "tickler" into your future file to ensure that this won't be overlooked next year.

An excellent procedure—one that will repay your efforts many times over—is to institute a follow-up file or calendar for items to take care of during the year. One obvious example would be to remind your client to make his estimated tax payments on time. In this capacity it pays to review his record before the end of the year to see if sufficient estimated tax payments have been made. If there is a sizable underpayment, and the client is employed, you can save him some penalties by having his employer withhold additional tax before the end of the year. Any tax withheld is treated as if it had been paid equally throughout the year and will reduce or eliminate any underpayment penalty.

Another personal—and effective—expression of professional concern can take place when you become aware of legislation pending that may affect your client. This can be at both the federal, state, and local level. If this legislation is enacted, why not get in touch with your client immediately to discuss what can be done on his behalf? He will appreciate—and let his friends know too—that you don't get this type of individualized treatment from the large, national tax services, not to mention the IRS (actually there is some noticing that occurs, but people need to be signed up to the various IRS email blast lists which not everyone is aware of).

Another way to show personal interest is to forward an occasional news item or magazine article relating to a client's particular business, side interest, or hobby.

If you employ assistants, it's a good idea to assign each client to an individual who can then become familiar with that client's problems and concerns. Of course, you run the risk of building too close a relationship between the two. In the event the assistant leaves you and sets up his own business, he may take the client with him. On the other hand, we feel the benefits outweigh the possible dangers. One way to minimize the risk is to make sure that you also meet with the client occasionally. At least give him a call or otherwise maintain the relationship—letting him know that you are there and well aware of what's going on with him. This also gives the client a direct outlet to raise concerns if he doesn't like how the assistant is dealing with his taxes.

## The Confidential Nature of Tax Work

In the course of your tax work, clients will confide in you business and personal matters that they wouldn't tell their wives, children, or even their best friends. You will probably never cease to marvel at the varied and unexpected bits of information that are revealed to you.

Needless to say, this special, privileged status imposes the burden on you of keeping all such business and personal matters in your strict and inviolate confidence. Never—but never—discuss clients' affairs with anyone. The slightest hint or suspicion that you are a gossip can do irreparable harm to your entire practice. Likewise, a well-earned reputation as a tight-lipped professional who does not—advertently or inadvertently—divulge any kind of information can be very advantageous to your practice.

Every tax practitioner has, at one time or another, been subject to adroit questioning by individuals trying to elicit personal or financial information about relatives, friends, neighbors or competitors. When this happens to you—as it surely will—your best defense is to be completely uncooperative. Your interrogator will soon get the message, abandon his fruitless efforts, and acquire new respect for you.

Never assume that a client's wife, relative, or business associate is acquainted with his business affairs. For instance, you may be preparing Mr. Smith's tax return and find that you need to know whether some stocks on which he reported dividends are owned by him alone or belong jointly to him and his wife. You try to call but he's not at home, and the filing deadline is approaching. Don't ask the information of Mrs. Smith. It may be that she is not even supposed to know that her husband owns stocks.

In this regard, it is important that you acquire the habit of never leaving any completed or incomplete tax returns or other working papers on your desk or open on your computer screen where others can see them. Whenever a return is finished or temporarily set aside always put it into a closed file folder. Many tax specialists make it a practice to not even divulge who their clients are. You may also come across individuals who, for one reason or another, do not want it to be known that they are coming to you.

In the case where you are confronted by administrative or law enforcement investigators, some may or may not serve you with a subpoena first for information they are seeking. Some may simply want to see specific documents. In any situation, whether a desire for a casual conversation or an outright notice, defer any discussion until you have talked with your lawyer. Do not discuss details and politely tell the investigator that you will contact him through your attorney. This allows you and your attorney time to figure out what's going on and for your attorney to get an idea of what the investigator is after. Often, people just have casual discussions, particularly with federal investigators, wanting to appear as helpful and not having anything to hide. Doing so automatically makes the person a legal witness to whatever case is going on, and it can possibly make the person a party or target of the investigation as well. Saying nothing and communicating through an attorney avoids this accidental problem from occurring.

When dealing with similar businesses chasing after the same market, confidentiality is extra important if you are serving several competitors at once or are trying to convince your clients to refer you to their competitors. The last thing you want is for a rumor or statement to get out that you leak confidential information to one business about another. That could make you lose all related business clients.

## Creating a Public Image

A most valuable asset to develop, and one that will engender client loyalty, is to present yourself as a meticulous and responsible executive. You keep your word, you meet appointments on time, and you fulfill your promises.

Here are some practical suggestions to help you create and reinforce a "positive public image" of yourself and of your practice:

- Immediately confirm every appointment in writing. For example: Tuesday, a new client phones you and makes an appointment for next Monday at 4:30 P.M. As soon as you get off the phone, send this client a card confirming the time, the place, and advising him of what to bring along. Aside from the actual reminder value (which in itself is worth the effort), you have immediately established yourself as a person who is caring and meticulous in every detail.

- You promise to mail a form or paper to a client by tomorrow morning. Try your best, even if it's greatly inconvenient, to keep your word and have the item in the mail as promised (or don't make the promise). More important than the document or form is the fact that you are dependable. You must become known and accepted as reliable, both in tax knowledge and in fulfillment of your promises.

- Make sure to be on time, or even a few minutes early, for every appointment. This shows the client that you consider the meeting important, not a secondary or incidental affair.

- Carry your briefcase and handle your working papers with obvious care. Never allow the client to get the feeling that his documents are "just another piece of paper" you're handling. Remember that your service consists of far more than just filling out forms. Even if tax work is only a part-time occupation, don't allow your work or attitude to reflect a feeling of unimportance. Remember: if you attach importance and dignity to your work, so will your clients. On the other hand, if you treat your work casually, your clients will assume the very same attitude.

- Never pass along to a client a paper or form that contains any error, even of a trivial sort. Your office must convey your accuracy and attention to even minor details, even when they have no direct bearing on income tax work. Watch your spelling and grammar as well as the cleanliness of your documents when preparing letters, reports, or statements. If you work with a computer, make regular use of the grammar and spell-check features. And don't assume the software is always correct, either. Many times word-processing spell-check tools misinterpret a word, leaving it in a document incorrectly.

- Bear in mind that the average client has no way of assessing the technical capabilities of his Tax Consultant. He often judges the total scope of his consultant's knowledge and expertise by observing how he handles other details: Do his papers look professional or sloppy? Is she well organized or is she hopelessly off-schedule? Does she have confidence in what she does, or not? Therefore, these seemingly "external," even inconsequential concerns carry an added measure of significance.

- While tax laws are too complex to demand that you have all the answers at your fingertips, it is important that you be sufficiently well versed so you can discuss common tax problems with confidence. This is not to say that you cannot inform a client that you are in doubt over a particular point or that a matter requires further research. On the contrary, such honesty can build confidence between you and your client. But generally, you should be familiar with your subject and be prepared to answer basic questions regarding a client's return.

- You will be doing business with many personal friends, neighbors, and acquaintances, and it becomes all-too-easy to meet with such clients in informal settings, or in comfortable, informal attire. Nevertheless, if you desire to be perceived as an experienced professional, it is advisable to dress for business meetings in business attire. This is especially important when meeting with new or prospective clients. Also in this regard, we should reiterate that the place you select in your home as a conference area should not interfere with other household activities. You can well imagine that a string of personal phone calls, a parade of people, or a blaring TV will do little to create an air of professionalism in your client's mind. However, a room arranged with business in mind—set apart from family and with explicit instructions to household members that you are not to be disturbed during business hours—will make a favorable impression, and set the tone for the importance of the meeting about to take place.

A wise person once remarked:

> "Almost everyone looks at you with the same eyes with which you look upon yourself."

If you consider your work important—if you dress, speak, and act accordingly—it is almost inevitable that your clients will view you, and your work, in the same light.

### How to Handle a Client's Tax Questions

You may find that clients will visit or call to ask for your advice on a pending or completed transaction or business deal. It may not seem important at the time, but the manner in which you handle the inquiry can have a lasting impact on your relationship with a client, and this, in turn, can affect the growth and development of your practice.

Here are some suggestions from experienced practitioners that can help you improve the quality of such client exchanges.

1) **Make sure you have all the facts:** The client may not be aware of all the facts she has to consider. She may ignore a certain detail thinking it's trivial, yet it may be vital to arriving at a proper assessment of the transaction. Therefore, you have to make sure you gather all necessary information. Remember: if your advice or opinion proves wrong, your client may put the blame on you—not on himself.

2) **Give clear-cut answers. Don't hedge.** Take all the time you need to consider a problem, but once you have an answer state it clearly and concisely. If you are in doubt, say so. Even the most experienced professional is not embarrassed to

admit that he does not know the answer to a particular question. If the concern is one of a tax rule interpretation make sure you inform the client of all possible, or likely, interpretations.

3) Consider the client's tax knowledge in your reply. Don't try to impress a client who is only vaguely familiar with tax law and procedure with a long, detailed account of how you came to your conclusions. In other words: adapt the amount of detail you provide in your dealings with a client to his particular level of understanding.

4) Try to offer alternative suggestions. If you must advise or caution against a proposed financial move at least try to devise a way of accomplishing the same client objective with even more advantageous tax results. Nothing will endear you to a client more than your ability to legally work your way around a specific obstacle.

5) Finally, prepare a written memo of every important discussion, and send a copy to your client. Recording your recommendations has several advantages: it will serve as a safeguard against misinterpretation, it will help crystallize your thinking, and—above all—it provides a clear record of all that has transpired. This comes in handy if the client ends up in trouble and then tries to blame you for giving him bad expert advice.

In writing, briefly summarize all the facts that bear upon the situation, set out the details of the problem, and then state your answer, or any alternatives you suggest. Incidentally, a full written account will certainly help justify a fee for your consultations or a larger fee at tax return time.

**Think of quality service as a product.**

1) It's easy to think of a purchased product as something that either works well, tastes good, or is attractive in appearance, but you can also picture a "service" rendered as a type of product.

2) Service is provided as soon as—and for as long as—you are in touch with your client.

3) Service is "experienced" by the client for as long as he or she is in touch with the practitioner or his office help—either in person, over the phone, by fax, e-mail, or via conventional mail.

4) Like an electrical circuit, when there is contact between practitioner and client there is a flow of service that consists of solving tax concerns and satisfying personal expectations—financial or otherwise.

In a survey designed to find out what clients expect from "financial service" professionals, researchers discovered that clients are concerned with the following:

- Reliable help: Especially in areas where most clients feel they do not understand the complexities and subtleties of certain financial procedures, they want to work with someone who is competent and trustworthy.
- Equal treatment: Clients, regardless of how big or small their income, believe that everyone should be treated equitably, in terms of time, sincerity, and undivided attention.
- Response to individual needs: Clients expect prompt and continuous assistance, especially when problems arise.
- Reasonable rates: Clients expect that fair fees should yield good service.

**Personal Appearance**

Considerations of personal appearance are crucial to success in any profession, but are especially important when you provide others with a service, because in a professional service YOU are the product that customers look at and assess.

Personal manner and appearance convey to others important information about your own sense of well-being and self-worth. Try to become aware of how others perceive you, and then, if necessary, take whatever reasonable steps you can to develop an image that enhances your professionalism. The rule is: if you don't envision yourself as a professional and behave like one, others won't either.

Here then, are a number of suggestions relating to manner and appearance:

- Be mindful of your appearance both in and out of the office. Make sure your clothes are neat, clean, and pressed, and your shoes shined.
- In terms of style, a conservative selection of business clothes is a safe choice to ensure a professional image, as opposed to unconventional or loud colors and styles. Remember: accountants and tax practitioners, like bankers and lawyers, are expected to be on the conservative side.
- Be aware of how you walk, sit, and carry yourself. Good posture is important. It communicates confidence, so sit up. Don't slouch.
- Eye contact and gestures are important. You should have normal, casual eye contact, but don't stare at clients; it will make them uncomfortable. Occasionally nodding in agreement is a sign that you understand what your client is saying.
- Smile when appropriate: a pleasant, welcome smile is a good icebreaker. It also conveys warmth, sincerity, and confidence.

# Chapter 8: Expanding Your Practice

- Your voice, too, should elicit professionalism: be relaxed and natural, but speak clearly, personably, and not too loud, but loud enough to be heard.

## In Conclusion

Since this chapter contains such vital information, it pays to emphasize and reiterate certain points in order to raise your level of awareness regarding the importance of quality service. Thus, here are a number of considerations worthy of your attention and periodic review:

1) Be honest. Never try to fool a client or oversell your capabilities.

2) Exhibit integrity: be dependable, keep appointments, and keep to your word. Otherwise, don't make promises you can't fulfill.

3) Take pride in your work. Approach your practice with an air of respectability and responsibility. Treat your time and efforts seriously—as if your business and reputation depend on it—as indeed they do.

4) Be patient with clients: spend extra moments with them if and when you can—answering questions, informing, explaining, putting them at ease. These extra moments are an investment that will pay off in clients that will remain loyal for a lifetime. In this regard, remember: quality service does not cost—it pays!

5) Exhibit both depth of knowledge and breadth of knowledge. Know your own profession well. Be ever on the alert for changes in tax legislation or other information that may affect your services to your clients. The more you know about your own subject—your own tax business—the more professional you are. This is depth of knowledge. You should also exhibit a sincere interest and understanding of the work involvements and activities of your clients. Through reading and a little research, become familiar with the basics of what they do. Not only will this enhance your own understanding of the world, and improve the quality of your client relationship, but it will also enable you to service him better professionally. This is what is meant by breadth of knowledge.

6) Train your staff well. They should be competent, courteous, and a reflection of all the policies that you are particular about. Make sure they are informed about the services you render, well trained regarding their own tasks, and familiar with general office procedure so that work and communications can flow through your office effectively and efficiently.

7) There is a basic difference between a business that is product oriented and one—like a professional tax practice—that is service oriented.

8) A product—be it food, furniture, or a house—is something tangible: you can smell it, see it, touch or hold it. But a service, very often, regardless of how

great the client benefits may be, falls more into the realm of the intangible, the immeasurable, and it's harder for clients to perceive the time and effort which is expended on their behalf. Therefore, the quality of your service—your own appearance, your office appearance, the courtesies and amenities, the way you treat and remember clients—all these features play a more pronounced role in service professions because these are aspects of your practice that are more "tangible." These are the facets of your practice that clients can more easily relate to, understand, measure, picture, and even hold on to.

9) These considerations should not infringe, in any way, upon the competence and skill of your technical know-how. It is only meant to point out the importance of courteous and respectful quality service, which, we could say, is the "heart" of your practice, whereas properly administering the intricacies of taxes and tax law is the "mind" of your practice. Both—heart and mind—are necessary if you are going to project the overall positive image of a tax professional.

10) Remember: when you focus on current clients, and gain their trust, confidence, and satisfaction, they will not only remain loyal to you but will recommend you wholeheartedly to others as well.

# Chapter 9

# Tax Return Procedure

*The art of personal efficiency... involves weaving the cables of constructive habit so that right action will become automatic. In sports and in business—good habits mark the champion.*
**Wilferd A. Peterson**

*Little by little does the trick.*
**Aesop**

Step one in preparing a client's income tax return involves the client interview. During the interview you should try to gather all the data you need to prepare the return, thereby minimizing any time you might spend backtracking or requesting additional follow-up material. Many practitioners prepare a special form in advance listing all the items they might need. This form becomes part of every initial interview.

Make it a practice, then, to always process and complete all tax returns as quickly as possible—without sacrificing the quality on which you built your reputation.

If possible, have your clients make a pre-scheduled appointment before coming in. This will save them waiting time and it will put you at ease as well. Get a desk calendar or an appointment book, or use this convenient feature on your computer, and record the date, day, and hour of any scheduled meeting. Many smartphones and mobile devices coordinate with your desktop computer's calendar via an Internet website, making it easy to see your schedule and make on-the-run changes as needed. This allows you quick access to your pending appointments even when not sitting at your desk. Obviously for those cases that involve more extensive transactions, you will have to allot more time.

Many tax consultants do not wait for their clients to contact them every season. Instead, they write or call their clients in advance, and set a convenient time to meet. Bear in mind, though, that except for rural areas, you will not be able to make appointments if it is too early in the season. In fact, if your reminder letters go out too soon you increase the chances of your clients not responding to you, so you have to learn how to precisely time this sort of correspondence.

## Client Information You Will Need

When making an appointment with a client, advise him in advance of the records, documents, and figures you will need to properly prepare the return. You don't want clients to have to come back for a second visit just because they forgot to bring the W-2 forms. Here is a general list of most (but by no means all) of the documents you will need:

- All W-2 forms received from the taxpayer's employers.
- All 1099's, 1098's etc.
- If the client owns rental property, he or she should bring a list of all rental receipts and expenditures.
- Complete itemized list of personal expenditures such as medical expenses, contributions, taxes and interest paid, casualty losses, child and dependent care expenses, alimony payments, and job related expenses (educational, work clothes, union dues, travel, transportation, and moving expenses, etc.). Ideally, the client will have added everything up on a spreadsheet or calculator tape, but this is not required. It does save a lot of meeting time though.
- In cases where a client sold any stocks, bonds, real estate or other property, you will need complete information such as broker's slips, or closing statements, etc. The best account information comes from the monthly brokerage statements or the year-end statement that covers the previous calendar from January to December. Also request any and all information regarding the original cost and date of purchase. You must impress upon the client the fact that the more complete his figures and records are, the better prepared your return will be, and the more money you may be able to save him in taxes. For estimating

---

*Remind them you need their 1099-Bs.*

*You need to know all of their stock transactions, even if there were no gains or losses.*

# Chapter 9: Tax Return Procedure

taxes on long-term investment sales, the client will need the purchase documentation from previous years to properly calculate owed taxes, so make sure the client knows this.

Also instruct your client to make note of doubtful items and to discuss them with you. Tell him to include any item that has even the remotest possibility of being an allowable deduction. Such a list may point to sizable deductions that are often overlooked because the taxpayer mistakenly assumes they are not deductible. Bear in mind that many clients are apt to forget or overlook deductible expenses, so you should really regard this list as your starting point for a more exhaustive search of such items. A thorough checklist (as found in most of the popular tax guides) will be very helpful for this purpose. If you take the time and trouble to make a careful inquiry for all legal deductions and tax saving possibilities, your efforts will be well rewarded.

> Ask if there were any out of the ordinary financial transactions during the last year.

In the case of a professional person or of someone in business, you must have complete records or statements of all business income and expenses. Even better, get their accounting books if available. If you can get such a list from your client, it will simplify matters considerably. Many taxpayers, however, keep scant records, if any, and you may have to reconstruct their deductible expenses from check stubs, bills, and vouchers. Naturally, you have every right to charge for the extra time and effort involved.

> Suggest using Quicken, QuickBooks, or other accounting software to help keep records.
>
> If they have a business (Schedule C) ask for the general ledger to help ensure all claimed expenses are business related and not personal.

If your client has complete records, it is not necessary that he bring along canceled checks and receipts to verify the various deductions. However, for reasons we will soon discuss, we recommend that you ask him to indicate next to each listed deduction whether it is based on a check, receipt, other form of proof, or simply on his own estimate. If the item is an estimate, ask for some brief notation of how he arrived at the stated figure.

Finally, you should ask every new client to bring along a copy of last year's return, and if available, of previous returns as well. This is especially necessary in the case of a taxpayer taking a depreciation deduction, since the depreciation rate should be consistent from year to year. Earlier returns should also give you a clue to additional deductions the taxpayer may be entitled to, or they may help you to point out possible deductions or tax saving opportunities that were missed. In the case of previous clients, you should have your own copies of previous returns to refer to.

The importance of the prior year tax return habit cannot be overemphasized, and it will give you a valuable advantage over more experienced and better-known competitors. Many accountants and tax consultants merely ask the client a few questions and fill out the return, without bothering to make a thorough search for tax savings. They thereby fail to give the client the full benefit of their expertise, and they also miss out on a possible fee and practice-building opportunity as well.

> Many items carry forward from year to year:
> - Net operating losses.
> - Capital losses.
> - Unused charitable deductions.

### Should you make use of a client questionnaire?

Many tax specialists prefer to use a pre-printed questionnaire when interviewing clients to reduce the likelihood of omitting important items. Others feel that such a questionnaire gives the meeting an assembly-line look and detracts from the all-important personal touch.

Some practitioners have found a compromise solution. They distribute questionnaires to clients before they come in. This helps them gather the necessary information, assuring them that nothing has been overlooked, while it facilitates the return procedure. Mailing such a questionnaire to all previous clients at the beginning of the season, along with a friendly cover letter, can be a helpful reminder, and also serves to invite the client back—and hopefully—early in the season.

However, keep in mind that questionnaires are only as good as their instructions. If the forms are not clear in what a client should write on the form, the information won't be useful. The best way to make sure your instructions work is to test them on someone who is not a tax preparer or an accountant. With a first read, the test person will quickly identify what makes sense or what doesn't. However, don't assume the test person will identify the problem correctly. You will need to make sure the person describes to you what he thinks the instructions say. Then you will know if they will work or not on the average client.

Always be sensitive and use tact in questioning a client. Instead of asking, *"Are you still married, Mr. Jones?"* you could say, *"Your wife's name is Betty, isn't it?"* Or, rather than ask whether a client's sick mother is still alive, say something like, *"Now last year you claimed an exemption for your mother..."* Leave it to the client to confirm your current information rather than seem probing.

Another instance that requires delicate handling is the case of female clients nearing the age at which they are entitled to an additional standard deduction, or they may be affected by one of the other age-related provisions. Instead of asking, "Are you 65 yet, Mrs. Brown?" simply ask for her birth date and do the figuring yourself. Even though the question is factual, people still have sensitive egos, especially about their age.

In other words, in certain sensitive areas, it pays to be discreet.

### Reviewing Last Year's Return

It is generally a good idea to quickly run through last year's tax return. You then become familiar with the client's tax picture and you reduce the risk of omissions and oversights. It also helps to point out and explain to the client any necessary changes due to new or changed regulations. Suppose an important deduction always claimed by your client is suddenly eliminated due to legal changes, it is better to show her that

# Chapter 9: Tax Return Procedure

she can no longer do so, than to explain this fact after she questions the unexpected jump in her tax bill.

Oftentimes, during the preparation of a return or even before you start, a client may ask: *"Well, how does it look? Will I have to pay additional tax or will I get a refund?"* Unless the situation is quite obvious, do not hazard a guess. You may have to eat your own words. This is particularly appalling when you assure the client that everything is fine and he can count on a nice refund, and then you find yourself having to inform him that you miscalculated, resulting in the embarrassing explanation that instead of a refund he has to pay additional taxes. Do everything you can to avoid such embarrassing moments.

## Preparing the Return

Once you are sure you have all the information you need you can start on the return. Indeed, if you use a computer you could begin to enter the information even before and fill in as you go along. But you'll generally find it more efficient and less error-prone to assemble all the data first.

On the other hand, if you prepare tax returns manually (and a surprising number are still being done that way) you have little choice but to hold off until you are completely ready. You don't want to risk having to do an entire return over because of one missing or overlooked piece of information.

No matter which method you use, look over last year's return (or the 'pro- forma', if your software provides one) to make sure that the basic client information has not changed, or to note any changes. Then carefully go over the information your client provided.

> Unless you plan on only preparing a handful of returns consider purchasing tax software. In selecting a software program try them out. Many offer a trial version. Make sure you are comfortable with it, and can use it with relative ease.
>
> Make sure the software company offers support for any complex issues that may come up.

### For manually prepared returns we recommend the following procedure:

Fill out the first draft of the client's tax return using the form and method you have chosen. Go over all calculations and check carefully for errors. Such mistakes, if carried over to the final return, are particularly embarrassing. If you are filling out the form by hand using a pencil for the draft copy will facilitate corrections and erasures.

Make an exact copy of the corrected form first. This is the copy you file with the IRS and it should be neatly written in ink, or typed. Attach all necessary IRS schedules, statements, and W-2 Forms, if your client is employed.

As you gain experience, you will find it more convenient to prepare the simpler returns directly on the tax forms. For the more complicated ones, you may first want to assemble the data on a worksheet and then transcribe it directly to the return forms.

However, we suggest that in preparing more complex returns, you prepare a pencil draft first to facilitate changes and corrections.

Remember, when your return is neat and legible, it gives it a professional look and promotes accuracy, helping reduce IRS audits and questioning.

Most tax practitioners prepare three copies of each return, accompanying schedules, and the various attachments. One set is for your own office files, one is for the IRS, and one is for the client. Your having a copy is a safeguard in case the client loses his. Such a procedure is therefore highly recommended.

There is another important advantage to having a copy of every return available in your files. Very often, a client will call you with an urgent question that he needs answered immediately. He may have received a routine IRS inquiry, or have a simple tax problem, or he may want to know why all of his fellow employees received refunds while he paid an additional tax (he already forgot about the extra income he had last year, from which no tax was withheld). You will agree that a response of..."Hold on a minute while I get your file" is preferable to..."Well, I don't know; I would first have to see your return."

With copy equipment being so efficient and effective, most practitioners opt for this method over any other. Incidentally, any good quality copy is acceptable for filing, as long as the signatures are affixed **after** the copy is made.

Before filing the return or delivering it to the client, make sure you proofread it carefully. If you have more than one person preparing returns, it's a good idea to have the proofreader be someone who did not prepare the return. This will automatically serve as a check on the first person's work.

> Most, if not all, tax software has a "once over" feature that checks and flags for possible errors, questionable transactions, or issues on a return.

**A note of warning:** Some practitioners feel that computer-prepared returns do not have to be checked over. Unfortunately, this is not so. Computers are unforgiving, and the slightest misstep or omission can easily result in a return that's off by hundreds or thousands of dollars. So exercise caution—especially until you've developed the "feel" that alerts the experienced tax professional when something is amiss.

The proofreader should also be instructed to make sure that all required schedules and attachments (such as wage statements, supplementary explanations, etc.) are attached to the return. You do not want to have pieces of the return floating around your office after it has been filed or given to a client.

One of the more common errors to occur in filing a return is the inadvertent omission of one or more of the supporting schedules or statements. This triggers a delay in processing the return and it may, occasionally, even trigger an audit. One way to avoid this problem is to inconspicuously number all forms and attachments in sequence. Then, when collating the return, it will be easy to see if one or more of the numbered sheets are missing.

While many practitioners mail the completed return to the client for his signature, some personally deliver the return, while others ask the client to pick it up. The last two methods enable the practitioner to collect his fee when handing over the return. On the other hand, doing so may mean spending valuable tax-season time in conversation with the client. Nevertheless, where a client is habitually late in paying his bill this procedure should be considered.

When delivering the return to the client, make sure to give her explicit instructions as to what she should do. Tell her where to sign, where to mail it, and when. Tell her whether a check is to be attached, and if so, for how much, and how the check is to be made out. If it is a joint return, make sure the spouse signs it too. Many practitioners use a written or printed sheet containing these instructions. If the return is mailed to the client rather than handed to her, such an instruction sheet becomes more of a necessity.

Many consultants ask each client to mail his or her own return to the appropriate tax authority. This puts the responsibility squarely where it belongs—on the client. On the other hand, if you undertake to mail the return, and for some reason it does not arrive, or the client does not receive his refund fast enough, she may suspect that you delayed, or never mailed the return.

We do, however, suggest that you follow up with the client a few days before the filing deadline—by phone, mail, or e-mail—to make sure the return actually went out. Clients will also appreciate the personal concern on your part.

A practice followed by some practitioners, and one we highly recommend, is to not only provide pre-addressed envelopes (typed, rubber stamped, or printed) for mailing the return, but to also pay the proper postage on the envelope. This provides the kind of special service the client remembers, and which indicates to him that you are doing professional, quality work. The postage is a small charge compared to the entire fee collected, but it can go a long way towards proof of customer service. This stamped envelope, of course, enables the client to mail his return immediately after signing it without having to hunt for stamps or worry about having sufficient postage.

Such thoughtful consideration on your part can only help your practice to grow—both in quality and in quantity. It's a small investment that can bring a handsome return.

# A Brief Look at Electronic Tax Services

Many practitioners employ the methods discussed above, but the trend for filing returns is undeniably in the direction of computerized electronic services. In this section we will discuss the IRS e-file.

The IRS e-file is a way to file a tax return electronically to the IRS using an Authorized IRS e-file Provider. With this method you do not have to worry about the return being lost or delayed in the mail. Upon receipt of all return information, the IRS quickly and automatically checks for errors or other missing information. The error rate for electronic returns is less than 1 percent. Within 48 hours of electronic transmission, the IRS acknowledges receipt of the return. Only IRS e-file options provide this assurance. Best of all, perhaps, is the fact that IRS e-file means fast refunds—in fact, refunds take half the time as when filing with paper and are even faster with Direct Deposit.

## The Basics about IRS *e-file* System

Any tax professional that is accepted into the electronic filing program qualifies as an "Authorized IRS *e-file* Provider." He or she also becomes an ERO, the Electronic Return Originator, who is authorized to file a return electronically to the IRS. So as a tax professional you can prepare a client's tax return as well as electronically file the return.

You also sign the electronic return by either using a Self-Select Personal Identification Number (PIN) for *e-file*, which results in a completely paperless return, or by actually signing a signature document—Form 8453.

> There are cases of returns being rejected for reasons of:
> - Fraud—if someone already filed a return under the same social security #. Contact the IRS Fraud Unit and you will need to file a paper return.
> - Mismatched Information—S.S. #, DOB, and names must match or return may be rejected.

After signing the return using a Self-Select PIN, or Form 8453, the designated ERO transmits the return to the IRS for processing. At the IRS, the return is automatically checked by computers for errors and omissions. If, for some reason, it cannot be processed, it is sent back to you for further clarification. You then resubmit the file and within 48 hours the IRS acknowledges receipt and acceptance of the file for processing. If a refund is due, your client can expect to receive it in about three weeks. If taxes are owed, it can be paid by check, direct debit (automatic withdrawal) directly from your bank, or by credit card.

An ever-growing number of tax professionals offer IRS e-file to their clients, and in most states (perhaps, soon, in all states) state returns can be filed with federal returns at the same time. With regard to charges for electronic filing, some practitioners do charge a fee for providing this service, while others do not.

In any event, the electronic service—along with being the current trend—is also the fastest and most accurate way to file a tax return.

# Chapter 10

# Streamlining Your Office Procedure

*Time is a man's most precious possession—his most precious commodity. To take a man's time is to take a portion of his life. To give a man some of your time is to give him a portion of yours.*
**Margaret E. Mulac**

*The time to repair the roof is when the sun is shining.*
**John F. Kennedy**

Many tax practitioners, as well as other professionals, believe that their sole concern should be to attract as many clients as possible. They feel that once they have a steady clientele their problems are over, and the rest will somehow take care of itself. This simple assumption leaves out the fact that someone has to do the work for the clients to pay. It is a concept that is far from the truth, for unless you institute effective office procedures at the very start, you will find yourself constantly engaged in an uphill struggle. As your workload increases, you will find yourself steadily overwhelmed with just the paper work alone. So the time to plan for an orderly, manageable flow of work—in and through your office—is at the beginning, before it ever becomes a problem.

This chapter begins with the concept of "managing your office information," primarily by way of a filing system. We begin by discussing the more conventional way of filing which is still very much in use, and then move on to discuss computerizing your office information. Many practitioners find themselves using both systems to various degrees—each according to that practitioner's personal style and needs.

## Your Office Filing System

Every office has a habit of generating countless pieces of paper, and filing is a process for organizing and storing such information. It is often referred to as "the memory bank of any business." Therefore, readily retrieving and replacing information is an essential key to effective office procedure. A good filing system, at the heart of your practice, shows that you are well on the way to operating a smooth running tax facility.

Speaking in general terms, filing procedures include:

- Your client files
- Your tax forms, schedules, and related office supplies
- Your personal files and reference materials

In most offices, client files are maintained in alphabetical order by a client's last name, even though some larger firms using computerized services are converting to an account numbering system. However, for most purposes, you will find that the alphabetical system is the fastest and easiest to use. We suggest you use a legal size folder for each client; in this folder you keep all copies of his tax returns, related worksheets and papers, communications, and everything else pertaining to his case. Wherever you can, clip or staple items together; that will make working with the file even easier.

In the case of a business, if it is not incorporated, the file should be kept under the client's name; if it is a corporation, file it under the corporate name. Partnership papers should be filed under the partnership trade name. A great time saver is to mark the client's social security number or business ID number prominently on the outside of the file. This not only guards against mix-ups where clients have similar names, but also gives you access to the number at a glance; because very often all you need is the client's number.

Remember, however, to protect client information in your filing system, particularly social security numbers. A business can be held responsible and liable for any negligence in allowing someone's financial information to land in the wrong hands and be used for fraud or theft. If there is no ability to hold onto the files anymore or they need to be removed, then at least thoroughly shred the documents and folders with the sensitive data on them.

# Chapter 10: Streamlining Your Office Procedure

It is important to keep filing procedures as simple as possible. This may not be of such vital importance as long as you run a one-man office and have everything at your fingertips, but as you add office assistants a complicated filing procedure can become hopelessly confusing. Therefore, it is important to be consistent throughout. Whatever filing system you choose for client information, use that system exclusively. Don't intersperse name, subject, or number files within one system.

Generally speaking, federal, state, and city tax returns should be filed together, unless the papers are so bulky that separate folders are required. Even in that case, all tax returns for each year should be kept together.

As for the sequence of material inside a general folder, it can either follow a "date" sequence or an "alphabetical" sequence—whichever you find more useful. But again, be consistent in whichever you choose.

Some practitioners use color-coded files: the regular manila for individual returns, and various colored ones for different types of business entities. Color-coded files are also helpful in preventing and locating misfiles.

Another handy type of folder to use is the one with built-in fasteners, to assure you that no papers get lost or misplaced. When using file folders with built-in fasteners, some use the right hand fastener for all current material (i.e. items still being processed), and the left hand fastener for all completed work (copies of all returns, and so on). Eventually, as the left hand side fills, the material is transferred to storage files.

As we mentioned earlier, it is imperative that you keep all worksheets, notations, and other pertinent supporting material in your client's file. These documents become very important when trying to figure out how a number was arrived at months or years after the fact. We also recommend that you indicate all supplementary schedules on your file copy of the return, or on your working papers: the nature of substantiating evidence (or an explanation of how an estimate was arrived at) available to support the claimed deduction in the event of an audit. Although only a small percentage of returns are audited, there is always the chance that any particular return will be the one so honored.

There is no better way to prove your competence, thoroughness, and foresight—to both client and IRS examiners—than by having this vital information at your fingertips if and when the need arises. More information about preparing for and handling IRS or state tax examinations will be found in a separate chapter later.

If, in time, a client file gets too thick and overburdened, break it down into sub files. Create another folder to avoid important papers getting crushed or becoming illegible.

A good filing system should also include a schedule for finally discarding unnecessary records, or at least of relegating such material to an inactive file. In businesses this is called a "retention schedule." With this in mind, try to keep all records, including your working papers, for at least seven years. In most cases, however, records can be moved out of the active files after two or three years, when the likelihood of an audit becomes remote. If file cabinets become overcrowded, you can obtain inexpensive fiberboard transfer files for inactive records. These storage files can be stacked or stored on shelves, at a considerable savings in the cost of filing equipment.

> When returning files, have the client sign a note stating that the files were returned.

Make sure to return to every client all material that is not required in your file. First of all, this prevents your files from becoming bulky and clogged. Secondly, it eliminates many frantic calls from clients in search of a particular document. There is always the chance that an important paper may get lost or misplaced in your office. To protect yourself, always put a note on your client's records stating what was returned to the client along with when it was returned.

**Note to computerized preparers**: Suppose you have all your returns on computer, should you still produce and retain paper copies? What about supporting documents, worksheets, notations, etc.?

Most practitioners will agree that a file copy of every return prepared should be printed out. When a question arises about a return or any particular item, you may find it preferable to access or review it on paper than on the screen.

With regard to long-term retention of return copies, the jury is still out: Some destroy them after a year or two when their likelihood of being needed becomes more remote; others hold on to them indefinitely. Our feeling is that if you're short on filing space and you have a truly reliable backup system in place for your computer files you can probably discard the returns after a year or so. Otherwise don't touch them. We've heard too many horror stories about crucial files inexplicably disappearing into cyberspace.

Supporting documents, worksheets and other pertinent papers should be filed away and retained for as long as they may be relevant.

### A Few Filing Tips

1) Straight cut folders, where the exposed tab runs the entire length of the folder, are the most versatile, and can be used in shelf or cabinet filing. Any size label can be used and it can hold various pertinent information because the tab is so large.

2) Make sure you label each folder properly and legibly so others can also readily refer to the files, and be sure to label file drawers properly as well.

3) You may find that a separate personal file for your own documents and records will work more effectively if you use an alphabetical system, by subject (i.e. Advertising... Bills... Car... Checking Account... Entertainment... Insurance... Medical... Office supplies... Speeches... etc.—the list goes on, each practitioner according to his needs).

4) Try to designate a specific time of day or week to sort, file, or discard unneeded papers.

## Tracking Computer Files

We are still quite far from a "paperless" office, but so much information is likely to come your way on a daily basis that you will certainly benefit from "electronic help" to organize and keep on top of the information you will need at your fingertips—when the time comes to retrieve it. When you purchase software. or a "software suite" which contains a variety of convenient programs, make sure that "information management software" is part of the package.

In the course of any given work week you may come across names, ideas, articles, facts, people, resources, and other contacts that may prove beneficial to your practice. You'll want to keep track of this information (or ultimately discard some of it). The right software provides the solution to this problem. Here again, as we mentioned in a previous chapter, it will be helpful to speak to colleagues or computer experts to find out which software will serve your needs best. Some of the software programs come with well-organized, predefined structures for entering and keeping track of specific information; while others allow you to more freely enter all the information you want and let you organize it in the way that best suits you. You may want to test some of these programs first hand before you decide on which to purchase. The good news is that today's software is easier to learn and easier to use, and you can more readily tailor it to fit your particular needs.

Here are some tips that may help you with your computer files:

- Create a file for each of your clients. Each file should then contain your client's name, address, phone numbers, fax, e-mail address (if applicable), notes, and any other pertinent information.

- As your client base grows, you may want to further subdivide these files into "past" and "current" or "active" and "inactive," or in some other way—such as the type of work they do.

- Try to keep your computer and paper records related to each other, so if you use certain category names for one, try to keep a corresponding system with the other.

- Just as with paper files, try to eliminate clutter by clearing out unnecessary electronic information on a regular basis.
- Keep disks you use frequently within reach of your computer. There are special cases and disk storage units to serve this purpose. Always remember to back up the contents of your hard drive onto some other format—disks or CD-ROM drive.

Whether you are working with paper files or computer files, certain principles are always in place: Set up a regular time for putting information where it belongs; use equipment and supplies—be it folders, filing cabinets, or software programs—that make storing and locating the information you need quick and easy.

## Time Management: Making Good Use of Your Available Time

We all have the same amount of time each day to work with and no more. The difference comes in, however, in how each of us handles this precious resource. Although some seem to make better use of their time at work than others, there are principles and techniques you can master to help improve the way you handle your time. We will discuss some of these techniques in this section; it will be worth your while to give them a try, for here are the skills that bear directly on your professional progress.

### A Time Log

*Make sure you are getting paid for the "time" you put in to a client.*

*Consider time spent for:*
- *Follow up work,*
- *Answering correspondence,*
- *Amending returns (due to the client's error).*

Keeping a temporary time log will allow you to see how you are currently spending your time. For a week or two, try to keep track of what you are doing. List your work activities and record how long it takes you to perform each activity. Also make note of interruptions, breaks, how long they took, and if they were necessary or if those activities could have been handled in some other way.

Keeping such a time log of your work habits will give you a reasonable picture of how you are presently handling your work day. After a week or two, examine your records. Study them, evaluate them, and see if and where there are areas that could benefit from some measure of improvement. Then, when you implement any time-management techniques, you will be in a better position to apply them to specific areas of weakness. This may be an exercise that you want to repeat every year, just to ensure that you are continuously using your time wisely.

### Planning Ahead

The technique we will examine more closely is simply referred to as "planning ahead." We will break the material down into three parts:

- Listing activities,
- Setting priorities, and
- Scheduling.

Bear in mind that the problem with using time is not what to do. We usually have enough things to do to occupy our time. The problem is really one of how to get all the jobs done timely. To accomplish this the technique of "planning ahead" can be a great help. Setting aside some measure of time to plan now can save you hours of confusion later.

## Listing Activities

Plan your day in advance by beginning your workday with a written list of all you intend to take care of that day. Depending on the type of person you are, you may find it easier to do this early in the morning before the workday begins, or perhaps on the previous night, before you retire. But do not get into the habit of devising this list once you get to your office or work area. This particular technique is more effective when you arrive at work with the list complete, and you already know exactly what you have to do.

In this regard, planning ahead serves you like a blueprint serves a builder: once your plan is on paper—laid out in front of you like a blueprint—it becomes your challenge to structure the day in a way that best approximates that design. Of course, all this is easier said than done, but having it in writing, in the form of a plan to carry out, provides you with direction, a pattern, a formula…a map to follow, if you will. Having your plan in writing also makes the tasks more concrete and tangible. In a way, it is as if they are already somewhere along the way to completion. Having written them down means you've already started working.

Another benefit to devising lists is that you will develop the good habit of actually "visualizing" the day ahead. Later, as you raise your sights and develop a longer-range view, you will better envision the week ahead, the month ahead, and even the year ahead. In conjunction with this you can make use of any number of helpful calendars—from pocket size to wall size to computerized—depending on what serves you best. On these convenient calendars that provide you with "a day at a glance," "a week at a glance," or "a month at a glance," you can chart or fill in the various tasks you know you have to do.

Developing this kind of "vision" is a beneficial by-product generated by the power of planning ahead.

## Setting Priorities

The next step is really a refinement of the list you made in the previous section.

Obviously, not all the things you may have listed are of equal importance. Some items may be pressing and carry a higher level of priority or urgency, while others can be pushed off for a day or more, though it might be nice to take care of them today. To determine which items fall into which category, you have to go over your list and prioritize—to indicate high, medium, or low levels of priority. Then you know which items must be taken care of first and which can follow later.

## Scheduling

Now that you have listed and prioritized your daily or weekly tasks, you still have to schedule the tasks into your time of day.

> Schedule appointments and leave enough time to accomplish the actual work.

To "schedule" a task is to determine when to do it and how much time to give it. Of course, with time and experience you will become an ever-better judge, able to determine with relative accuracy how much time to allot to certain activities. You will also become intimately familiar with your work habits, able to assess when in the day you accomplish the most and when you accomplish the least. All of these considerations will affect the way you finally schedule certain tasks.

> Be prepared for "crisis management." Client may call with an urgent situation, and you may need to re-schedule other work.

You will also quickly learn that you cannot control the entire day. Hardly anything works out exactly as we plan it, so you will have to factor "flexibility" into your schedule. You will have to leave some room for the unexpected, slots of in-between time to take care of certain "unforeseeables." This must also include some quiet time for yourself: to rest, return calls, respond to the mail, or catch up on other unfinished chores.

Planning ahead can be a helpful technique in streamlining your office procedure, and like any worthwhile habit, it will involve some initial investment of time to properly cultivate. However, once you have mastered the system, you will see that making the list will only take minutes each day, but these are minutes that will literally save you hours.

There are a number of excellent software programs available that can help you with scheduling (both tasks and appointments) and time management, creating lists of things to do, keeping track of unfinished projects, and reminding you of upcoming due dates and deadlines. However, they require the same amount of self-discipline, investment of time and dedication as the more traditional methods. Unless you put in the necessary time, effort, and attention to make the required entries and keep them current, the most sophisticated programs in the world will be of no use to you.

## Tax Preparation and Efficient Use of Time

When performing the actual tax document preparation make sure you have all the required papers and documents such as W-2 Forms, 1099's, etc., as well as all supplementary data such as rental income, expenses, securities transactions, and so on. This will help you avoid the common practice of interrupting work on one return because vital information is missing, then switching to another return, and then having to go back to the first one. This is a time-consuming routine, because every time you switch from one client's file to another's, you have to stop and reorient yourself.

Try to anticipate "peak season" workloads by doing as much work as possible beforehand. Some practitioners even prepare tax return kits for each client before the season begins. In this kit they assemble all the anticipated tax forms this client will need, and other worksheets or information that the previous record shows will be required. Some go even further and "head up" their work-sheets and schedules with the client's name, social security number, and taxable year—in order to speed work along during the tax season. You can also prepare carry-forward schedules in advance, for capital losses, charitable contributions, and investment credit carryovers.

> **STOP**
> Leave time to relax and clear your head throughout the day. It helps!

Avoid wasting time searching through files by making sure that all related records are stored together.

Make a preliminary list of all forms and additional information you will need for a particular return. This too, will help avoid annoying interruptions while the information is gathered or forms obtained.

Here is an idea to help ensure that you have all the necessary forms on hand. Every time you use one of the less common forms, make a note of it on a special list. Before the next tax season pull out this list. If you retained these clients, you will most likely need the same forms again, so with your list as a guide, order sufficient quantities of the various forms you need.

Some practitioners find that they increase efficiency by evenly dividing their day, setting aside one part for client interviews, and using the other part to work—without interruptions—preparing returns.

### Time Management: a Few Practical Tips

1) It's part of human nature to drift toward easier tasks, postponing the more difficult, problematic assignments. But this usually tends to aggravate the work situation. It's psychologically advantageous to deal with the more difficult matters first; then you tend to feel so good that you become more effective at everything else you do that day. With the burden lifted, you are more efficient in the way you handle your other jobs.

2) Be organized: Here is one vital area where time and space intersect. By knowing where things are, you will be amazed at how much time you save, not having to hunt every item down.

3) Unnecessary interruptions can disrupt your momentum and dilute your efforts and powers of concentration, so you have to develop a method of handling interruptions. If you have an assistant that person can screen calls or take messages for you. If you work alone, then you can leave a polite message on an answering machine at certain hours of the day. But you must develop a strategy that enables you to devote certain blocks of time to uninterrupted work.

4) To overcome procrastination, try to establish deadlines for yourself—for both beginning and ending a task. Also, reward yourself and others (i.e. family members) at certain points of progress or at the completion of a task.

5) In dealing with mail the goal is to handle each piece of correspondence one time only. If at all possible, do what has to be done right away, rather than reading it, putting it down, and then having to start over with it at some later point in time.

6) When you open a piece of mail try to ascertain immediately where it belongs, whether in the circular file or some other appropriate bin or file. For example, put all checks away where they belong for later deposit.

7) If it is something you can handle on the spot—with a brief note or telephone call—then do so. If you can't, try to develop the habit of putting everything in its proper slot immediately, to be taken care of in its appropriate time, rather than repeating the cycle of having to senselessly read and re-read your mail, thereby wasting precious time.

8) Economize your movements: If you have errands to run or traveling to do, try to plan your day so that you can take care of as many stops as you can on a single outing, whether it's trips to the post office, the bank or the office supply.

If you happen to be waiting somewhere for a period of time—for example, in a dentist's or in a client's office—you may find that there are certain tasks you can take care of while you wait: sorting, calculating, bills, making brief notes, scheduling, or composing a letter—especially with laptop computers. Waiting time can be put to productive, creative use to handle important or subsidiary tasks that might otherwise cut into prime working time.

Remember our discussion earlier about the virtual office concept on a cloud platform? It's during dead times when you're in transit that such tools provide their greatest value and flexibility. By being able to reach office files and client information from just about anywhere with a fully-equipped laptop and a broadband air card, you can continue working and billing your time even when sitting on a train commuting or at the airport

# Chapter 10: Streamlining Your Office Procedure

waiting for a connection. Even marginal time can help you get more work done in the day, increasing your revenues in the aggregate.

## What Records to Keep

- You should keep a master record (large or medium sized index cards work well) for each client, listing his name, address, telephone number, date you prepared his return, form of return, amount of the fee, and date of payment. These cards will be very valuable to you the following year. You may want to send reminders or post cards to this list, or you may want to advise them that you moved or have a new telephone number. You will also be able to tell at a glance how much you previously charged each client. Of course, today, you may find it far more convenient to keep such files in your computer, or you may wish to use both: paper files as well as computer files. Redundancy is a good practice to be in, especially as a backup for an information loss. Just don't keep the paper cards and computer in the same place. For example, if the office burns down they both get destroyed, regardless of redundancy.

- You may also want to make special notations on some of the cards for future reference. For example: "Wasted time because of incomplete records." "Ask client to bring more detailed lists." "Complicated return, increase fee next time." "Recommended some new clients. Acknowledge." The list can go on…with notations and reminders reflecting each client's situation. You will also find this file to be a veritable gold mine in case you want to sell or merge your practice. These files can either be attached to client folders, or sorted alphabetically in a separate file.

- One form many practitioners and tax firms use is a Master Control Sheet on which they list each client or return, showing the initial interview date or first contact with the client, any follow ups required, date return was completed, fees, etc. This gives you an immediate profile of each client. As your practice grows, such a form can be quite helpful, and with the aid of your computer, these files can be easily updated and modified.

- We also suggest the use of an individual client calendar on which to note the date each client was interviewed in previous years. This enables you to follow up on a client if you haven't heard from him at about the same time in the current year. It's a great help at bringing in clients, and avoiding that last minute rush.

- As a tax practitioner you will be intimately involved in the bookkeeping of others. At the same time you must realize that it's imperative to keep accurate records of your own if your business is to succeed.

> Most tax software programs allow you to print customized lists of information, in a variety of formats.

> Don't use your personal bank accounts for the business.

Aside from providing you with your own income tax information, maintaining accurate records offers you valuable information that can help you see developing trends in your practice. Examining and comparing your records from year to year will reveal to you your practice's strengths and weaknesses. Armed with such vital information you can better chart the future of your practice.

> Make sure to use appropriate software to track the financial information for your tax preparation business.

So for your own income and expense record, be sure to get a good, easy-to-use cashbook, or utilize this feature on your computer. Simply list all receipts for each day with the names of the clients, along with expenditures and brief explanatory notes, if necessary. At the end of the day or week, transfer the totals to a separate "summary page." It's also a good idea to do your own bookkeeping regularly, so that paperwork and confusion do not get out of hand.

## Keep Records of Communications with Clients

In the course of your practice you will make and receive innumerable phone calls—both to and from, and on behalf of—your clients. It is highly recommended that you keep a record of these calls, especially the more important ones. Some clients require an inordinate amount of time on the phone, and unless you keep a record, you will never be compensated for this time. Furthermore, you will receive a lot of information over the phone and unless you record it immediately you may forget it. In addition to causing you embarrassment, you may have to do much of the work over again. So if you choose to write such information down, it may be worth your while to keep a telephone log.

> Print out and file, or back-up, email correspondence with clients. It is a great way to document what the client said or sent you.

A telephone log is charted paper that allows you to keep a careful track of who called, when they called, the length and reason for the call, what resulted from the call, and you can also make note of any long distance charges, to get reimbursed, if that's appropriate. On the other hand, some practitioners use a tape recorder or attach a recording device to the phone to record such information. In that case you should advise the client that the conversation is being taped. In some states it can be a felony to record a conversation without the other party's explicit permission.

Like many doctors, some practitioners establish special telephone hours during which time they do business over the phone. At other times, calls are answered by a secretary or an answering machine that records the information, or assures the client that the call will be returned as soon as possible. This avoids interruptions and also enables you to better serve that client by pulling out his file and looking over his papers to refresh your memory, before you return the call.

### Complete All Work As Soon As Possible

One of the more common human shortcomings that may interfere with the efficient functioning of your tax practice is the tendency to procrastinate—to put off completing a return until the last moment.

When a return is prepared, let's say, in February, and a question arises requiring further research, or you find yourself in need of more information, you then have plenty of time to do the research or obtain the missing data. On the other hand, if you are rapidly closing in on an April 15th deadline, or are in the midst of the pre-deadline crunch, you may be tempted to skip or abbreviate the necessary research or even prepare the return on the basis of incomplete information.

Now if a client, in spite of your urging, insists on bringing you his material at the last moment, he has only himself to blame if he does not receive the superior service you are prepared to give him. But the client who comes to you before the rush starts, who makes it a point to assemble all relevant information and documents early in the season, has every right to insist that you give his return the most thorough and painstaking attention possible. He deserves no less!

Hand in hand with the tendency of putting off a return until the last moment is the habit of many to begin working on a return and then leave it incomplete for days or even weeks at a time. What happens all too often is that, to save time, the tax consultant takes down basic information and then puts the whole folder or file away until he has a more opportune moment to complete the return. However, when he finally does get around to it, he must go over all the information, reorient himself with the client's facts and circumstances, and try to reconstruct what was said or done until this point in time. Not only is this wasteful and inefficient, but you invite costly error, and the risk of overlooking or forgetting vital facts and information.

In short: the best time to prepare a return is immediately or as soon as possible after the client interview, or after you receive the necessary information. If you must interrupt because some facts are missing, make every effort to obtain the information as quickly as possible, so you can proceed with the return while all the information is still fresh in your mind.

## Getting the Most Out of Your Telephone

The telephone with its incessant ringing and disregard for your schedule can be both friend and foe. Employed judiciously, it is a tremendous timesaver and goodwill builder, but without proper safeguards, it can be a disruptive and annoying intruder.

First of all, make sure that you—or whoever else answers the phone in your office—cultivates a pleasant telephone personality. Remember that the phone is an extension of yourself and your office. Clients and prospective clients contact you more often by phone than in person, which means that it can create impressive amounts of good or ill will. No matter how busy you or your secretaries are, and regardless of how ill-mannered or unreasonable the person on the other end of the line is, every call must be treated graciously and politely.

At the same time, you owe your clients your full attention while you are with them. If a call comes in during a conference or interview, try to keep the call as brief as possible. Better yet, tell the caller you will return his call as soon as you are free—and make it a point to do so. It can be annoying to an immediately present client to have his conversation with you constantly interrupted by phone calls. Even worse, he may suspect that you'll be charging him for the time you are spending on the phone with someone else.

If you have a secretary, let him screen your calls and explain tactfully that you are presently engaged and will call back shortly. Likewise, if you have to call a client on a matter that may take more than a few minutes, ask him first whether he has the time to talk now or whether you should call him back later.

## Business Correspondence

Handling correspondence is an important part of regular office procedure. Some overlook it as a mundane chore, but every piece of communication reflects on a tax office and its professionalism.

> Try and use email (short, sweet, and to the point), and you can print it out for your records to document who said what, complete with the time and date.

You will often be called upon to communicate your thoughts in writing—either with letters you initiate or letters you respond to—so this is an essential skill, the mastery of which will help you immensely in the smooth running of your practice.

Remember too: the letters you send—their style, content, and appearance—are extensions of your office personality. They are your thoughts and voice enclosed in an envelope, and in some cases, the impression a letter makes can spell the loss or gain of an important client.

Here then are some practical thoughts and guidelines to help you write more effective business letters:

1) You can write a good business letter and still sound natural and relaxed. You can deliver your message in a businesslike manner, without sounding stiff. For example: Instead of writing "according to our records," use "I received your letter." Instead of "due to the fact that," use "because." Instead of "in the amount of," use "for." Instead of "at the present time," use "now."

2) Be pleasant and positive in your writing. Sprinkle the letter with courtesies. Effective correspondence can go a long way to strengthening a business rela-

tionship. Instead of writing "We have received your recent forms," use "Thank you for the forms you sent." At the same time, be tactful and diplomatic when relaying unpleasant messages.

3) Be personal: use the pronouns I, we, and you, whenever appropriate.

4) Before you start to write, be clear about the purpose of your letter: what do you want the reader to know or do? Spend a few minutes thinking about the purpose, jot down some notes or make an outline; then turn it into a rough draft. The final letter will then be much easier to write. Obviously, a word processing program (that may even include a number of letter templates) makes letter writing even easier—almost painless.

5) Once you have written the letter, be sure to check it for accuracy. Review all facts and figures to make sure they are correct, and proofread the letter for mistakes in names, spelling, and grammar.

6) Remember: although style, content, and form are important, the real effect of your letter depends upon the words you choose to convey your message. Keep your words clear, simple, and to the point. Write in a friendly tone: businesslike, but not overly formal.

7) Surround the letter with balanced, ample margins, and try to center your letter on the page. If your letter is brief, don't put it high on the page. If your letter is long, don't cram it all onto one sheet. Use an additional sheet of paper—even for one paragraph.

8) In business replies, try to be prompt. Don't make your clients remind you repeatedly of their requests.

## A Parting Thought to this Chapter

Maintaining efficient office procedure calls for the coordination of various talents and skills. At first you may wonder how all these components will ever fall into place, but with time and experience it will become one seamless effort: harmonious, second nature, almost automatic. Effective office procedure is like developing a good habit: by giving it time, practice, and proper attention, you develop the traits and skills that make managing an office as routine as driving your car. And just like your car, once your office is in gear, and you know how to guide your vehicle you'll be advancing with certainty on the road to success.

# Chapter 11

# Hiring Staff Members

*A leader does not say, "Get going!" Instead, he says, "Let's go!" and leads the way.*

*He helps those under him to grow "big" because he realizes that the more "big" people an organization has, the stronger it will be.*

*A leader does not hold people down; he lifts them up.*

*A leader has faith in people. He believes in them, trusts them, and so draws out the best in them.*

*A leader uses his heart as well as his head. He is not only a boss; he is also a friend.*

*He has a sense of humor. He is not a stuffed shirt. He can laugh at himself. He has a humble spirit.*

*A leader can lead. He is not interested in having his own way, but in finding the best way. He has an open mind.*

*A leader keeps his eyes on high goals. He strives to make the efforts of his followers and himself contribute to the enrichment of personality, the achievement of more abundant living for all, and the improvement of civilization.*

**William F. Pederson**

## Introduction

Even if you are still months away, it pays to give thought and take practical steps toward achieving maximum efficiency and productivity during the busy tax season. With all the laborsaving devices a modern office can have, the most valuable are those that extend your precious time.

In this chapter we will discuss a number of ideas designed to give you—the tax professional—more time to perform the tasks that only you can do best, thus relegating other important, but tedious and routine work to others. In hiring office help, you want to find someone who can take care of paperwork and other details, leaving you to ply your craft and deal personally with your clientele.

Regardless of how many clients you serve, all necessary tax office work can be classified as either:

**a)** Routine clerical tasks, or

**b)** Skilled, technical, professional work.

It follows then, that wherever possible, all or most of the tasks in the first category can and should be delegated to others. This enables you to concentrate on the work that requires your specialized training and expertise.

## Using an Office Assistant

Even the smaller tax practitioner can employ—to good advantage—the services of an assistant to perform the following tasks:

- Act as receptionist while you interview or prepare the return of another client.
- Make appointments for you. Most appointments are established by phone and by using an appointment book your receptionist should have no trouble setting up and keeping track of your appointments. Just make sure the receptionist records and double-checks the information so that it is correct, legible, and contains no scheduling conflicts.
- Take care of many vital but routine office tasks such as addressing envelopes, collating complete returns into sets, inserting and mailing, billing clients, etc.
- Answer routine questions. An informed assistant can easily answer many of the calls you receive, especially in those hectic weeks prior to April 15th: Where do I send my federal or state return? When will I get my refund? How much tax do I have to pay? How do I make out the check? Such calls are interruptive and eat up a lot of time, especially if they come in the middle of an important

discussion or interview. Having someone else handle these calls will enable you to give your clients your undivided attention, and will earn you the respect of your callers as well.

- Follow-up calls. Usually, there are a number of clients whose returns cannot be completed immediately; they may be lacking information or documents the client did not bring along. It is most advisable that you call the client after a day or two if the information did not arrive. A simple "tickler" file, which the receptionist is in charge of, can accomplish this.

- Have your assistant prepare all necessary copies of forms and other documents.

- If your receptionist can type or use a computer, let her prepare all supporting documents—schedules, explanations, statements, and other correspondence.

- Train your assistant to handle the files—preparing the file folder for a new client, filing all completed copies, and retrieving client copies of previous returns in advance of each scheduled appointment.

Each of these tasks considered alone may only amount to a matter of minutes, but you will soon realize that if you eliminate 10 to 15 minutes worth of interruptions per hour with a client, the quality and quantity of your services will greatly improve. You will then be able to give your clients the full attention and concentration they deserve.

Your first office assistant will probably work only part-time and even then, only during the tax season. Your helper may be a spouse, another family member, a high school or college student, or even a full time secretary in need of additional income. But always make sure to hire a responsible, mature, intelligent person. Then, the first thing to impress upon any prospective employee is that all client matters are strictly confidential. Gossip—about any client, in or out of the office—is absolutely forbidden.

Next, take time off to train the employee in all the duties you expect him or her to perform and then delegate as much work as possible to them. Let the assistant handle all filing, retrieval of files, appointments, and so on. Bear in mind that the longer the individual works in your office—assuming the work is satisfactory—the more valuable he or she becomes as a member of your organization. If you encourage the assistant to take on more responsibility, he or she will be able to relieve you of more routine tasks. At the same time, clients will get to know and trust him or her as well. Therefore, do everything you can to hold on to a good, trained and trustworthy employee.

Keep in mind, as well, if you have a valuable assistant who performs well, you may want to enhance the person's salary or benefits over time to retain him or her. Don't take for granted the hard work the person provides if he or she truly helps your office succeed. Even assistants can see when things are working well due to their influence, and they will seek employment elsewhere if they feel unrecognized over time.

If the extra help you need is to simply get you through the busy tax season, then you might also consider hiring someone through a temporary employment agency. The understanding here is that the work is of a temporary nature: there are no employee benefits or other peripheral issues to consider, and you get a qualified helper without having to go through the procedure of advertising or interviewing. Furthermore, the agency is seeking to please its clients, so if a particular individual is not working out well you can simply call for a replacement.

To get your money's worth from a temporary employment agency, be as precise as you can in describing the work you want done. Reliable agencies have extensive files and will do their best to find you a worker with whom you will be satisfied. In fact, it often occurs that a "temp" becomes thoroughly familiar with the procedures in a particular office setting, and if the "chemistry" is right this individual may become a permanent employee. That said, you will need to pay a "finder's fee" to the temp agency to be able to permanently hire the placement. This allows the temp agency to receive some income for what otherwise would have been earned from the person had he continued to work as a temp.

## Hiring Full-Time Professional Help

As your practice grows and develops, the quantity of work you must perform will expand as well. When it reaches the point where you need more than just clerical assistance, you'll need to consider employing a qualified tax assistant, or at least train someone to handle the less involved tax returns.

If you prefer a trained, experienced professional, you may locate a retired accountant or other tax practitioner willing to do part time work. For leads and contacts we suggest you ask other local practitioners or put a small ad in your local newspaper.

The role of a professional assistant is to interview clients, and to prepare the simpler—or even more complex returns—depending on his or her competence. It is also important to choose an individual who is not only technically proficient, but also someone who can relate and properly deal with your clients. At the same time, be sure this individual is well-trained and up-to-date on all new tax developments.

If you happen to come upon the right person, you may find that in the long run it is more economical and practical to train the assistant yourself—provided you have the necessary patience and instructional skills to do so.

Whichever course you pursue, you should realize that hiring full-time professional help (or helpers) marks a genuine turning point in the development of your practice, and is therefore a matter you should consider with care. An employee, though he or she may differ from you in significant ways, is nevertheless an extension of yourself and your tax practice. Your clients' attitudes toward your practice will be strongly influenced—favorably or unfavorably—by their contact with your assistants, so hiring someone should not be rash, desperate, or a spontaneous gesture. It calls for a definite approach and plan of action.

Here, then, is a sequence of steps you may follow to help locate and recognize good, prospective office assistants.

## Writing a Job Description

It isn't enough to have a vague idea of what you want hired help to do. The more specific you are, the better off everyone will be. So first try to identify your needs and define the tasks you want someone else to do. For example, when seeking clerical help the description may include…typing, billing, handling mail, filing, handling incoming calls, writing letters, making appointments, general book- keeping, etc. If you can be more specific within these categories, that's even better.

Categories can be broken down in percentages to help identify which ones make up most of the time of the position. For example, the total position work is 100 percent. Beneath that could be a list that states the duties of an office assistant as such:

- 40% Phone communication—answering phones and client or external calls to the office, taking messages, directing callers to specific information, and scheduling appointments.
- 40% Filing paperwork—maintaining the office file system, managing client information in folders, purging old folder material with supervisor's approval and coordination, shredding confidential material.
- 20% Other duties as required—etc.

It would then be a good idea to prioritize these tasks as well, with the most important items at the top of the list. Which are primary duties, which are secondary or even expendable duties? You may not find someone to handle all the jobs on your list, but if you can get someone to capably handle the most important ones, that may be good enough.

Then write a brief job description—including job qualifications you require—spelling out the duties, responsibilities, conditions, and requirements that constitute the offer you are proposing. This precise description will be a helpful guide to you and job candidates as you proceed through the hiring process. It provides everyone with clarity regarding what the job entails, and helps avoid later misunderstandings. You can also, and should, use this description as a basis for your want ads, or the information you transmit to employment agencies. That way there's no miscommunication in terms of what you wanted for a hire and what the applicant understood the job was for.

## Recruitment

You are now in a position to recruit applicants. There are numerous employee resources available to you: secretarial agencies, employment agencies, government agencies, educational facilities (for example, schools that train the kind of employee you want), putting a "Help Wanted" ad in your local newspaper, or posting notices on select bulletin boards. You can also send the word out among friends, relatives, other practitioners, other employees, or post your request on an appropriate computer site.

Whichever venue you pursue, you will have to be ready to receive prospects, either with a filled-out application form that records basic, essential information, or with a resume. When you sift through such material you can begin screening out acceptable from unacceptable applicants. Carefully examine the filled out forms, questionnaires, or resumes for tell-tale signs:

- Is the information neat or sloppy? Is it clearly written or incoherent?
- How is the grammar and spelling?
- Is the writing "to the point" and functional—highlighting skills, experience, and abilities; or does it "beat around the bush" and speak about secondary concerns and hobbies?
- Does the writer's tone reflect a positive, serious, and ambitious note, or is it merely casual and flippant?

## Interviewing an Applicant

Even after you are left with your most impressive applications, you cannot hire someone without conducting a well-planned interview. You need to know how applicants present themselves, and how they conduct themselves in conversation.

- You can prepare for your interview by writing out appropriate questions in advance. Such questions might include: What were your responsibilities in your last job? What did you like or not like about your job? What did you like or not like about your boss? Why did you leave? Aim for questions that are "telling," that go beyond a simple "yes" or "no" response, and reveal something about the person you are with. This way you can get a feel for the way this person thinks and looks at things. Ask questions that go into details and specifics—that touch upon skills and situational encounters.

- Conduct the interview privately. Most applicants are somewhat nervous at such encounters, so try to put the person at ease by offering a drink, or by first engaging in some light conversation. In such a comfortable setting the candidate's replies will tend to be more candid and meaningful.

- Aside from the questions you ask and the answers you receive, you should also observe the person's style of presentation—his or her manner, appearance, and dress—and discreetly jot down information you will later want to consider.

- At the end of the interview, graciously thank the applicant, and inform him or her that you will soon be in touch. When you do call back—with one answer or another—thank the applicant again, and briefly explain the decision you came to. However, before you reply at all, make sure you contact references—both listed and unlisted—and ask former employers very specific questions: Was the person punctual, polite, and efficient? Would you hire this individual again?

- In the course of an interview, some employers will give actual tests to applicants reflecting various job related skills, to get an even better gauge of a candidate's performance level.

- Although it is difficult to measure certain important attributes in an interview (i.e. motivation), this is still an important and necessary step in seeking a reliable, prospective employee.

## Selecting the Best Applicant

It may seem obvious, yet it's important to point out that you are primarily looking for someone who can do the jobs you need to have done. Don't pick candidates for peripheral reasons—a winning smile, good manners, or a way with words—if they lack the skills you require.

Also, do not look for a mirror image of yourself, or for someone who handles everything just as you do. Different personalities lend themselves to different kinds of work, with various likes and dislikes; and tasks that you find tedious, another will find challenging. Of course, there should be harmony and compatibility, but you are not searching for a carbon copy of your attitudes and skills. You want people who have the drive and the ability to get your work done.

At this point, take your choice applicants and thoroughly consider all pertinent material: written forms, phone conversations, interviews, and references. The closer you come to fitting the applicant exactly to the job, the happier things will be for everyone concerned.

You should make your selection carefully, but also do it as soon as you can. Good candidates have probably applied for other positions as well, and may get hired before you make up your mind.

Finally, don't throw away any of the prospect files you were seriously considering. They may be of use to you later on, if a present employee does not work out and leaves you, or if your practice expands and you need more help, these files may come in handy.

## Training and Orientation

Misunderstandings between an employer and an employee can cause resentment, office tension, and loss of productivity. One excellent way to reduce such misunderstanding is to hire a new employee and clear the air of all questions and concerns beforehand. Either orally or preferably in writing, make sure the employee clearly understands what he or she will be expected to do, and what you will provide in return for that service.

Among the points to cover are the following:

- A list of job duties
- Date and time the job will begin
- Length of the work day and work week
- The amount of pay for the work, stated in terms of pay per hour, week, month or year
- The day of the week or month the employee will be paid
- Fringe benefits, if any
- Whether there will be paid vacations, and length of vacations, sick days, "personal days," holiday policies, a list of such holidays, and maximum number of paid sick days
- Time of reporting to and leaving from work, and overtime policy
- Attendance and emergency leave policies
- Work rules, office rules, and dress code
- Lunch time, break time, and personal calls policy
- At what intervals the employee will be considered for a pay raise
- Warnings, discipline, and termination policies

The more clearly all these areas are addressed (in writing), the less chance there is for office friction, confusion and disagreements.

After hiring and orientation you still have to train your new employee. This is really an ongoing procedure, but there is still a "breaking in period" of on-the-job learning-by-doing.

Here are some guidelines to help you through this initial "period of adjustment":

- Prepare the employee by first putting him or her at ease. Be patient and encouraging. Find out what he already knows and then proceed to tell him precisely what you are going to teach him.
- Present new tasks in steps—one manageable step at a time—showing the employee what has to be done, never demanding more than he can master at one time.

- Supervise as the employee explains and shows you his own performance of that task. It's altogether natural to make mistakes, just correct the employee's errors and periodically check on his work.

To help motivate an employee, delegate tasks that encompass greater degrees of responsibility: for example, to oversee a job from start to finish, rather than giving out pieces of repetitive work. This makes the job more interesting, complete, and satisfying to do.

- With time, you have to give your workers enough authority to carry out tasks on their own. This also offers them greater freedom to err, so you will have to periodically check on their progress. But it's counterproductive to stifle your workers. If you have good, capable workers trust them and employ their skills.

- Encourage all staff members, or trainees, to read tax related periodicals, announcements, and news releases in order to keep abreast of information that pertains to your work; and if you have the time discuss as many client problems and returns with them as possible, exposing them to a variety of tax situations.

- For the first six months to a year under your supervision, if you see that your employee is capable, you can advance him to more responsible levels of tax work. Your staff member will also gain a lot of valuable experience if you let him do the research on the tax problems you are working on. Just make sure you check the work until you are certain that you can fully rely on his findings.

- One question to resolve is whether to let the trainee do his studying and research work on his own time or on your time. The general trend is to permit studying on employer time, to encourage as much independent study as possible.

- As your relationship with employees develops, remember: Everyone is different in significant ways—in goals, attitudes, and personalities—and that no one is perfect. Everyone is subject to moods, ups-and-downs, and unexpected problems, all of which may affect performance on the job. Come to understand this within yourself, by way of your own strengths and weaknesses; then your patience, understanding, tolerance, and treatment of others will go much easier.

## Working With and Supervising Others

At this point, with one or more people working under you, you have technically become a "manager." Managing others—even one other person—adds a significant change to your base of operations. For one thing, being a manager may call for interpersonal skills and abilities that you haven't had any reason to cultivate until now. After all, you were trained to operate an effective and efficient tax practice, and now—as your practice grows—you are being asked to properly supervise those who are under your hire.

Here, then, is a set of reliable guidelines to help you oversee anyone who works for you:

- As the employer you should set a good example. Show up on time and dress appropriately. Your own conduct, appearance, and attitude will set the tone for your staff. Be a model of what you expect, and your employees will pattern themselves after you.

- Maintain a healthy, positive, productive outlook, and let your actions and words convey this message to those who work for you.

- Office morale can be affected positively or adversely by an incident that may seem quite insignificant to you, but which is very important to your employees. Don't overlook this factor, and try to treat all incidents with fairness and understanding.

- Express orders properly—with decency and respect. A simple "please" and "thank-you" are almost always in order. Give clear instructions and deadlines, whenever appropriate.

- Maintain a healthy sense of humor, and most of all, be able to laugh at yourself.

- Don't use obscene or vulgar language, and never make jokes at an employee's expense. It's demeaning to the employee, to yourself, your professional image, and to your practice as a whole.

- The traditional phrase "firm but fair" is appropriate in your office setting. Be sure your employees know the rules you expect them to work by, and then enforce those rules in a just and consistent manner.

- Be rational, patient, pleasant, and calm. Use self-control at all times. Things are bound to go wrong occasionally, even get out of hand, but you must try to remain cool, calm, and in control. This may seem like a tall order to fill, but it's preferable that you remain part of the solution, and not become part of the problem.

- Be sure to always acknowledge an employee's good work. In other words: give credit where credit is due. Let an employee know that you take note of, are actively aware of, and fully appreciate what he or she is doing. In fact, such praise can be lavished openly, even while others are around.

- On the other hand, if criticism is in order, take care of that softly and in private. When you criticize, make sure it is constructive and not destructive: focus on a specific action and don't be critical of the person as a whole. Never insult or "put down" an employee—publicly or privately. Afterwards, document what was discussed and keep a copy in your supervisor's file. This will be handy if you need to take further action later and need to be specific about patterns of deficient performance. If you gave instructions on how to improve, make sure to follow-up in writing with the employee via an e-mail or memo, spelling out what is expected.

- When you make a suggestion or request, give your reason for it, if possible. You will get a lot more cooperation from your staff if they know what they are doing and why they are doing it.

- Impress upon clients that you have full confidence in your staff. This not only reassures the client, but boosts your office morale as well.

- Don't hesitate to discuss a problem with an employee or ask for his input and advice if you think he is qualified. This will enhance your assistant's self-esteem and sense of loyalty to your practice.

- Let employees use their own methods, as long as they achieve the desired results. The employer who incessantly meddles into every office routine destroys his employee's initiative and incentive.

- Keep communication lines open and be a good listener. Be available so that employees can come to you with questions and concerns. Encourage workers to discuss problems and offer ideas.

- Express a personal interest in your employees. Let them know that they are not just cogs in an office wheel, but important and valued members of a close-knit team.

- Remember: happy, satisfied employees will do substantially more and better work than frustrated, disgruntled employees.

- Where you have a problem employee, act quickly and decisively. Left to sit, a bad employee will begin to negatively influence others in the office if there are more than one subordinate. In most cases, employees are at-will, which means an employer or employee can quit the labor relationship immediately without reason, so if need be let the person go and hire a replacement. We will discuss this more below.

To briefly summarize: managing "human resources"—exhibiting leadership—involves far more than just issuing orders. It calls for interpersonal skills, proficiency in communication, empathy, and a broad perspective. You want to direct your employees in such a way that the necessary jobs get done, but in a positive and uplifting manner—not in a begrudging way. Toward this end it would be helpful to generally improve your own understanding of human behavior, and in particular, to understand the factors that motivate and energize an employee to do a good job.

## The Art of Firing

Like it or not, the time will come when you'll have to lay off an employee. This is never a pleasant experience, whether you let an individual go due to downsizing, consolidating, because of poor job performance, dishonesty, personality problems, or for some other reason.

As noted earlier, when dealing with an indolent or disgruntled employee, it is important to move fast. A poor worker with an unhealthy attitude, unsatisfactory motivation, or low performance level can affect the morale of an entire office. So if and when the time comes—and it has to be done—do not postpone the procedure: be prepared to move fast and at the earliest possible opportunity. Putting off such matters with further deliberations can wreak emotional havoc on your own state of mind, and severely undermine your work efforts.

The fact that you're feeling unpleasant—even guilty—about disciplining an employee or following through on a termination is a normal human reaction, but in your office you will have to keep that reaction to yourself. If you did whatever you reasonably could do for this worker in the way of corrective efforts and they failed, then it is not your fault that he or she has to be fired.

The following suggestions may not soften the blow, but will still be of help to you:

- Communicate the message in person—yourself! If you hired the person, then it is your responsibility to relay the notice of termination as well. Do not give this job over to someone else.

- Be prepared. Have all the information you need on hand: the explanations and reasons for the firing, papers, payments—whatever is coming to the employee—so you don't have to drag the ordeal out longer than necessary. Be tactful in how you relay the information in order to reduce tension, bitterness, or resentment. Where the termination is of an at-will employee, a reason is not required. In fact, many businesses simply just tell the person it's not working out and they have to go. The less said about why in these instances is better. This may be frustrating or confusing to the terminated employee, but it protects your office legally from giving out too much information that could later be used against you if the former employee sues for unfair treatment.

- Where the employee has a satisfactory work history and is being discharged for reasons that are not his fault, declare your willingness to provide recommendations to any prospective employers. Better yet, why not act as a "matchmaker" by trying to line up a job—or at least some interviews—with fellow employers. Your concern would certainly be a great morale booster for the entire staff.

When it's all over, try to assess the situation in terms of how and where things went wrong, so you can at least try to avoid this sort of circumstance in the future.

Hiring staff members, when it is done with care and an open mind, can be a genuine educational experience. It makes you aware of how complex office procedure can be, and how you can effectively streamline that procedure. Working with staff is a constant lesson in human interaction skills, and it poses a constant challenge as well. The benefits, however, are extraordinary: for when people master the art of teamwork and cooperation—the accomplishments can be far-reaching and truly inspiring.

# Chapter 12

# Fees and Billing

*It's good to have money and the things money can buy, but it's good to check once in a while and make sure you haven't lost the things that money can't buy.*
**George Horace Lorimer**

## Factors to Consider

The subject of "fee setting" is of great interest to both veteran and new tax practitioners. If you're a seasoned tax professional with a well-established practice you'll wonder: am I charging enough or should I raise my fees to produce more revenue? So, whether you're a newcomer to the tax profession or a veteran who has always worked for others and now finds yourself venturing into your own practice, setting proper fees is critical to your survival.

On the one hand, you do not want to drive business away by charging too much. On the other hand, you have to be adequately compensated for your time and skill. Bear in mind that if you charge too little, the quality of your work will inevitably suffer. Thus, in the long run, undercharging will not benefit your clients.

Before deciding on a fee schedule, you must consider a number of factors. The most important ones are discussed below:

1. **The average level of fees charged for similar work in your community**

   This amount will depend, to a great extent, on the severity of competition, the general economic level, and the size of your community. Fees tend to be higher in better income areas and are usually somewhat higher in larger cities than in small towns.

   To begin, we suggest you find out how much other consultants charge for a simple itemized and non-itemized Form 1040. If you can get a few such figures you will be able to gauge the relative fee level in your area.

   In many communities you will find several tiers of tax professionals. There are established, professional public accountants, CPAs, and non-CPAs whose major source of income is routine, year-round accounting work. Many of these individuals or firms expand their offices, hiring additional staff members during the season to accommodate the many clients who come in only once a year to have their returns prepared. The fees generally charged by this group are, as a rule, relatively high, with CPAs at the upper end and non-certified accountants somewhat below that bracket. They consider tax work a profitable sideline and therefore assume a "take it or leave it" attitude toward the client. But, being established professionals, they command larger fees. At the other extreme, you find the relatively untrained, mass production "tax experts." Their primary attraction is a low fee, although most clients end up paying considerably more than the advertised amount. H & R Block and other chains are usually somewhere in the middle.

   If such a situation exists in your community, we suggest that you establish your fee level somewhere near the large tax chains to start out. As a newcomer you cannot demand the same fee as a long-established professional. On the other hand, to equate yourself with the untrained, so-called "tax expert" can only serve to downgrade your reputation and public confidence in your abilities.

   It's important to remember that by virtue of your specialized professional training you are entitled to professional fees, providing you render a complete, professional service. Once you are established and become known as a capable tax specialist you will be able to raise your fees accordingly.

2. **The amount of work and time spent in the preparation of a return**

   If a client comes to you with a complete summary of income and expenses, you will charge less—other things being equal—than if you have to reconstruct his financial business history item by item. If you come to a client's home or business you are also entitled to extra compensation for your traveling time and trouble. Also consider: At the beginning you may be a little slow and may even make some time-consuming errors; it would be unwise and unfair to charge for time lost due to your lack of experience.

You will also find that it takes considerably longer to prepare a return for a first time client than for a client you have serviced before. Once you have accumulated certain basic information—familiarity with his business operations or other sources of income, special problems in connection with deductions and exemptions and so on—tax return preparation time will be drastically reduced. Since you expect the client to return year after year, you would be well advised to keep this in mind in setting your fee.

3. **The value of your services**

   Your service value provides you with your greatest opportunity for sizable fees. If the client can be shown that your efforts and input resulted in sizable tax savings for her, she will not object to your fee. In fact, it will be considered a cost to obtain the savings on a regular basis. Especially valuable in this respect is a tax refund; with care and patience you should be able to provide such savings and get refunds for many of your clients.

   With a little practice you will be able to tell, in most cases, which of your clients offer opportunities for worthwhile savings. For example, the returns of lower income workers with no outside income or business activities are usually not complicated, and you can't expect a big fee from them. On the other hand, there are business and professional people, investors, taxpayers with income from real estate rentals and sales, sales representatives, and others who use their car on business. Such clients often provide you with a variety of opportunities for large deductions, and you should spare no time or effort to ferret out any and all possible savings.

   Most tax professionals set a minimum fee for a relatively simple standard deduction return. For itemized returns requiring additional schedules or statements, or for more complicated and time-consuming work, they charge for each additional form or schedule. In such cases we suggest you submit an itemized bill to explain your charges. Also, for corporation, partnership, and estate tax work, compensation is usually much higher than for individual income tax work, since more specialized knowledge is required.

4. **The client's income**

   Another factor to consider when setting a fee is the size of the client's income. At first glance it may seem unfair to charge a higher fee just because a client has a higher income. The rationale for the additional charge, however, is that there are many instances where the tax practitioner is not fully compensated for the amount or difficulty of the work involved simply because he realizes that the client can't afford it. Furthermore, the chances of an audit generally increase with the size of a client's income, which means that greater attention and care must be given to a higher income return.

In setting fees, both the consultant and the client should be aware that the taxpayer is paying for the consultant's professional skill and knowledge as well as for her time. A well-trained professional tax practitioner will certainly be able to prepare a return in a way that will save the client considerably more than the fee entails. Obviously, the reason even "tax-savvy" taxpayers hire a professional is because they realize they cannot do the job as well as a professional can. The professional tax consultant should in turn be amply paid for her time and expertise.

With a little experience you should be able to judge how high a fee you can set, without making the client feel you are overcharging. But until you are well established, it's wiser to undercharge rather than overcharge. Bear in mind that as a beginner you usually have less expense, less overhead, and less bargaining power with clients.

## Fees for Extra Services

Every practitioner has a number of clients who repeatedly contact him throughout the year, with questions, financial concerns, or tax related problems. The extra time spent on one such client during the year, in addition to the time spent preparing his return adds up to a sizable amount, frequently overlooked when the tax return fee is established. Many practitioners keep a running log for such clients, entering every phone call, research study, letter or memorandum written, and so on. These items are tallied and an extra charge is made, or the return fee is appropriately increased, to cover the additional time and work.

You will often find that problems arise in the course of preparing a client's return—calling for specialized research. If the problem is of a general nature, many practitioners feel that the time required for the extra research should simply be absorbed as part of one's general responsibility to "keep current." But if the problem is a specialized one, you have every right to expect payment for the additional time and effort. Also, if you spent time with or for your client in conducting year-end tax planning before the tax return season, you are obviously entitled to an additional fee.

Quite often, in connection with preparing a tax return, a client will ask you to perform some non-tax work for him as well. The tasks put in your lap may range from obtaining a refund for an unused plane ticket to helping straighten out a dispute with the electric company. In any case, if it involves an appreciable amount of time you should get paid for it.

## Fees for Tax Examinations

Inevitably, some client returns will be selected for IRS and state tax examinations. This, of course, entails extra work on your part, either in representing the client at the audit or in helping him prepare for it. While a few tax practitioners do this type of work without extra charge, the great majority certainly do charge extra for such services, and we wholeheartedly concur.

If you simply absorb the additional time spent on audits you will eventually have to increase your fees to make up for the lost time. This, of course, means that all clients—audited or not—will have to pay extra. Moreover, a practitioner who represents a client at an audit or spends time preparing for it without charging extra conveys the impression that the audit is really due to his fault or negligence. This, in most cases, is not true, as we will explain later in the chapter dealing specifically with this subject.

In truth, many seasoned tax consultants not only charge for representing clients at audits but also charge a premium fee, because audits call for specialized skills. Fortunately, these are skills you can easily acquire and put to very profitable use. Fees for preparing or representing a client at an audit are generally charged on a time basis, though a minority of practitioners charge a fixed minimum with an additional charge if excessive time is required. In any event, if you succeed in saving your client a substantial amount of money, a proportionately higher fee is entirely justified.

## Fee Schedules

Virtually all national or regional tax services, as well as many accountants and independent tax practitioners, use a fee schedule as a basis for setting prices. In many cases the fee schedule is intended to show only the minimum fee for a particular type of service, return, or schedule. These fees are often adjusted upward as the situation demands.

You will find a suggested fee schedule in this book's Appendix.

# Chapter 13

# Collecting Your Fees

*The pessimist sees the difficulty in every opportunity; the optimist sees the opportunity in every difficulty.*
**L.P. Jacks**

*You can't escape the responsibility of tomorrow by evading it today.*
**Abraham Lincoln**

## Overview

You will find that a great majority of clients will pay your fee upon receiving their return or shortly thereafter. But without a doubt, you'll come across some individuals who are always late in paying their bills. The following suggestions should help accelerate the collection process.

- First and foremost, make it a practice to submit a formal bill that either accompanies the tax return or that arrives shortly thereafter. It is axiomatic to all collection efforts that the sooner the bill is received the sooner it is paid.

- As tactfully as you can, try to obtain payment when the return is delivered. For this reason, many practitioners do not mail returns to clients but have them pick up their returns in person—at which time the bill is presented. A good opportunity for payment is when the client must write out a check for additional taxes due, or for estimated taxes. While the checkbook is still in hand, it's easier for the client to write you a check as well. If he is short of funds, you could suggest a post-dated check, but tell him you would like to avoid the bother of having to send statements.

- Unless you expect immediate payment when the return is delivered or picked up by the client, we suggest that you include a self-addressed stamped envelope. Moreover, we think that an envelope with a postage stamp is preferable to a business reply envelope. Somehow people find it harder to disregard an envelope bearing a valid stamp as opposed to an unstamped reply envelope. Indicate on your bill that you expect payment within 10 days (or 30 days, at the most) after receiving the bill. It also helps to have a clear due date on the bill.

- Some clients will claim, "I'll pay the bill as soon as I receive my refund." This practice should be thoroughly discouraged. You're essentially letting the client walk out the door with free services and a promise. Like any professional, you are entitled to compensation upon completion of your service: i.e. when the return is prepared and handed to the client. Once your fees become subject to a tax refund, any number of things can happen, and you may receive payment very late or not at all. By agreeing to wait for a refund you are, in effect, guaranteeing the refund, which you should avoid at all costs. The only exception to this is where both the bill and the tax refund are substantial, and you know the client is simply unable to pay at the present time. Even then, we suggest that you and the client agree on a deadline (perhaps 90 days) at which time you are paid regardless of the refund. Better yet, suggest that the bill be paid in installments, with the understanding that the entire balance be paid if the client receives his refund before all of the installments are due.

- A growing number of accountants and tax consultants accept one or more of the major credit cards in payment of their services. The quicker collection will more than offset the small service charge.

- Make sure to remind the client either by phone or by mail, no more than 30 days after the due date, if his bill is still unpaid.

- If you serve the client on a year-round basis—preparing his quarterly business tax returns or sales tax returns—you should expect payment on a quarterly basis, or even monthly, if the fee is large enough.

**How to Bill**

There are various schools of thought concerning how much itemization, if any, should be put on a bill. Current practice runs the gamut from the casual sentence, "For services rendered in preparing Federal and State individual tax returns", to an explicitly detailed bill listing every form, schedule, phone call, and other service rendered.

## Chapter 13: Collecting Your Fees

The most common practice probably lies somewhere in between. Obviously, if you detail the bill the client will better understand your charges. On the other hand, you don't want to appear overly mercenary or picayune. However, if you do prepare detailed bills, make sure to keep a copy in your files, for clear reference, in case your client questions you, and as a basis for billing in the future.

**How to Handle Complaints about Your Fees**

Of course, the best way to handle complaints is to avoid them. But short of charging so little that no client will ever object, you really have no way of forestalling all complaints. In the case of bills that are larger than usual, you can minimize complaints by drawing up an itemized account explaining the work you performed. This is most effective where special services were rendered to a client.

Another approach is to explain to the client in person—either at billing time, or when the complaint arises—exactly how much work, research, time, and skill went into preparing his return. Some practitioners will take out the client file, go through all the paperwork, and point out exactly what was done.

Some tax consultants offer a discount to all clients who pay their bills within a specified time, such as within 10 or 30 days. Others feel this method lacks professionalism. It may also help to remind your client, in writing or in person, that your fee is fully tax deductible.

Be sure to take note of any comments the client makes about the fee on his record for future reference. If you know that a particular client is sticky about the fee (and assuming you want to keep him), you will be more careful next time in setting the fee, or at least in making sure you fully explain the charges when drawing up the bill.

Sometimes an entire return must be redone because the client omitted some important information. It is perfectly proper for you to charge for the additional time required, but make sure to note this fact on the bill and in your records so you won't inadvertently charge an extra fee again next year.

As a general rule, whenever you present a bill that appears higher than the normal fee, take the initiative and explain the reasons for it. Do not postpone your explanation until the client raises questions about the fee. Some clients may pay the bill without a word, but with a silent vow to never return again.

## Some General Thoughts about Fees and Collections

A knowledgeable practitioner once remarked,

> *"There is one sure way to recognize an inexperienced or unsuccessful professional: he's the one who usually tries to bypass or minimize the subject of fees. This apologetic attitude about fees can give the client the impression that you are afraid or ashamed to talk about them because they are out of line."*

In other words, if a client questions your fee, don't go on the defensive. Point out that even though he may get cheaper service elsewhere "you generally get what you pay for." Explain that you provide professional, personalized, reliable service; that you are available all year and not just at tax time, and that the savings in taxes and aggravation far outweigh the relatively minor difference in the fee.

Finally, you should consider dropping those clients who remain stubborn, even after you explain the reasons for your fee. Remember, those who pick a tax practitioner primarily on the basis of fees are not the ones who contribute much to your practice in the long run. Their loyalty is skin deep. They will probably drop you as soon as they find someone cheaper, and any clients they recommend will probably also expect an extra low fee from you.

A mathematician named Pareto theorized that people and businesses generally spend 80 percent of their time on 20 percent of the customers. This concept became known as the Pareto Rule. What you want for your office is to make sure that the time spent is on the 20 percent or more that produce your office revenues consistently. Don't end up spending most of your time on those that produce little revenue.

Very often, a client will ask you in advance about your fee. If you quote your minimum fee—though you emphasize the fact that it is just a minimum—you will find it difficult to present a larger bill, even where you had more work than anticipated. In effect, you will generally find that your minimum fee becomes the maximum. But if you did quote a fee and then find that there is a lot more work involved than you had expected, it helps to give the client a breakdown of the additional time and charges. You could also, when quoting an estimate, advise the client that the fee will necessarily be larger if—in preparation of the return—you run into any unusual problems that require extra work or research.

In cases where you were successful in saving your client a substantial amount of money, we suggest you attach a memo to your bill explaining exactly what you did and approximately how much you saved. This will not only enhance your professional image and the client's respect for your abilities, but will also justify a larger fee.

## Some Additional Billing and Collection Tips

The following suggestions should help you streamline your billing and collection procedures. If properly carried out, they should result in faster and easier collections, while maintaining the good will of your clients:

1) Bill clients immediately upon completion of the work. If you wait they may forget the extent and efficiency of your services. Worse, you may forget to bill them getting too busy with something else!

2) Use round dollar amounts. Even if you base your fees on flat time rates don't send a bill for $235.85. Pennies make your business look petty.

3) In writing out a detailed bill don't use technical abbreviations. Their meaning may be clear to you or someone in the field, but will likely mean nothing to your client.

4) Make sure to charge for long-distance phone calls or for other out-of-pocket expenses (unless the amount is inconsequential in relation to the fee). These charges can quickly and substantially add up.

5) Make sure to follow-up on every unpaid bill after 30 days. Be courteous but persistent if payment is not forthcoming within a reasonable amount of time.

6) Add a handwritten note to the bottom of the reminder statement, to give the payment request a sense of urgency.

7) If the bill is large, suggest a partial payment to the client, but try to get a definite commitment as to when you can expect payment of the balance.

8) Make sure to bill for non-tax work—especially if it was time consuming. Some clients are under the impression that tax practitioners don't charge for non-tax related work.

9) If you think the fee will be more than the client expects, prepare him beforehand. Explain the fee by calling his attention to what is involved: the amount of taxes saved, the extent or difficulty of the work performed, the research required, etc.

10) For efficiency in billing and follow-up notices, consider multiple-set, snap-apart statement forms. The second and third copies can serve as reminders.

11) Instead of mailing a reminder notice, email or fax it. Faxes somehow convey a sense of urgency, without being unduly pushy. If the bill is seriously overdue, add a handwritten note indicating that the client should see to this matter at his or her earliest convenience.

# Chapter 14

# Obtaining Additional Income from Clients

*There is no royal road to anything: One thing at a time, all things in succession. That which grows fast withers as rapidly; that which grows slowly endures.*
**Josiah Gilbert Holland**

*Knowing when not to work hard is as important as knowing when to.*
**Harvey Mackay**

## Overview

While preparing income tax returns for individuals and businesses can be a very lucrative occupation, it is largely, but not entirely, seasonal. The figures vary, but in the past, many small to mid-sized practices handle about 70 percent to 75 percent of their annual return volume during the January-April season, another 15 percent to 20 percent during the May to October extension period, with the balance (mainly fiscal-year business returns) the rest of the year.

If this suits you, that's fine. However, if you, like many others, are looking for a year-round business with steadily growing, annual earnings then you are in an excellent position to expand your services and revenues into a profitable, full-time, yearly source of income.

This chapter will alert you to a number of such opportunities. Bear in mind, these are not get-rich-quick schemes that will put thousands of dollars into your pocket overnight. What we present here are practical, proven, ideas and service opportunities—both traditional and nontraditional—that you can use to boost and further develop your practice.

Some of these opportunities will come knocking on your door; that is, clients or prospective clients will initiate the contact and ask for them. Others will require your initiative in one of two ways:

1) Clients or potential clients looking for a service provider have to be made aware that you are capable and available, and

2) They have to be made aware of their need for your particular services.

It may take time and patience to develop a really lucrative practice, but if you are willing and prepared to put in the necessary effort and perseverance, your eventual success is almost guaranteed.

Basically, once you go beyond preparing tax returns, the types of additional services you can offer fall into two categories:

1) Taxes (federal, state and local) related matters, and

2) Non-tax related matters.

We will discuss tax related matters first. This is probably the area with the quickest return in relation to the time and effort you invest.

Besides the preparation of a yearly tax return, many taxpayers find themselves in need of assistance with tax questions and concerns at various times throughout the year. A number of returns and information reports affecting many taxpayers—especially people in business—are due in the course of any given year. In addition, decisions and transactions must be made, which may have a favorable or unfavorable effect on taxes. The average taxpayer is not familiar with the intricacies of tax law and is only too glad to shift this particular burden into the lap of a competent and reliable tax professional. That advisor can most certainly be **You**!

Therefore, invite and encourage your clients to consult with you about the tax effects of every important transaction they may be involved with: the purchase or sale of stocks and bonds; the purchase, sale, and improvement of real estate; large business expenditures, changes in business, contributions, and so on.

Make it a point to assist or advise your clients of your availability for counsel throughout the year and not just during tax season. Needless to say, you must stay up-to-date on current tax law and related developments, and make sure your clients are well aware of this.

The most profitable area in the tax field is probably tax planning. This is true both in terms of financial remuneration—and more importantly—in terms of increasing your client base, enhancing your professional image, and building a genuinely successful tax practice. Obviously, tax planning involves in-depth tax work that goes beyond the routine service rendered by the average tax consultant.

Tax planning calls for a continuous, abiding interest in the client's financial and personal situation combined with a thorough knowledge and understanding of tax law and an awareness of likely changes in the field. Tax planning requires knowledge, imagination, a sympathetic attitude, and creativity.

Tax planning, more than anything else, results in client referrals from associates or from friends of clients who are in the same business or profession or who have similar jobs. This, of course, enables you to get a lot of extra mileage out of one initial effort because you can apply the same or similar ideas, suggestions, or techniques to a number of clients in the same or similar circumstances.

As one professional in the know put it:

> *"A competent, dedicated tax consultant is in a position to become as indispensable to his clients as the family doctor once was to his patients...provided he maintains a close, personal, working relationship with his clients."*

This means that you should get to know your clients—in a professional as well as a personal context—and thereby become more aware of financial developments in their business, professional, and personal lives.

## Expanding Your Tax Services

Bear in mind that there are various levels of tax planning, requiring various levels of skills. Keeping abreast of current tax literature, studying a few of the annual tax guides that spell out the more common tax saving ideas and steps, plus reading a good book or two on tax planning (make sure it's current) should equip you to properly service most clients.

Wealthier taxpayers—especially those with income (and losses) from varied sources—often require more sophisticated, customized, long-term planning with multi-year "what-if" projections. This, of course, demands correspondingly higher fees. There is tax-planning software also available that makes this task much easier and quicker. If you have—or are taking steps to acquire—the knowledge and skills to serve this extremely lucrative market you can expect to increase your income substantially.

Some practitioners use the slower, post tax-season months to pull out client files, one by one, and examine them closely for any tax saving opportunities. Even if only one out of ten such examinations results in a tax advantage for a client your time will have been well spent.

Another opportune time for tax planning is in the last 30 to 60 days before the close of the year—either the calendar year—or the fiscal year for some clients. Some tax consultants have a practice of sending out a routine form letter to all clients with an income above a certain level—perhaps $50,000 or $60,000. In keeping with the adage that "an ounce of prevention is worth a pound of cure"; this reminder informs clients that tax saving moves made before the end of the year may far outweigh any tax savings you can attain for them later, during tax return time. If you can specify areas of particular interest—either to that client or areas that have witnessed important changes during the year—then your letter will have an even greater impact.

Obviously, even if your client does not respond to your invitation, it still serves as a valuable—and perfectly ethical—reminder to call you when tax time comes along.

Another area to mentally prepare for is that of out-of-state returns. The preparation of out-of-state returns is an especially big business near military installations and in and around border areas where a good portion of the population commutes to work in another state. By the same token, tax consultants working in these areas will pick up quite a bit of business from residents of neighboring states who travel to work.

While the tax preparation fee normally covers both the federal and home state return (plus local tax, if applicable), preparing out-of-state income tax returns calls for an additional fee. In fact, most consultants charge proportionally more for out-of-state returns.

Taxpayers who moved during the year from another state or worked out-of-state are often unaware of their filing responsibilities and must be informed of these requirements. An individual who resided in several states during the year may need to file in each state, depending where his income was earned in the tax year.

It's a good idea, therefore, to familiarize yourself beforehand with the forms and instructions of those states you anticipate filing for.

## Extra Income from Handling Tax Examinations and Disputes

It is virtually impossible for a tax consultant with any size practice to entirely avoid IRS audits and controversies. Inasmuch as this type of work often requires thorough research and personal negotiations with IRS agents, the fees charged for such services, are generally 25 percent to 50 percent higher than comparable time spent in the preparation of a return. If handled properly, this work can turn into an important source of additional income for you.

Another source of extra income for tax professionals is in the area of state tax audits. With the almost universal application of state income taxes and with ever increasing state tax rates, the incidence of income tax audits by state tax departments is steadily increasing. There is also more cooperation between the IRS and state tax administrations whereby the audit load is divided between the Federal government and the various states. Under this program, some tax returns that would have normally been examined by the IRS are assigned to state tax auditors instead. Any deficiencies that turn up on the state tax return are reported to the IRS, which in turn, revises that individual's Federal Income Tax Return to reflect the disallowed deductions, additional income, etc., as determined by the state.

For this reason, clients should be cautioned to approach a state audit with the same care they would give a Federal examination, even though the dollar amounts are usually not as high. Here again, if you prepared the return originally, you will most likely be asked to defend it as well.

## Social Security Counseling

Anyone engaged in tax practice for any length of time will at some point be asked to assist clients or their relatives in Social Security matters. Since it was first introduced, the old Social Security Act has mushroomed into a gigantic benefit program that intimately affects the lives of nearly all Americans. Moreover, about half of the population now pays more in Social Security taxes than in Federal income taxes with the percentage due to increase in the future.

With more individuals becoming aware of their immense stake in Social Security, the demand for help in this area is sure to increase dramatically in the next few years, and it would be worth your while to become more familiar with this vital area.

Here is a sample list of the type of services you may be called upon to render:

- Assist with application for Social Security benefits.
- Help clients decide whether to file for reduced early retirement benefits.
- Help clients avoid or reduce loss of benefits because of excess earnings.
- Help clients obtain necessary documents for benefit applications.
- Assist with pre-retirement planning.
- Counsel self-employed individuals on how to obtain maximum benefits.

- Design retirement plans to allow clients to earn income without jeopardizing their benefits.
- Help dependents and survivors collect maximum benefits.
- Help clients avoid problems in applying for disability benefits.

This list could easily be extended, but it does give you a sample of the opportunities for service—and earnings—in this particular field.

For many types of assistance, such as helping with applications or filling out reports, very little in the way of specialized knowledge is required. However, those who desire to seriously take on a Social Security practice should make an in-depth study of the pertinent Social Security laws and regulations—especially those affecting coverage, computation of benefits, and loss of benefits. The greatest demand for services and greatest opportunities for substantial assistance is in the area of disability benefits. We can assure you that your time and effort will be well rewarded.

## Operating a Year-Round Payroll Tax or Business Tax Service

Operating a year-round payroll tax or business tax service is a major source of income for many tax practitioners. As you know, any business employing one or more workers is required to file numerous federal and state wage reports and returns. There are federal and state withholding, Social Security and unemployment insurance taxes, disability benefit taxes, compensation insurance, and a host of other related tax returns and reports that have to be filled out. Very often there are federal excise tax returns, state or local excise and sales tax returns, various census reports—plus other returns, statements, and reports too numerous to mention—that every business, large or small, is required to submit.

The alert practitioner—able to secure a few such business-tax accounts on a monthly or yearly basis—can net a comfortable, steady, annual income. The fee for this service, which usually includes preparation of the proprietor's own income tax returns, depends on the size of the business and the number of employees involved. It may range from $400 to $800 per year for a very small business, to $200 to $400 or more per month for a larger business that employs even more people. You can also anticipate being asked by many of your clients' employees to prepare their income tax returns as well; or at least, as part of your advertising strategy, make your services available to them.

If you are able to maintain a part-time bookkeeping service in connection with your tax service, so much the better. Many small businesses do not have enough work to hire a full-time or even part-time bookkeeper and would be glad to let you handle the work. Remember: when you provide bookkeeping and tax services, you are in a good position to obtain your clients' recommendations for similar work at other firms.

Many tax specialists first get involved in bookkeeping through the back door, so to speak, but then discover it to be a lucrative area that can yield a nice, steady, annual income. What often happens is that a few small business clients come to you to prepare their returns. While questioning them, you find that they have few, or even no, records, which means that either they or you have to go through the lengthy process of reconstructing the figures in order to get the data you need for the return. Since every business is required by law to keep accurate records, it is usually an easy task to persuade these individuals to A) engage someone to do the bookkeeping for them, and B) let you be the one to handle that responsibility. Small entrepreneurs are characteristically impatient to get on with their business and abhor the "paperwork" aspect, so that factor should be of help to you.

To operate such a service all you have to do is set up a simple manual, or better still computerized, record-keeping system designed to provide the figures and other data required by the particular client. There are a number of excellent software packages available that can help you in this regard. Then, depending on your client's needs, and amount of time he has available, either he or you will periodically enter the necessary data. The amount of detailed work you have to do and the size of the enterprise you are servicing will determine whether your work is to be done on a weekly, monthly, or even quarterly basis. As a rule, most bookkeeping accounts are handled monthly, but if you have to do all the entries, or even make out the payroll and accounts payable checks, then your services may be required weekly.

Some public bookkeepers keep their clients' records in their own office and obtain information from their clients through daily or weekly report sheets. These may be picked up or mailed, or more conveniently, faxed or e-mailed.

In trying to sell a client on your bookkeeping service emphasize the fact that you will then obviously be in a much better position to prepare an accurate, "tax-saving" income tax return because his books are in order, and you are entirely familiar with his operation. Furthermore, it will be much easier for you to substantiate the figures on the tax return, in case of a tax audit.

Here's a suggestion: When preparing the tax return for a new client, one who may be a candidate for either a payroll tax or a bookkeeping and tax service, take extra pains to do an outstanding job. Make sure the return is not only technically accurate and correct, but also show your client that every possible tax-saving opportunity was indeed explored and, if possible, implemented. This will be a clear indication to him of the personalized, dedicated, and professional service he can expect as a client of yours throughout the year.

A good way to get new clients for this purpose is to compile a list from your classified telephone directory of a few hundred small business establishments in or near your community, and send them a printed card, letter, or brochure offering them this range of services. Your advertising should state that you would be glad to visit anyone interested to further discuss your services, without obligation. Enclose a business reply card for this purpose and then follow-up with a second and third mailing a few weeks apart. The best time to get new accounts is from December to February, so concentrate your efforts in those months.

Particularly good prospects for either a business tax or a bookkeeping and tax service are new businesses that have not as yet hired anyone to fill these needs. You can learn more about new business establishments through your local paper and by keeping your eyes and ears open. Another way to obtain the names and addresses of new firms is by visiting your county or town clerk's office periodically. In some jurisdictions this may be the county recorder's office. All new firms using a trade name must register there. (In most states this requirement also applies to new partnerships, regardless of whether or not a trade name is used).

Contact these new businesses by mail, or preferably in person, a short time after their opening and again, a week or two before the next quarterly payroll tax return is due.

Since most new business proprietors are reluctant to invest too much in what they perceive to be "unnecessary" expenses, some practitioners offer a special low introductory rate for the first year. Remember, if the business grows, as is often the case, your workload and fees will grow with it. Always bear in mind that a few small clients can quickly lead to some exceedingly lucrative accounts.

## Non-Tax Related Income Opportunities

Individuals involved in work of a public nature are often asked to assist in preparing various official and semi-official papers and documents. Therefore, the range of services you will be called upon to perform is virtually limitless.

To give you some idea of this, there are many older individuals who need help with such simple matters as filing claims for Medicare reimbursement. There are low-income individuals who need assistance in obtaining welfare payments, food stamps, Medicaid, and various government subsidies and loans. Then there are insurance claims, accident reports, and local real estate tax matters such as senior citizen exemptions. The list goes on.

While the fees for such services may not be high, they can add up to a comfortable and dependable year-round income, and many of those you help will turn into loyal tax clients and sources for further referrals as well.

We also suggest that you obtain a commission as a Notary Public. While notary fees alone rarely amount to a major source of income, many reports, statements, and applications do require notarization. So being a Notary can help you secure and develop more business connections.

Being a Notary does require a separate examination and licensing. You will also be restricted in most jurisdictions to a flat fee and to having to maintain a Notary journal as well as related records. This is so that any records you authenticate as accurate can be legally confirmed after the fact based on your journal and records. For more information on how a Notary works, most states' Secretary of State's office oversees the Notary registration, licensing, and regulation. Much more detailed information can be found on these government agencies' websites.

In the last few years the federal and state governments have become involved in numerous additional programs affecting much of the population—especially lower income individuals and families. This trend is going to accelerate as taxpayers demand and receive more assistance and services from the federal, state, and local governments, and the resulting paperwork is going to be staggering. This means there will be a greater demand for those ready, willing, and able to help the average citizen cope with the increase in forms, applications, reports and statements to fill out. As you gain expertise with the various programs and their accompanying forms, you can expect the demand for your advice and services to escalate as well.

One thing you can clearly see from the various suggestions offered above: there are a lot of avenues and opportunities out there in need of your professional services; a great deal depends upon how imaginative and enterprising you choose to be.

# Chapter 15

# Ethical Responsibilities of the Tax Consultant

*The thing that must survive you is not just the record of your practice, but the principles that are the basis of your practice.*
**Bernice Johnson Reagon**

*Integrity without knowledge is weak and useless, and knowledge without integrity is dangerous and dreadful.*
**Samuel Johnson**

*Truth is given, not to be contemplated, but to be done. Life is an action, not a thought.*
**F. W. Robertson**

Aside from the legal requirements and responsibilities just discussed, the reputable tax professional should also be aware of the moral and ethical responsibility involved in handling a client's tax affairs. One common concern is to what extent you should go to ascertain whether the return you are preparing for your client is a true and correct one. The American Institute of Certified Public Accountants (AICPA), the national professional organization of CPAs, issued the following rules and guidelines. This statement considers the responsibility of the CPA to examine or verify certain supporting data or to consider information related to another client when preparing a client's tax return.

While non-members are not bound by these rules, you may still wish to use them as a guide in your own practice. Be sure to familiarize yourself with IRS Circular 230.

**Certain Procedural Aspects of Preparing Returns**

1) In preparing or signing a return, the CPA may in good faith rely without verification upon information furnished by the client or by third parties. However, the CPA should not ignore the implications of information furnished and should make reasonable inquiries if the information furnished appears to be incorrect, incomplete, or inconsistent either on its face or on the basis of other facts known to the CPA. In this connection, the CPA should refer to the client's returns for prior years whenever feasible.

2) Where the Internal Revenue Code or income tax regulations impose a condition to deductibility or other tax treatment of an item (such as taxpayer maintenance of books and records or substantiating documentation to support the reported deduction or tax treatment), the CPA should make appropriate inquiries to determine to his or her satisfaction whether such condition has been met.

3) The preparer's declaration on the income tax return states that the information contained therein is true, correct, and complete to the best of the preparer's knowledge and belief "based on all information of which preparer has any knowledge." This reference should be understood to relate to information furnished by the client or by third parties to the CPA in connection with the preparation of the return.

4) The preparer's declaration does not require the CPA to examine or verify supporting data. However, a distinction should be made between (1) the need to either determine by inquiry that a specifically required condition (such as maintaining books and records or substantiating documentation) has been satisfied, or to obtain information when the material furnished appears to be incorrect or incomplete, and (2) the need for the CPA to examine underlying information. In fulfilling his or her obligation to exercise due diligence in pre-

paring a return, the CPA ordinarily may rely on information furnished by the client unless it appears to be incorrect, incomplete, or inconsistent. Although the CPA has certain responsibilities in exercising due diligence in preparing a return, the client has ultimate responsibility for the contents of the return. Thus, where the client presents unsupported data in the form of lists of tax information, such as dividends and interest received, charitable contributions, and medical expenses, such information may be used in the preparation of a tax return without verification unless it appears to be incorrect, incomplete, or inconsistent either on its face or on the basis of other facts known to the CPA.

5) Even though there is no requirement to examine underlying documentation, the CPA should encourage the client to provide supporting data where appropriate. For example, the CPA should encourage the client to submit underlying documents for use in tax return preparation to permit full consideration of income and deductions arising from security transactions and from pass-through entities such as estates, trusts, partnerships, and S corporations. This should reduce the possibility of misunderstanding, inadvertent errors, and administrative problems in the examination of returns by the IRS.

## Another problem arises in the following situations

Suppose you gave a client advice on a tax matter such as a proposed transaction or form of business organization. Then, a change in the law, new Revenue Ruling or court decision, affects your previous advice or even makes it inapplicable. Must, or should, you notify the client of these developments?

There is no question that you will enhance your standing in his eyes if you take the time and trouble to advise him of the change. But, whether you actually have a moral or ethical responsibility to do so is open to question. Here again, we draw on the guidelines provided by the AICPA to its members. We realize that these guidelines may not be entirely appropriate to your situation but they should surely help you to define your own course of action.

## Form and Content of Advice to Clients

This statement discusses certain aspects of providing tax advice to a client and considers the circumstances in which the CPA has a responsibility to communicate with the client when subsequent developments affect advice previously provided. The statement does not, however, cover the CPA's responsibilities when it is expected that the advice rendered is likely to be relied upon by parties other than the CPA's client:

1) In providing tax advice to a client, the CPA should use judgment to ensure that the advice given reflects professional competence and appropriately serves the

client's needs. The CPA is not required to follow a standard format or guidelines in communicating written or oral advice to a client.

2) In advising or consulting with a client on tax matters, the CPA should assume that the advice will affect the manner in which the matters or transactions considered ultimately will be reported on the client's tax returns. Thus, for all tax advice the CPA gives to a client, the CPA should follow the standards in SRTP No. 1 relating to tax return positions.

3) The CPA may choose to communicate with a client when subsequent developments affect advice previously provided with respect to significant matters. However, the CPA cannot be expected to have assumed responsibility for initiating such communication except while assisting a client in implementing procedures or plans associated with the advice provided or when the CPA undertakes this obligation by specific agreement with the client.

4) Tax advice is recognized as a valuable service provided by CPAs. The form of advice may be oral or written and the subject matter may range from routine to complex. Because the range of advice is so extensive and because advice should meet special needs of a client, neither standard format nor guideline for communicating advice to the client can be established to cover all situations.

5) Although oral advice may serve a client's needs appropriately in routine matters or in well-defined areas, written communications are recommended in important, unusual, or complicated transactions. In the judgment of the CPA, oral advice may be followed by a written confirmation to the client.

6) In deciding on the form of advice provided to a client, the CPA should exercise professional judgment and should consider such factors as the following:
    - The importance of the transaction and amounts involved
    - The specific or general nature of the client's inquiry
    - The time available for development and submission of the advice
    - The technical complications presented
    - The existence of authorities and precedents
    - The tax sophistication of the client and the client's staff
    - The need to seek legal advice

7) The CPA may assist a client in implementing procedures or plans associated with the advice offered. During this active participation, the CPA continues to advise and should review and revise such advice as warranted by new developments and factors affecting the transaction.

8) Sometimes the CPA is requested to provide tax advice but does not assist in implementing the plans adopted. While developments such as legislative or

administrative changes or further judicial interpretations may affect the advice previously provided, the CPA cannot be expected to communicate later developments that affect such advice unless the CPA undertakes this obligation by specific agreement with the client. Thus, the communication of significant developments affecting previous advice should be considered an additional service rather than an implied obligation in normal CPA-client relationship.

9) The client should be informed that advice reflects professional judgment based on an existing situation and that subsequent developments could affect previous professional advice. CPAs should use precautionary language to the effect that their advice is based on facts as stated and authorities that are subject to change.

What happens when you feel that existing rules or regulations do not accurately interpret the law? In addition to the legal implications already discussed there are ethical considerations as to how far you may go in disregarding official IRS pronouncements.

We will once more rely on the AICPA for guidance in this area.

**Tax Return Position**

1) This statement sets forth the standards a CPA should follow in recommending tax return positions and in preparing or signing tax returns including claims for refunds. For this purpose, a "tax return position" is (1) a position reflected on the tax return as to which the client has been specifically advised by the CPA or (2) a position as to which the CPA has knowledge of all material facts and, on the basis of those facts, has concluded that the position is appropriate.

2) With respect to tax return positions, a CPA should comply with the following standards:

   a) A CPA should not recommend to a client that a position be taken with respect to the tax treatment of any item on a return unless the CPA has a good faith belief that the position has a realistic possibility of being sustained administratively or judicially on its merits if challenged.

   b) A CPA should not prepare or sign a return as an income tax return preparer if the CPA knows that the return takes a position that the CPA could not recommend under the standard expressed in paragraph .02a.

   c) Notwithstanding paragraphs 2a and 2b, a CPA may recommend a position that the CPA concludes is not frivolous so long as the position is adequately disclosed on the return or claim for refund.

   d) In recommending certain tax return positions and in signing a return on which a tax return position is taken, a CPA should, where relevant, advise the client as to the potential penalty consequences of the recommended tax return position and the opportunity, if any, to avoid such penalties through disclosure.

3) The CPA should not recommend a tax return position that:

   a) Exploits the Internal Revenue Service (IRS) audit selection process; or

   b) Serves as a mere "arguing" position advanced solely to obtain leverage in the bargaining process of settlement negotiation with the Internal Revenue Service.

4) A CPA has both the right and responsibility to be an advocate for the client with respect to any positions satisfying the aforementioned standards.

5) Our self-assessment tax system can only function effectively if taxpayers report their income on a tax return that is true, correct, and complete. A tax return is primarily a taxpayer's representation of facts, and the taxpayer has the final responsibility for positions taken on the return.

6) CPAs have a duty to the tax system as well as to their clients. However, it is well-established that the taxpayer has no obligation to pay more taxes than are legally owed, and the CPA has a duty to the client to assist in achieving that result. The aforementioned standards will guide the CPA in meeting responsibilities to the tax system and to clients.

7) The standards suggested herein require that a CPA in good faith believe that the position is warranted in existing law or can be supported by a good faith argument for an extension, modification, or reversal of existing law. For example, the CPA may reach such a conclusion on the basis of well-reasoned articles, treatises, IRS General Counsel Memoranda, a General Explanation of a Revenue Act prepared by the staff of the Joint Committee on Taxation and Internal Revenue Service written determinations (for example, private letter rulings), whether or not such sources are treated as "authority" under section 6661. A position would meet these standards even though, for example, it is later abandoned due to practical or procedural aspects of an IRS administrative hearing or in the litigation process.

8) Where the CPA has a good faith belief that more than one position meets the standards suggested herein, the CPA's advice concerning alternative acceptable positions may include a discussion of the likelihood that each such position might or might not cause the client's tax return to be examined and whether the position would be challenged in an examination.

9) In some cases, a CPA may conclude that a position is not warranted under the standard set forth in the preceding paragraph, 2a. A client may, however, still wish to take such a tax return position. Under such circumstances, the client

should have the opportunity to make such an assertion, and the CPA should be able to prepare and sign the return provided the position is adequately disclosed on the return or claim for refund and the position is not frivolous. A "frivolous" position is one that is knowingly advanced in bad faith and is patently improper.

10) The CPA's determination of whether information is adequately disclosed by the client is based on the facts and circumstances of the particular case. No detailed rules have been formulated, for purposes of this statement, to prescribe the manner in which information should be disclosed.

11) Where the particular facts and circumstances lead the CPA to believe that a taxpayer penalty might be asserted, the CPA should so advise the client and should discuss with the client issues related to disclosure on the tax return. Although disclosure is not required if the position meets the standard in paragraph .02a, the CPA may nevertheless recommend that a client disclose a position. Disclosure should be considered when the CPA believes it would mitigate the likelihood of claims of taxpayer penalties under the Internal Revenue Code or would avoid the possible application of the six-year statutory period for assessment under section 6501(e). Although the CPA should advise the client with respect to disclosure, it is the client's responsibility to decide whether and how to disclose.

Finally, every practitioner encounters situations where he discovers errors or omissions made by another practitioner. Is he morally or ethically bound to bring the matter to the client's attention? Suppose he does, and the client refuses to correct the error, should or must the practitioner alert the IRS or state (or local) tax authorities?

Here's what the AICPA has to say on the subject, and we strongly endorse their position, whether you are an AICPA member or not.

## Knowledge of Error: Return Preparation

1) This statement considers the responsibility of a CPA who becomes aware of an error in a client's previously filed tax return or of the client's failure to file a required tax return. The term "error" includes a position taken on a prior year's return that no longer meets these standards due to legislation, judicial decisions, or administrative pronouncements having retroactive effect. However, an error does not include an item that has an insignificant effect on the client's tax liability.

2) This statement applies whether or not the CPA prepared or signed the return that contains the error.

3) The CPA should inform the client promptly upon becoming aware of an error in a previously filed return or upon becoming aware of a client's failure to file a required return. The CPA should recommend the measures to be taken. Such recommendation may be given orally. The CPA is not obligated to inform the Internal Revenue Service, and the CPA may not do so without the client's permission, except where required by law.

4) If the CPA is requested to prepare the current year's return and the client has not taken appropriate action to correct an error in a prior year's return, the CPA should consider whether to withdraw from preparing the return and whether to continue a professional relationship with the client. If the CPA does prepare such current year's return, the CPA should take reasonable steps to ensure that the error is not repeated.

5) While performing services for a client, a CPA may become aware of an error in a previously filed return or may become aware that the client failed to file a required return. The CPA should advise the client of the error (as required by Treasury Department Circular 230) and the measures to be taken. It is the client's responsibility to decide whether to correct the error. In appropriate cases, particularly where it appears that the Internal Revenue Service might assert the charge of fraud or other criminal misconduct, the client should be advised to consult legal counsel before taking any action. In the event that the client does not correct an error, or agree to take the necessary steps to change from an erroneous method of accounting, the CPA should consider whether to continue a professional relationship with the client.

6) If the CPA decides to continue a professional relationship with the client and is requested to prepare a tax return for a year subsequent to that in which the error occurred, then the CPA should take reasonable steps to ensure that the error is not repeated. If a CPA learns the client is using an erroneous method of accounting, when it is past the due date to request IRS permission to change to a method meeting the standards of SRTP No. 1, the CPA may sign a return for the current year, providing the return includes appropriate disclosure of the use of the erroneous method.

7) Whether an error has no more than an insignificant effect on the client's tax liability is left to the judgment of the individual CPA based on all the facts and circumstances known to the CPA. In judging whether an erroneous method of accounting has more than an insignificant effect, the CPA should consider the method's cumulative effect and its effect on the current year's return.

## Knowledge of Error: Administrative Proceedings

1) This statement considers the responsibility of a CPA who becomes aware of an error in a return that is the subject of an administrative proceeding, such as an examination by the IRS or an appeals conference relating to a return or a claim for refund. As used herein, the term "error" includes any position, omission, or method of accounting, which, at the time the return is filed, fails to meet the standards set out in SRTP No. 1. The term "error" also includes a position taken on a prior year's return that no longer meets these standards due to legislation, judicial decisions, or administrative pronouncements having retroactive effect. However, an error does not include an item that has an insignificant effect on the client's tax liability.

2) This statement applies whether or not the CPA prepared or signed the return that contains the error; it does not apply where a CPA has been engaged by legal counsel to provide assistance in a matter relating to the counsel's client.

3) When the CPA is representing a client in an administrative proceeding with respect to a return which contains an error of which the CPA is aware, the CPA should inform the client promptly upon becoming aware of the error. The CPA should recommend the measures to be taken. Such recommendation may be given orally. The CPA is neither obligated to inform the Internal Revenue Service nor may the CPA do so without the client's permission, except where required by law.

4) The CPA should request the client's agreement to disclose the error to the Internal Revenue Service. Lacking such agreement, the CPA should consider whether to withdraw from representing the client in the administrative proceeding and whether to continue a professional relationship with the client.

5) When the CPA is engaged to represent the client before the Internal Revenue Service in an administrative proceeding with respect to a return containing an error of which the CPA is aware, the CPA should advise the client to disclose the error to the Internal Revenue Service. It is the client's responsibility to decide whether to disclose the error. In appropriate cases, particularly where it appears that the Internal Revenue Service might assert the charge of fraud or other criminal misconduct, the client should be advised to consult legal counsel before taking any action. If the client refuses to disclose or permit disclosure of an error, the CPA should consider whether to withdraw from representing the client in the administrative proceeding and whether to continue a professional relationship with the client.

6) Once disclosure is agreed upon, it should not be delayed to such a degree that the client or CPA might be considered to have failed to act in good faith or

to have, in effect, provided misleading information. In any event, disclosure should be made before the conclusion of the administrative proceeding.

7) Whether an error has an insignificant effect on the client's tax liability should be left to the judgment of the individual CPA based on all the facts and circumstances known to the CPA. In judging whether an erroneous method of accounting has more than an insignificant effect, the CPA should consider the method's cumulative effect and its effect on the return which is the subject of the administrative proceeding.

# Chapter 16

# Tax Audits and How to Handle Them

*Nothing in life is to be feared. It is only to be understood.*
**Marie Curie**

*Whatever course you decide upon, there is always someone to tell you— you are wrong. There are always difficulties arising, which tempt you to believe that your critics are right. To map out a course of action and follow it to an end...requires courage.*
**Ralph Waldo Emerson**

## How and Why a Return is Selected for an IRS Audit

Every tax return filed is checked for mathematical accuracy and completeness.

If any mathematical errors are found, or if some vital information or required attachments are missing, the taxpayer will receive a notice, either correcting the error or asking for the missing data.

Next, the IRS computer screens the return to determine its "audit potential." The return's audit potential is rated on the basis of a mathematical formula called the Discriminant Function System (DIF), under which various weights are assigned to different entries on the return. The exact characteristics that will flag a return are, of course, kept secret. But generally speaking, any income tax return that shows larger than usual personal deductions for the amount of income reported, especially in such categories as contributions, medical expenses, etc., as well as certain types of business expenses—particularly large travel and entertainment expenses—is a likely candidate for an audit. Nevertheless, if the examiner—on the basis of his experience and judgment—feels that the return appears to be in order, it will be returned to the file; if not, the return is forwarded to the IRS Audit Branch nearest the taxpayer's residence.

In addition to the computer-screening test, the IRS also annually selects a certain percentage of returns at random for further examination. The exact percentage varies from year to year. In the last year for which figures are available the range was from less than one-half percent for returns in the under $20,000 income group, to almost 9 percent in the case of returns reporting more than $100,000 in income. The percentage is also higher for returns showing itemized deductions than for standard deduction returns and for returns with Schedule C business income.

The IRS further conducts ongoing taxpayer compliance programs in which it annually examines almost every taxpayer in selected groups, businesses or professions, in a particular area. Often targeted are taxpayers such as doctors, cab drivers, waiters and others who receive a portion of their income in cash.

There are other reasons that a return may be selected for closer examination—usually as a result of manual screening by IRS examiners. For instance, a taxpayer reporting poverty level income, but residing in a "high-class" neighborhood is a likely target. Or, the individual may have had his return done by a tax preparer that is suspected, or being investigated, by the IRS for unscrupulous or fraudulent practices.

Other factors that may trigger an audit are large refund claims, the taxpayer's prior history, discrepancies between the return and information documents filed with IRS (W-2s, 1099s, etc.), or information received from informers. In recent years the IRS frequently conducted so-called "financial status audits" and "economic reality checks" to flush out unreported income. Agents would examine in detail the taxpayer's assets, living style, and estimated expenditures to determine whether they match the income reported on the return. The 1998 tax law restricts these techniques to situations where the IRS has other indications of unreported income.

According to current government figures, of the more than 96 million returns filed in a recent year, 1.7 million, or 1.8 percent, were selected for audit. Of these, roughly two-thirds were picked because they matched the computer profile for returns with high audit potential. The balance was selected manually or in connection with one of the various enforcement programs.

But no matter what the percentage odds are, you can expect that some of your clients will be audited and the great majority will turn to you for assistance. If you are new or relatively inexperienced in this area you're likely to be somewhat apprehensive. The following discussion, advice, and hints should alleviate your apprehension. Whether you are a novice or a seasoned practitioner, these suggestions will help you face the IRS with confidence and substantially improved prospects.

## Reassuring Your Clients

Your first task is to reassure the client that the selection of his return does not necessarily mean that anything is wrong, that there is any negligence or error on his part or yours, or that the IRS suspects him of cheating. Explain the selection process to him, emphasizing that the return may have been picked at random, or that he may be in a particular class of taxpayers being checked.

Make it clear to him that an individual (especially with more than average income) whose return has never been examined may very well have been overpaying his tax. This observation is particularly appropriate when you are dealing with a new client.

To remove some of the dread a tax examination brings on, it may help if you acquaint your client with the official "IRS Statement of Principles of Tax Administration," which are supposed to guide all IRS employees in their dealings with the public:

> *"The function of the Internal Revenue Service is to administer the Internal Revenue Code. Tax policy for raising revenue is determined by Congress.*
>
> *With this in mind, it is the duty of the Service to carry out that policy by correctly applying the laws enacted by Congress; to determine the reasonable meaning of various Code provisions in light of the Congressional purpose in enacting them; and to perform this work in a fair and impartial manner, with neither a government nor a taxpayer point of view.*
>
> *At the heart of administration is interpretation of the Code. It is the responsibility of each person in the Service, charged with the duty of interpreting the law, to try to find the true meaning of the statutory provision and not to adopt a strained construction in the belief that he is 'protecting the revenue.'*
>
> *The Service also has the responsibility of applying and administering the law in a reasonable, practical manner. Issues should only be raised by examining officers when they have merit, never arbitrarily or for trading purposes.*
>
> *Administration should be both reasonable and vigorous. It should be conducted with as little delay as possible and with great courtesy and consideration. It should never try to overreach and should be reasonable within the bounds of law and sound administration."*

### Types of Examination

The IRS has two examination procedures, and the type of procedure selected depends largely on the type of return and size of income. Individual returns, especially those in the lower income brackets, are normally selected for office examination (formerly called an "office audit"). This means that the taxpayer (or his representative) is requested to appear at the nearest IRS office at the designated time and date, together with the required records and further substantiation. Sometimes, an office examination is handled by correspondence and the taxpayer is requested to send the required data by mail. This method is usually employed where the desired data or substantiation is not extensive.

A field examination (previously called a "field audit"), where the IRS agent comes to the taxpayer's business, office, or home is usually confined to business tax returns or high income individual taxpayers. Occasionally, a field examination is set up where the IRS suspects that a taxpayer with a small reported income lives in a lavish style, way out of proportion to his reported earnings. Then the examiner—besides checking taxpayer's books—will take a closer look at the type of home the taxpayer lives in, his manner, and standard of living, etc.

In the usual case, though, where you are dealing with an individual, non-business return, your client will be involved in an office examination. Assuming that the taxpayer was asked to personally appear at the IRS office, several possibilities arise:

1) The client can go by himself.
2) You can go with the client.
3) You can go alone as the client's representative (subject to the rules of practice previously discussed).

The route to choose depends on the complexity of the return, the number of issues involved, and equally important, the nature and temperament of the client.

If it's a relatively simple return, and all, or mostly all substantiation is available, there is really no need for you to go to the examination unless the client is temperamentally unfit to go by himself. There are individuals who, for some reason, become extremely agitated, frightened, or antagonistic when confronted with IRS agents. Others get themselves into trouble by talking too much.

If it is decided that you will represent the client, the next question is whether or not to take him along. Here again the previously mentioned factors should be taken into account.

If the client is temperamentally suitable and willing to go, we suggest that you take him along. For one, it may hasten the examination because there will be a number of questions and issues raised that only he can answer. There is also a psychological advantage to his being there. Frequently an agent may doubt a client's statements or representations. He may even suspect some of the records as being "doctored." Nevertheless, he will usually hesitate to call the client a "liar" to his face, while he will have no such reservations in his absence. Likewise, if the client is obviously unsophisticated in these matters, or convincingly appears as honest and trustworthy, it may help to put some of the agent's doubts to rest.

## Find Out What the IRS Wants

Your first step in preparing for the examination is to find out exactly what the IRS is after. In most cases, the letter advising the taxpayer of the examination gives that information. The letter may request substantiation of contributions, medical expenses, rental expenses, and so on.

But your quest should go beyond that. Oftentimes, one or two items on the tax return triggered the examination, and if these can be explained and substantiated to the satisfaction of the examiner, you may have smooth sailing with the rest of the return.

You can sometimes, but not always, get this further information by simply calling the examiner in charge and discussing the matter with her. In fact, many experienced practitioners routinely call the IRS agent when a client is audited to discuss the matter with her. Ostensibly, many call to set up an appointment or to change the appointment, but their real purpose is to determine what the agent is really after. If the agent is unknown to you, and you plan to either accompany the client or represent him at the examination (more about that later), it won't hurt if you speak to her beforehand and try to establish some kind of personal rapport with her.

Generally, the IRS agent will not discuss a client's return with you, unless she has on file a Power of Attorney, Form 2848, or a written statement from the client authorizing you to act on his behalf.

If you are lucky, you can determine during your preliminary conversation whether she is the "fault-finding" type who will insist that you show proof for every penny claimed, or whether she is the more broadminded type who will concentrate on the big issues and not spend much time fretting about petty items. Fortunately, there are more of the latter type around. At the same time, you can try to impress the agent with your knowledge, expertise, and professionalism. From the beginning you should impress the agent with the understanding that you have every intention—and are capable—of backing up the return, and that you have full confidence in your client's position.

## Preparing for the Examination

Now let's get down to the crux of the matter. Assuming you have a fair idea of what the IRS is after, it is up to you to help, coax, perhaps even needle, your client into providing the necessary information. After all, the return is his, not yours, and it is imperative that your client understand that the responsibility squarely falls on his shoulders, not yours. You can help and assist him in every possible way, but it is his task to assemble the necessary bills, receipts, checks and other supportive items.

Some clients take the attitude: "My tax consultant prepared the return, let him worry about it." Needless to say, this is an unhealthy, counterproductive attitude and you should seek to eradicate it, not when the return is examined, but when it is initially prepared. By the time the return is examined, it is usually one or more years after the return was filed.

We suggest that you assemble the return under examination—as well as all related documents, copies of previously audited returns, etc.—into a separate file and keep them all together. Never mix audit papers with your current year's worksheets or returns.

What do you do if the client is unable to produce any kind of substantiation for a large expenditure? Here, a full explanation may be helpful. In one case, for instance, a very sizeable deduction for medicines and drugs was reduced to $50 because the taxpayer was unable to show receipts or checks. The tax consultant then prepared a letter explaining that one of the taxpayer's children (identified by name) was required to take regular daily anti-allergy medication, at a certain cost per week. He also listed the name of the drug, the dosage and the name of the physician. Other drug items were similarly explained with the result that the full deduction was reinstated without further question.

As a rule, the more proof you can furnish in the way of names, dates, exact amounts, reasons, and explanations, etc., the better your chances are of seeing the questioned deductions go through. However, while preparing for the examination, if you come across weak spots in the return—items you feel you will have a hard time substantiating or defending—by all means, tell your client right away to avoid disappointment later on. It is better for you and the client if he expects the worst and then is surprised to find that it turned out better, than if he is confident at first only to experience great disappointment later.

Incidentally, if someone else, or if the client himself, prepared the return under examination, you have a good chance to convert that taxpayer into a regular client. Don't criticize the previous preparer, but show how you would have maintained a stronger position with the IRS if you had prepared the return—given the precautions you normally take.

## Coaching the Client for the Examination

Let's assume the client decides to attend the audit by himself, rather than have you accompany or represent him. A little coaching session with you beforehand will greatly enhance his chances at success.

First and foremost, make sure the client understands that he has to be cooperative, not belligerent. Human nature being what it is, the taxpayer's stubbornness and defiance will tend to make the agent more suspicious and more determined to dig into every item under examination. It may even invite him to raise new issues. At the same time, it is essential that you advise your client not to volunteer any information unnecessarily. Let him answer the questions, furnish the requested data and records, but no more! Many taxpayers invite trouble, for in their eagerness to be extra helpful or impress the agent, they unwittingly provide him with possibly incriminating information. As mentioned previously, if, in your judgment, the client is either too belligerent or too talkative, it is better to dissuade him from going to the examination, or at least make sure that you accompany him and try to keep him under control. If the client is intelligent enough and knowledgeable you can also brief him on some of the points discussed in the next section.

## How to Deal with the IRS Agent

In dealing with an agent who is examining a client's return, bear in mind that his job is to protect the interests of the Treasury by carefully examining the return to determine whether it shows the full legal tax liability. As a result, the average agent develops a rather suspicious nature. However, it would be wrong to treat every examiner from the start as an adversary. In fact, the IRS in recent years has taken pains to keep the previously antagonistic client-agent atmosphere out of examinations and conferences with taxpayers.

IRS agents, like all human beings, vary in nature, temperament and attitude.

Although official policy dictates that they are to determine the tax due with reasonableness and fairness, rather than squeeze out every possible dollar, some are more zealous or technical at this than others. In general, however, if you give the agent the feeling that you are dealing with him in good faith, there's a good chance that he will reciprocate and treat you and your client in a similar manner.

It is therefore up to you to avoid turning the agent into an adversary. Be friendly, without indulging in undue flattery. Treat him in a businesslike manner and show respect, realizing that he has a job to do. On the other hand, your attitude should clearly be that it is your job to protect the taxpayer, and that you are not afraid to do so. In other words, establish at the outset an atmosphere of mutual respect. This is especially important if you live in a rural area or small town, since you are likely to come into contact with the same few agents time and again. Therefore, it is wise to establish good rapport as soon as possible. Keep in mind too, that agents, among themselves, indulge in a certain amount of "shop-talk" discussing cases, taxpayers, and tax practitioners. This means there is a good chance that an agent you haven't met as yet has already heard about you—especially if the job you do is out of the ordinary.

Having attended to the preliminaries, the agent will go over the items in question one by one. If the return is "tight" and you have sufficient documentary evidence to support your position, then you have little to worry about. If, however, as in most cases, some or many items are in the "gray" area, you will need tact, diplomacy and a certain amount of psychology to come out ahead.

Although IRS agents are specifically enjoined from engaging in any "wheeling and dealing," it frequently takes a considerable amount of bargaining—give-and-take—to arrive at a satisfactory settlement, particularly when a number of issues are involved. In such cases, it pays to be persistent, but not petty, to ensure the best possible deal for your client. In other words, make it understood that you are willing and anxious to bring the matter to a prompt conclusion, that you will be reasonable where you feel he is right, but you will not permit your client to pay more tax than you think he is obligated to pay.

Some experienced practitioners, in advance of the audit, classify all items in question into three categories:

- Items they are prepared to concede,
- Items over which they will not concede, and
- "Negotiable" issues.

Group 1 includes those issues you feel are hard or impossible to defend, over which the IRS is going to win anyway, and for good measure, you might also throw in a few minor or inconsequential items.

Experienced negotiators feel it is good psychology to let the opponent have a taste of victory at the beginning. This will convince him that you are a reasonable person and may put him under some pressure to reciprocate by demonstrating that he too can be reasonable.

It will help if you try to put yourself into the client's shoes, to better understand what he is up against and what his options are. Until recently it was an open secret (despite repeated denials by the IRS) that agents worked on a "quota" system. In other words, every agent was more or less expected to "raise" a certain amount of money in additional tax assessments. The more efficient he was in this respect, the faster he advanced. Lately, the emphasis on money-raising ability has abated somewhat, and agents are now urged to conduct "quality" examinations even to the point of discovering and correcting errors made by taxpayers in which they overpaid their taxes (but don't rely on it).

Nevertheless, it is the general consensus by those in the know that agents are still given to understand that they must, to some extent at least, justify the time spent on an audit. In fact, the IRS, in its annual budget request to Congress, usually asks for funds to hire additional auditors on the grounds that each and every dollar spent on their salaries produces X amount of dollars in additional revenue. This means that the longer an agent spends on an examination, the harder he will try to come up with a correspondingly large tax deficiency. It is therefore in your interest to give the agent all the help you can so he may conclude his assignment as fast as possible.

You should also be aware that even though agents are under some pressure to produce money for the Treasury, they are also under pressure to close as many cases as possible. Knowing this can sometimes give you a psychological edge, where all issues have been resolved except for one or two items. As a rule, most agents are anxious to settle such cases to conclude the examination. This is especially true where you have convinced the agent that there is a point beyond which you will not go to reach a settlement.

Here are some additional hints suggested by seasoned tax professionals:

1) Never hedge when answering an agent's question. Say "yes" or "no," or "I don't know." You need not hesitate to admit that you don't know the answer to a question.

2) Never impugn an agent's motives or attack him personally, even if you feel he is being stubborn or arbitrary.

3) If the agent is forced to give in on a hotly contested issue, permit him to do so in a respectable manner.

4) Do not negotiate in front of outsiders. It will make the agent only more determined to show his competence and bargaining ability.

**The Issues Involved**

In general, tax controversies fall into two categories. In one, there is a question of law or interpretation; in the other, there is a question of fact. Where there is a question of fact, did the taxpayer really make the expenditures deducted, or did he actually support the claimed dependent?…there is no better way to arrive at a quick and favorable solution than by demonstrating to the agent the care with which you prepared the return (assuming you prepared it). If you followed our previous suggestions about preparing your substantiations at the time the return is made out, your task will be an easy one.

Where the question is one of law or interpretation, you probably explained to the client in preparing the return (again assuming you prepared it), that the particular point is open to debate, and it is now up to you to convince the agent that you are right. This usually calls for a certain amount of research on your part, and this is where the tax services and other research and reference materials come in handy, because they cite previous rulings and court decisions on similar or related questions.

Finally, bear in mind that in questions of law or interpretation the agent operates along rather rigidly prescribed rules. He does not really have too much leeway. He may secretly sympathize with your client and feel that a certain deduction should be granted, but if the official IRS position on this item is "no," then his hands are tied. A common error committed by many taxpayers (and even some practitioners who should know better), is to try and convince an agent that a certain rule or regulation is unfair. You must understand—and share this understanding with your client—that the agent does not write the rules. His job is to enforce them, and he has very little say in the matter.

However, where questions of fact are involved, the agent has considerably more authority. She is expected to use her judgment, and as far as the IRS is concerned, if she considers an item substantiated, her decision is generally final.

## Preparing the Documentation

In order to substantiate a claimed deduction (this is the area where most problems lie) you must prove:

1) That the expenditure was actually made, and/or
2) That it is allowable.

The most common and accepted substantiation of expenditures are canceled checks, but sometimes the agent will want to see the bills, or invoices too. In the case of charitable contributions, agents often want to see receipts, especially for larger amounts. If these are not available, you may get a letter from the organization confirming the gift. Bear in mind that for contributions of $250 or more made at one time the client is required to have a receipt on file. Losses due to casualty and theft can often be substantiated by photos, (especially in the case of fire, storm, flood, etc.), newspaper clippings, and police reports (in the case of accidents, thefts, and robberies). If nothing else is available, an affidavit from witnesses or others having knowledge of the circumstances should be submitted.

**Here is an excellent way to assemble and have control over substantiating information:**

Take a multi-column worksheet and enter the deductions in the first column (or other questioned items) as they were reported on the return. In the second column, enter the amount of substantiation you have available, and in the third column, make a note of the type of substantiation (i.e. checks, receipts, letters, etc.). In the fourth column, enter those items or amounts for which you have no substantiation. Use the remaining columns for notations or explanations as to how you arrived at the unsubstantiated figures. This lets you see, at a glance, your strengths and weaknesses—what you have in the form of proof and what you still need.

Whether or not you actually want to show this sheet to the agent depends on how well documented the return is. If all or most of the items on the sheet are substantiated, by all means let the agent see how well you did your homework, and if not, then keep it out of sight.

Needless to say, this worksheet approach will save you and the agent considerable time and will also help ensure that you or the client do not forget to bring any needed papers or documents. Another advantage of this system is that it helps put you, rather than the agent, in control of the order in which the audit proceeds. As we mentioned before, you can then start with the easy items and gradually work your way up to the tougher ones.

We strongly suggest that before you submit this documentation you examine it critically yourself, just as any agent would. Check if the documents are convincing and credible. Also check if the dates shown correspond with those on the return. All too often a taxpayer will happily furnish a receipt or other document to prove expenditures, only to have the agent discover that the check or receipt shows a different year than the one in question.

The reason we urge you to examine all proofs and documents with a critical eye is simple; careful documentation of the questioned items not only makes your case considerably stronger, but also engenders respect for you on the part of the agent. Conversely, too many rejected or weak items will undermine his confidence and may even cast doubt on the entire return.

Incidentally, preparing all this documentation with your client provides you with a good opportunity to educate him for the future. Show him how to avoid repeating such mistakes by proper record keeping, how to pay all deductible items by check, along with other similar precautions. It is unfortunate, but true, that many clients are not impressed with the need for strong documentation until they are faced with an audit.

This is also the time to emotionally prepare the client if the examination isn't going well. If he has resigned himself to the fact that he may be hit with a large deficiency the shock will be less painful if and when it comes. If the audit comes out better than expected, even if he has some additional tax to pay, he will be in a much healthier frame of mind. In fact, he may even cheerfully add up all the money he saved.

### The Agent's Report

At the audit's conclusion, the agent will write up his report proposing:

- (If you are lucky), either no change; or
- (If you are even luckier) a decrease in the tax liability shown; or
- (As in many cases) an increase in the tax liability.

The agent is required to explain all proposed adjustments to you or to the client, so don't hesitate to ask about every proposed change to fully understand what is involved. Ideally the changes are detailed in writing, if you can get such notes from the agent. If the agent's findings are agreed to, he writes up an agreement form (usually Form 870) which the client (or you, as his authorized representative) signs. Once the agreement form is signed, interest on any additional tax due automatically stops thirty days later. Or, the client can stop running up interest immediately by paying the deficiency at once. The IRS can take credit card payments at its office or you can make a related payment via its website.

On the other hand, if you don't agree with the agent's proposed adjustments, you can request, and usually obtain, an immediate conference with the agent's supervisor. You may sometimes find the supervisor to be a little more flexible, especially if you are already close to an agreement with the agent. If you do, the same procedure applies.

But a warning here is in order. If you have a weak case with respect to several issues and the agent gave in on all but one or two (or on a major issue while remaining adamant on minor ones), it may be wiser to settle directly with him. The supervisor may choose to pick up on those other issues, and that could make matters worse.

### Should You Settle With the Agent?

Suppose you don't agree with the agent or the supervisor: Should you settle anyhow, or is it advisable to strive for a better deal by pursuing the matter further?

The answer to this question depends primarily on:

1) The amount of money involved,
2) The strength of your case, and
3) The client's temperament and willingness to fight.

In other words, does he have the stomach for it, even if he has an excellent chance at winning?

If the amount involved is small, there is little reason to incur the expense, bother, and headache of going through the IRS appeals procedure. You might explain to the client that further appeals are apt to be expensive, time-consuming, and unless the strength of your case and the amount of tax at issue war- rants it, he ought to conserve his time and energy by settling. You should also alert the client to the possibility that if he appeals, the return will be reviewed by more skilled and experienced IRS employees, and as a result, additional issues or questions may arise. According to IRS statistics, more than 95 percent of all examinations are settled with the agent or supervisor; only a fraction of these disputes enter any stage of the appeal procedure.

Nevertheless, if the client, in your opinion, has a good case and the amount involved justifies the bother and expense, further appeals should be considered. The rationale is that there is enough money involved to justify the appeal even if—as is often the case—you are only partially successful. An appeal may also be warranted even if there isn't a lot of money at stake, if you expect to encounter the same problem repeatedly in future years. In any event, no matter how strong your case is, never assure a client that he or she is going to win. The most you should permit yourself is to appraise the case as being in his favor.

### Going Up the IRS Ladder—The Appeals Procedure

If you and your client are contemplating an appeal, or are undecided, you should of course refuse to sign the agreement form, but instead await the receipt of the official copy of the agent's examination report, accompanied by the "30-day letter." This letter gives you thirty days to either accept the proposed adjustment by signing the agreement form, or initiate an appeal within the IRS. If no response is made the taxpayer will then receive a Statutory Notice of Deficiency or "90-day letter" which means he has 90 days to either pay, or take his case to the Tax Court.

If you decide to appeal within the Service, you should not wait for the "90-day letter." Instead, during the period specified in the "30-day letter," make a request for an "appeals office conference," in accordance with the instructions accompanying the letter.

Remember: once the case reaches the "appeals conference level" you can't represent the client unless you are a CPA, attorney, or Enrolled to Practice before the IRS. However, anyone who prepared the return or has knowledge of the pertinent facts can accompany the client as a "witness."

### The Field Examination

The previous discussion relating to office examinations applies to field examinations as well. Since field audits normally encompass a larger area they usually take longer and require more advance preparation.

When the agent appears at the client's business or home he should be given a comfortable place to work and be treated politely. There is nothing inappropriate about offering him an occasional cup of coffee or other refreshments, but don't make him so comfortable that he'll be reluctant to leave and consequently be tempted to prolong the audit.

If lunchtime intervenes and you feel the examination is almost complete, don't offer to take him to lunch or have sandwiches delivered to his desk. An empty stomach may persuade him to finish sooner and settle the items in dispute on your terms. On the other hand, if he is going to stay all afternoon, you could offer to take him to lunch at a nearby restaurant. If you do, choose a place that is not-too-expensive, and let the agent pay his own bill if he insists. In fact, he is supposed to. Also, don't talk "shop" during lunch unless he broaches the subject first.

Some practitioners like to postpone discussing the really tough items until near quitting time. This gives the agent the choice of having to stay overtime and come home late for dinner (an unattractive prospect, especially since he doesn't get paid extra for it), come back the next day (which may interfere with his schedule), or try to settle with you and conclude the examination. Taking this route, though, does involve a risk, for the agent may decide to come back and spend another half or full day with you on the examination.

One important point: In case of a field examination, try to ascertain at once whether you are dealing with a regular or a "special" agent. Special agents work for the Criminal Investigation Division of the IRS and are used primarily for fraud investigations. So if a "special agent" contacts a client, the chances are he is suspected of fraud. Advise the client to hire an experienced attorney immediately and not discuss anything with the agent or disclose any information without first consulting his attorney.

Likewise, if in the course of preparing for the audit, you suspect tax fraud on the part of the client, you should by all means urge him to get a criminal defense tax attorney experienced in handling tax fraud cases. The topic and area of law is so complicated a regular criminal defense attorney won't be adequate. If the client asks you to suggest a particular attorney specializing in this type of work, you can ask among fellow practitioners or else contact the local bar association. In any event, once the attorney steps into the picture, you should let him handle the case completely and let him decide whether, and to what extent, he will need your services.

Under prior law the "attorney-client privilege" did not extend to accountants and tax practitioners. Thus the IRS, in the course of a client's audit, could subpoena all practitioner-client communications connected with the return. The 1998 IRS Restructuring Act extended the privilege to CPAs and Enrolled Agents, thus protecting the confidentiality of these records, except in the case of criminal investigations.

The procedure to follow if agreement is not reached in a field examination is generally similar to that of an office examination. However, unlike an office examination, a taxpayer seeking an "appeals office conference" must file a written protest if the amount in dispute exceeds $2,500. If the amount in dispute is less as in the case of office audits—a written protest is not required but is advisable—especially if difficult questions are involved.

We should also point out that regardless of whether the disagreement results from an office or field examination, the taxpayer can skip the Appeals Conference and go to court immediately. To go to the District Court or Court of Claims he must pay the deficiency and then sue for a refund. To go to the Tax Court, he simply ignores the 30-day letter, which would then be followed by the 90-day letter. As soon as he receives that letter he can petition the Tax Court. If he wants to speed the process, he can ask IRS to issue the 90-day letter immediately, and then petition the Court at once.

After your first few IRS audits, you will find that dealing with the IRS has lost its terrors and can even be quite enjoyable, challenging, and stimulating—not to mention involving considerable financial rewards. Furthermore, your success in steering clients through tax audits will prove to be a tremendous prestige and business builder.

## State Tax Audits

While the exact rules and procedures may differ, state income tax audits generally follow a pattern similar to federal tax examinations. State tax auditors will also be on the lookout for unsubstantiated deductions, unallowable items, and so on. Likewise, the suggestions given regarding conduct with IRS agents apply to state tax personnel as well.

Until recently, state income tax audits, except in the case of larger businesses or well-to-do individuals, were a rare phenomenon. Generally, the states used to rely on the federal government to bear the brunt of verifying income tax returns. Since taxpayers in just about all states are required to report any changes on the federal tax return to state tax authorities, the state would eventually get its share of any upward adjustments in an individual's tax return anyway.

During the past few years, however, close coordination has developed between the IRS and the various state tax departments. As a result, there has been some sharing of the audit load between the state and the federal government. It is not uncommon to find a taxpayer being audited in some years by the IRS and in other years by his state tax department. Any adjustments made by the state are passed on to the IRS and vice versa.

This means that although state tax rates are considerably lower than federal rates, it is just as important to fight any upward adjustment on the part of a state auditor, even if the amount involved is not that much. The reason is simply that any increase in the state tax liability automatically results in a much larger increase in the federal tax.

## A Final Word

It cannot be emphasized enough that the groundwork for successfully weathering an examination starts with the preparation of the tax return. You can avoid a lot of grief for your clients and yourself by taking the following precautions:

1) **Properly substantiate:** Working papers, notes, or memos retained with your copy of the return should show what source documents (i.e. checks, receipts, payroll stubs, invoices, etc.) are available to support the return if questioned. If items are based on estimates, make notes as to how the estimate was made.

2) **Professionally prepare:** The entire return should be neat and error-free, with no required data missing, and all required schedules and attachments included.

3) **Explain unusual items:** Properly explain any inconsistencies, unusually high deduction items, and other out-of-the-ordinary entries that could flag an audit on the return. At the very least, make a notation on your own working papers so you have an explanation if the return is questioned.

4) **Last but not least, make it a practice to forewarn clients:** Warn those whose returns show unusual income, or deduction items, or other uncommon features of a possible examination.

**To round out this chapter consider the following additional hints and suggestions:**

- When preparing for an examination try to anticipate all possible questions and objections the agent may raise. Remember that the agent may have to defend items he resolves in the taxpayer's favor, so help him.

- If an audit results in a large tax liability you can generally soften the blow somewhat by arranging for installment payments.

- If purely technical questions are involved, an examination may sometimes go smoother, without the client present, allowing you to talk directly to the agent on a professional level.

- Contrary to what many taxpayers think, last minute filing of tax returns will not avoid a possible audit. The IRS insists that all returns filed receive the same scrutiny, no matter when they are filed.

- In taking a client with you to an examination try not to leave him alone with the agent. He may inadvertently volunteer some damaging remarks or revelations.

- IRS agents will not recommend a tax consultant, but will often express an opinion about his or her qualifications if specifically asked. Obviously, their judgment carries great weight with many taxpayers, so it pays to make sure they have a good opinion of you.

## What about Fees?

As we discussed in the section addressing this subject, fees for representing clients at IRS or state tax examinations, and fees for preparing for such examinations, generally run higher than those charged for routine tax return preparation. However, recent statistics indicate that the differential has leveled off to some extent. While practitioners previously surveyed reported that hourly audit fees ran 25 to 50 percent above hourly tax return fees, that figure was reduced to below 20 percent by 1997. But part of the decrease may be due to the sizeable increases in tax return fees that took place in the interim.

You should also consider the amount of money involved, and finally, your measure of success at handling these controversies. Obviously, where a large amount of money is at stake, it helps to keep the client informed, to prepare him if he eventually has to pay, or to justify your fee if you succeed in saving him all, or even a fair share, of the proposed deficiency. At the same time, don't aggravate the sting of an unexpectedly large tax bill with an exorbitant fee.

In the case of new clients whose returns you did not prepare when billing them, consider the likelihood of their becoming a regular client of yours. If you charge them less now, you will very likely make the difference up many times over in the years to come.

Incidentally, a recent survey, undertaken by the National Society of Accountants of its own members, disclosed that more than 3 out of 4 tax professionals do charge an extra fee for representing clients at IRS examinations. Of these, about 86 percent base their fee on an hourly rate while the remaining 14 percent charge a minimum fixed fee. Average hourly rates range from $75 to about $110 with a median hourly rate of nearly $90, whereas minimum fixed fees reported ran from $150 to as much as $500 per audit.

# Chapter 17

# Assuring Your Advancement through Professional Self-Development

*For many years it has been part of my business to indulge in the analysis of businesses and the personalities who operate them. Without one single exception, successful business results from the power released by the positive attitude of mind. With scarcely a single exception, the failures analyzed have been dominated by the negative attitude. I have yet to find an outstanding successful individual who has a negative outlook. I have yet to find a failure who had positive qualities outweighing the negative. I have yet to find even one top executive, man or woman, who doesn't agree with these findings. Success adores the positive.*
**Douglas Lurton**

*People begin to become successful the minute they decide to be.*
**Anonymous**

In this world, very little stands perfectly still. Most everything is in flux: changing, evolving, hopefully progressing, and the ongoing strength of your tax practice lies in recognizing this fundamental fact of life. To succeed you will have to meet the ever-present prospect and challenge of change.

The changes that will concern you the most will come from two directions:

- **a)** the general tax picture—its rules and regulations—will undergo change, and
- **b)** your clients' needs and circumstances may change from year to year.

For your part, you must keep up with these changes, both in your field, and in your clients' lives. This is necessary not only to maintain, but to advance in your profession as well.

To a far lesser degree, you should also be aware of significant changes in technology that may impact upon your business. As we mentioned earlier, you need not purchase every new item that appears in the marketplace, but if there are tools and resources that have a considerable impact on the way you—or most tax professionals—do their work, then you will want to become part of that momentum in order to further develop your practice.

As a tax consultant, you sell your professional knowledge and skills. Your business does not lie in the stack of forms on your shelf, but in the education, training, skills, and competence you have acquired. And like a merchant who constantly restocks, renews, and upgrades his inventory to stay ahead in business, you too must strive to keep up-to-date, refresh your know-how, and sharp- en your skills, if you want to get ahead. In fact, due to continuous changes in our economy and concurrent developments in the tax field, keeping up-to-date becomes an absolute necessity.

To develop your practice and maximize your earnings you need to increase both in terms of quantity and quality, providing your clients with expanding services, which in turn, is an outgrowth of your ever expanding skills and knowledge in your field of expertise.

Most successful tax professionals can attribute a substantial portion of their growth in revenues to their existing client base. In other words, a percentage of your clients will sooner or later open or expand businesses, form partnerships and corporations, enter the professions, start to buy and sell properties, and engage in a host of other financial transactions and commercial ventures that call for an "in-depth" familiarity with taxes. While you may have the basic knowledge to handle this type of client, it is only through actual experience in the field, through continuous study, through continuous research in handling the various problems that arise, that you become truly proficient in the art of being a tax professional. This chapter will elaborate further on this point.

Finally, increasing your professional skills will provide you with a high degree of personal satisfaction: yourself image and self-confidence will genuinely expand, consistent with your ever expanding reservoir of knowledge, skills, and personal proficiency. You will become a reliable and recognized expert in your field, in a better position to answer to the needs of a growing clientele.

## Keeping Up-To-Date

As you know, tax law is in a continuous state of flux. Congress enacts new tax rules almost every year, the IRS issues new and revised regulations, the tax forms undergo annual revisions, and the courts keep re-interpreting the statutes. So whether you prepare ten income tax returns a year or a thousand, you owe it to your clients to keep abreast of any changes that may affect them.

Fortunately, keeping current in these matters is a lot easier than you may think. Once you have acquired a clear knowledge and basic understanding of the tax provisions as they stand today, you will have little difficulty following whatever twists and turns these rules take on in the future. The reason for this is that the **basic structure** and the **fundamental principles** do not change. For example, an airline pilot does not have to learn how to fly all over again, every time a new plane goes into service, regardless of how radical the new technology may seem, and in spite of how complex the new gadgetry in the cockpit may appear. Likewise, you will easily learn to cope with any changes in tax legislation, now and in the future, because all of it simply relates to a structure you are already quite familiar with. But you must make a point of continually keeping up with the changes.

Keeping current on changes in tax provisions—and how they impact upon your clients—remains a necessity. There is no excuse for any tax professional to prepare this year's return on the basis of last year's tax law.

One way to stay abreast of changes is to purchase—before the tax season—one of the annual income-tax guides, which are readily available at your local bookstore. There are also a number of good websites, periodicals and newsletters that can also keep you abreast of vital tax related information.

Once you have an established and profitable practice, you may want to subscribe to one of the privately published tax services (print, CD-ROM, or Online) that provide a detailed, continuously updated compilation of all current tax laws, regulations, rulings, and court decisions. Such a service is indispensable to anyone with an extensive practice, but in view of the expense involved (subscriptions range from several hundred to well over a thousand dollars per year), we wouldn't recommend it to the beginner.

Consider joining a professional association such as the National Association of Tax Professionals (NATP) at www.natptax.com, or the National Society of Accountants (NSA) at www.nsacct.org. They send out tax law updates to their members and offer forums where members can discuss questions or issues that may come up in their practice.

## How to Sharpen Your Skills and Broaden Your Horizons

If you are genuinely serious about your tax work, you should seek out every opportunity to add to your fund of knowledge and to improve your skills and competence. Any training program, regardless of how thorough it is, can only provide you with the basic foundations you need to enter your field of endeavor. However, once you begin to practice, you will find that your knowledge and expertise will grow along with you "on the job." In fact, the work itself is the best catalyst to assure ongoing development and growth. At the same time, you can also stimulate and accelerate the learning process in numerous other ways: by attending classes, by reading, by information online, and by keeping in touch with fellow practitioners—especially a mentor.

Most service related businesses offer periodic seminars and classes for those in the field. When you find such offerings in your area (or even nearby) it would be a good idea to attend them. For example, the IRS conducts special seminars or workshops for tax professionals. Just make sure the subjects covered are in areas of concern to you and your clients. It makes little sense to attend a conference on gift and estate planning (unless you intend to go into that area) if all you do is income tax returns for wage earners.

In addition to what you may formally learn, such classes and seminars are also good places to make friends, meet your peers, and exchange constructive ideas. People with more experience than you may offer valuable tips; you may meet consultants who will back you up—or vice versa—in a moment of professional need; you might even meet someone who will refer his overflow business to you. Just being in the company of those who share your professional aims and interests can be a productive and satisfying experience.

Another benefit of attending such gatherings is that you may, in turn, be prepared to share what you have learned with others. Perhaps you can give an up-to-date presentation of your own to clients (and non-clients) on vital, practical, and current tax related topics. Aside from its informational value, this can be an excellent promotional opportunity as well.

Reading pertinent material is an excellent way to grow professionally, but to be most effective it should be handled systematically. Try to designate a specific time of day, or a certain amount of time each week (we suggest 2 to 4 hours) to devote to this activity. In fact, try to integrate this into your daily or weekly work schedule. Peruse as much tax related material as you can, but then concentrate on those articles or subjects that are of specific interest to you and your clientele. Also, make sure you read to remember. Pay careful attention, underline, insert marginal notes, set aside anything you might need—whatever helps you retain the material you've just taken in mentally.

You will get more practical knowledge and retention out of what you read if you make a habit of applying what you learn to particular client situations. If you come across an idea that could reduce taxes for a particular client or clients make a note for yourself to do further research and get into it at once. You can well imagine the boost your practice will get if you come up with a few unexpected tax saving ideas for your clients.

Even if an article you read has no immediate practical import, file it away. Try to remember the salient points and keep them in the back of your mind. You never know when you may have an occasion to use such information.

It also helps to read "tax-related" material. Study the history of taxation, try to remember tax related anecdotes, stories, even cartoons. Your well-rounded familiarity with all aspects and facets of the tax world will further enhance your image as a tax professional. You may even incorporate some of what you've learned in newsletters, articles you submit, or in seminars and lectures you give.

Along with seeking ways to increase your tax knowledge and competence, make every effort to expand your knowledge and awareness of general current news, general business matters, and economic trends. Stay informed of what goes on in the world-at-large, and in the business world by reading journals devoted to such developments. All of this applies to your employees and associates as well. Their continuous professional development along these lines will enhance their job performance, and in turn, the overall reputation of your practice.

## The Information Explosion

For better or worse, we live in an age of "information overload," where a virtual flood of information comes our way daily through the various media. With mobile devices today that information flow has increased in capacity and availability day and night. We, the recipients of all these words and images, simply do not have the time or capacity to properly handle it all. Scanning information quickly has now become a required office skill. Therefore, to make optimum use of the time you designate for professional growth, you must routinely screen what is worth your while and relevant to you, from that which has little or no value, and is simply irrelevant.

- First, identify and locate the best available material worthy of your attention—be it in the area of general news, business news, or tax news. It may exist in books, on disk, online, video or audiocassettes, radio, television, or reference services. Then, develop the discipline to disregard all that is unworthy of your time and attention. Finally, with the material you selected to stay with, learn to seek out and focus in on the information, facts, and figures you need, and dispense with the rest.

- Over time, try to develop your own media mix. If one good weekly magazine and a local daily paper, or evening radio or TV program is sufficient for your general news intake then let that be enough. You don't have to read, see, and hear the same thing repeatedly day after day.

- If an occasional tax related text, a specific weekly or monthly tax newsletter or journal, or particular website is all you need to keep abreast of necessary tax news, then let that suffice.

- In all the material that comes your way—from mail, magazines, texts and tapes, to computer generated information—learn to skim the material, rapidly weed out the waste and redundancies, and zero in on the key points, those which matter most to you.

**Getting Into Deeper Tax Areas**

The majority of small, independent tax specialists confine their practices to individual income tax returns. This is obviously where the demand is, but there are millions of partnerships, corporations, trusts, and estates that also need competent tax assistance. Needless to say, practitioners who are equipped to handle these more complex tax situations stand to gain a greater financial reward.

If, at present, you are primarily or exclusively 1040-oriented, it is entirely up to you whether you want to delve into these more complex but lucrative tax areas. If you are content to stay with your practice as it is, there is certainly no need to expand into this field. On the other hand, if you seek broader opportunities along with a substantial increase in earnings, then you should consider advanced training programs. Such programs train and prepare you for the unique tax issues and concerns relating to partnerships, corporations, trusts, and estates. You can acquire the necessary training through evening courses at a nearby university, or if you prefer to study at home, you can train through the National Tax NTTS Higher Course in Federal Taxes. We would be happy to furnish you with full details upon request. Call 1-800-914-8138, or visit our website at **www.nationaltax.edu**.

Contrary to what you may think, a corporate and partnership clientele is not difficult to obtain. It's true that most incorporated businesses and partnerships employ year-round accountants, but there are many small business organizations operating in a partnership or corporate form that need few accounting services other than the preparation of their annual income tax and franchise tax returns. In fact, even corporations that do no business must at least file an annual state franchise tax return to keep from being dissolved by the state. The minimum fee for preparing even simple corporate tax returns can be quite impressive, so it does pay to be versatile in this area. However, we suggest that you take it one step at a time: make sure you are fluent in individual tax law and related procedures before you climb up to the next rung of the tax ladder.

### The Pre-Tax Season Warm Up

Another way to boost efficiency and increase both the quality and quantity of your output is to spend a few hours—before the tax season begins—brushing up on your tax knowledge. Briefly skim through your reference material, or a current tax guide, paying particular attention to any changes that have occurred since last year, both in the rules and in the annual inflation-indexed amounts (exemptions, standard deduction, minimum filing requirements, phase-outs, etc.). Remember that your clients expect you to be familiar with such routine matters. If there are areas you often encounter in which you feel weak, now is the time for corrective action.

Also, try to obtain the new tax forms as early as possible so you can familiarize yourself with them before the season's clients come around. It could be embarrassing to have a client watch you fumble with the mere entry of tax information. Keep in mind, too, that reviewing this material and being thoroughly conversant with the forms gives you a strong psychological edge as you enter the new season. It increases your self-confidence and enables you to convey an encouraging, positive attitude to your clients.

### Have You Thought of Specializing?

It's common knowledge that a "specialist" is held in higher esteem and commands greater fees than a "general practitioner." This holds true not only in medicine, law, and engineering but in tax practice as well. Many practitioners, as their practice and clientele increase, discover that a substantial portion of their earnings comes from specific industries, professions, or businesses. This is only logical since a satisfied client tends to recommend the services of his tax advisor to other friends, associates, and relatives, and very often they are in the same or a related line of work.

With time and experience, you will acquire a "fine-tuned" insight and proficiency for the unique concerns and specialized needs of these specific groups, and of the tax saving opportunities that apply in particular to them.

In fact, when you get a new client who represents a trade, profession, or business you never handled before, you will find it most helpful to do some research in that area for any special deductions, tax savings or tax problems relating to that particular field. If you come up with any tax saving opportunities, and inform the client about them, you can expect to soon hear from others in that particular line of work.

Developing such "specialized" expertise will greatly enhance your value and prestige among clients of that group, and the subsequent "snowball effect" will amount to more business for you.

We know of tax consultants who, by accident or design, have come to specialize in the returns and tax matters of teachers, theatrical personnel, doctors, dentists, and ministers—to name just a few. You can and should increase your proficiency in lines you already specialize in or would like to specialize in, by familiarizing yourself with that particular trade, business, or profession. One good way to do this is by reading up on the subject, especially in trade publications which, very often during tax season, contain tax articles of special interest to that audience.

Finally, if you really want to publicize your interest and expertise in a particular field, there is probably no better way than to publish a tax article in one of these trade journals. It demands research and effort on your part, but you will find it worthwhile. Getting an article into print is not as hard as you might think—especially when you have the financial interest of a particular clientele in mind. Simply contact the editor of the trade journal, advise him of your expertise in the field, and perhaps submit an outline of your proposed article. It's likely that the editor will be eager to cooperate. He or she may even make some valuable suggestions as to which topics to cover. If your article is well received, you will probably be invited back; in time you may even become a regular contributor. In the meantime, a clientele representing that line of work will be forming around you.

## The Future Growth and Development of Your Practice

If you are a relative newcomer, it may seem unrealistic just now, but it's a good idea to keep the future in mind—even from the start. It's been proven repeatedly that an individual who knows where he is going, and wants to go, is usually the one who gets there. Likewise, even if you are already well established, the fact that you are reading this book shows that you are sincerely interested in further growth.

As we have mentioned time and again, the foundation for success in tax work is technical competence combined with quality client service. But suppose you have already developed a personalized, professional service...where do you go from here?

The next logical step is to first decide for yourself how far you really want to go. If your ambition is to operate a part-time, seasonal practice that supplies you with a comfortable amount of extra income that's fine. You can be perfectly content with this type of practice and derive a great deal of satisfaction from it—as so many continue to do.

On the other hand, if you would like to see your tax practice become a high-volume, high-income business, then you should aim toward that goal, no matter how far you still have to go. This means consistently advancing your professional knowledge, missing no opportunity to obtain additional clients, and taking all possible steps to make your office as efficient as possible. A successful, well run, one-person tax practice can yield a very lucrative financial return.

Now let's take it to the next level. If you are really ambitious and anxious to expand, you should set your sights on developing a practice where the bulk of your tax work is done—not by you—but by your assistants. The reason for this is simple: as long as you are paid for your own services only—no matter how well paid you are—there is a built-in limit to the amount of business one person can handle. If, on the other hand, you have sufficient volume to warrant hiring assistants, your gross fees and net income will be limited only by the number of clients you can obtain and the number of assistants you can properly supervise—or have supervised.

Finally, if you feel you can obtain sufficient clients at other locations, you may reach the point where you will seriously consider setting up additional branch offices. In that case, make sure competent, personable assistants staff your branch offices. Otherwise, you may find your client base declining instead of increasing.

The growth of your practice will also depend, in part, on the growth and development potential of your community. A very likely source of clients, at least in the beginning, are taxpayers who recently moved into the area: newlyweds, those entering or opening a new business or profession, and others who have previously not needed—or had—professional tax assistance. Naturally, if you can plug into a community that is on the upswing you will have a greater pool of potential clients than if the area is in a state of decline, where residents are moving out.

Another factor to consider in this regard is that a growing, dynamic community undergoes rapid change with more people opening and expanding businesses, bringing in new industry, creating new jobs and positions, etc. Even though experience has shown that capable tax practitioners can succeed in a stable or even a declining community this is a challenge. Rather, when you step into an area that is "on its way up" you are very likely to get caught up in that momentum and develop right along with it.

## Stress Management and the Tax Practitioner

Until now our emphasis has been on "professional" self-development, but we feel it necessary to discuss another type of "development" as well: that of one's physical and emotional well-being. "Professional" and "personal" self-development really go hand-in-hand, and true success lies in the combination of these vital considerations.

A common concern of anyone involved in today's hectic business world is the matter of emotional, work-related stress, and how to deal with it effectively. To pretend that this type of stress does not exist or to deny that it affects one's work life, personal life, or family life is simply naive.

In a tax practice—or for that matter, in life—it is unrealistic to expect things to run smoothly all the time. They just don't. There are ups and downs, slow times and busy times (the peak season carries with it its inevitable stresses and strains), and there's always the possibility of an unexpected turn of events, so you have to be emotionally prepared for all of the above.

Any business can fail, and for any number of reasons, but one reason, unfortunately, may simply be an "inability to cope" on the part of the professional. In other words, you may know the intricacies and applications of tax law inside and out, and you may be better equipped to handle clients than any other office in town, but if you don't maintain a strong, emotional arsenal within then you may fail on that account alone.

Therefore, it is to your utmost advantage to develop positive living habits and positive personality traits, qualities that generate physical and mental well-being. Such habits will serve you well, not only in terms of meeting an April 15th deadline, but they will be of service to you and a personal asset, throughout the year, and throughout your life.

Here, then, are some practical tips relating to your overall well-being. They will help you cope with work demands as they arise, throughout the year. Fortunately, the range of options—and coping mechanisms—is great, and the real key is to establish and maintain healthy routines and positive attitudes.

**Exercise and diet are essential features to consider in an effort to maintain emotional harmony.** Try to develop a combination of both a cardiovascular workout and strength-training. And whether you like to swim, cycle, walk or run, at least endeavor to do so on a regular basis. Being physically fit does wonders for your self-esteem and increases your capacity for physical and mental work.

Hand-in-hand with exercise is the habit of eating nutritious meals at regular intervals. Eating foods that provide genuine energy and that strengthen you is essential. Try to avoid the whole fast-food syndrome, sweet snacks and repeated cups of coffee for quick pick-me-ups, and then a shot of alcohol for a calming effect.

**Don't isolate yourself.** Just as the body needs nurturing through exercise and diet, so does a person's emotional state need nurturing through constructive and satisfying relationships with others. Lacking a partner (or until you get a partner), the tax professional—working alone—needs to be aware of this vital dimension to his well-being.

You need to be able to talk to someone—a spouse or other family member, a mentor, a confidant, a spiritual advisor—for professional advice and personal development. It is important that, over time, you create a network of supportive friends and advisors to talk to. Spending time with such individuals on a regular basis can strengthen your knowledge, broaden your perspective, and improve your frame of mind. Without input from others, it's very difficult to know how you are doing and what you should be doing differently. You cannot possibly know all that there is to know. What you need are people who can give you constructive and encouraging feedback. Finding out how someone else coped in a similar problematic situation, or avoiding the mistakes that others made can be invaluable.

You may be interested to learn that local "support groups" have recently formed consisting of sole tax practitioners for the sake of regularly sharing information and advice. Groups meet periodically to discuss mutual problems and concerns, and members of such a group often call one another between meetings to discuss tax matters and questions that arise in the meantime. Such groups have also been instrumental in encouraging and helping new practitioners get off to a good start. Maybe you can be the first to start such a support group in your area!

**Try to pick an appropriate time of year (a slow season) to take a vacation.** A vacation that offers you a complete change of setting and pace, and provides freedom from job responsibilities can go a long way to alleviate stress and bring you back into emotional balance. If you can't take a full vacation then how about a mini-vacation? Sometimes a weekend or even a day away devoted to some favorite activity or hobby can do wonders for your state of well-being.

Then there are times, to be sure, when you just can't get away at all. But even then there are certain emergency measures you can take to regain your composure. For example, in a tense moment, close your eyes and let your imagination take you to one of your favorite places. Or relax with music or a magazine. Massage your forehead. Take a nap. Take a walk. Usually a break in activity brings with it a break in attitude as well, and some measure of relief from an agonizing encounter.

The important point here is to incorporate into your day slots of time that serve as diversions or relaxations. These "recesses" can help you reorient and re-energize in a positive and helpful way.

Remember, given the hectic pace and mounting pressures of our day and age, it is not always easy to juggle the many facets of an active tax practice—running the business, maintaining proper relationships, satisfying clients, meeting community obligations, and more. But fortunately, there are many good and wholesome ways to create a supportive and helpful surrounding environment. The choices range from exercise to hobbies, from sports and entertainment, to meditation and meeting with friends, music, reading, hikes, day trips—the list goes on. The key, however, is to be in touch with yourself: recognize your needs, your interests, your pleasures, and make time for them, in order to derive the requisite energy or benefit so that you may return to your tasks and responsibilities with renewed confidence and good will.

In reality, these ideas are not new. On the contrary, these are age-old principles. In the year 600 BC the philosopher Anacharsis said,

> *"Play—so that you may be serious."*

And more recently Thomas Fuller remarked,

> *"Refresh that part of yourself that is most weary. If your life is sedentary, exercise the body; if stirring and active, recreate your mind."*

The same holds true today…if not more so!

# Chapter 18

# Should You Consider a Tax Office Franchise?

*The art of work lies in making your work—you. It is putting the stamp of your unique personality on the work you do. It is pouring your spirit into your task. It is making your work a reflection of your faith, your integrity, your ideals.*
**William A. Peterson.**

*Most people don't plan to fail they fail to plan!*
**Anonymous**

Many people think of "franchising" as something relatively new on the American scene, but it's been around—in some form—for well over a century. There are now virtually thousands of franchises in the United States, and as the trend continues to rise we feel that a discussion of the franchise tax field is in order.

The franchising concept is basically a simple one. First, there is a "franchiser" who owns or possesses rights to a business: its name, its product, its methodology and procedure. This franchiser, without relinquishing ownership, is willing to extend or license the business name and all that goes with it over to someone else, the "franchisee", for a fee, and for an ongoing payment called a "royalty". There are all sorts of conditions attached to this arrangement, but the final legal contract or agreement is termed a "franchise."

When you, the franchisee, sign a contract with a franchising company, you become an added unit to that chain of businesses, and they spell out the terms and conditions under which you are permitted to operate that business extension. In effect, your contract is a license to function under the parent company's trade name and in accordance with their policies and procedures. In return you get a chance to operate a business already known for its name and a chance to earn profits from the same, after deducting the royalty payment and franchisee fee paid up front.

For franchising enterprises the concept is a promising one because it enables them to expand without the enormous sums of capital needed to form a chain store operation. Instead, the franchisee pays for the expansion. Furthermore, since each extension is independently-owned, the franchiser is dealing with a more motivated-to-succeed group than if each business operator was a hired manager under the owner's direct supervision.

The main advantage for the franchisee is the array of benefits he stands to gain from the relationship. Stepping into an established business with a widely recognized name, uniform products or services, proven, successful methods and procedures tends to reduce "the risk factors" involved in starting a new business.

Most people are more familiar with the product-oriented franchises:

- fast food outlets
- Ice cream parlors
- Doughnut shops
- Convenience stores
- Hotels and motels

However, there are an ever increasing number of service-oriented franchises available as well, including a variety of options for the tax professional. There are numerous factors to consider, but depending on your circumstances this may be a viable consideration for you. In any case, you should be aware that the option exists, and of some of the more common advantages and disadvantages inherent to this form of business arrangement.

## Advantages of a Franchise

1) A franchise may serve as a shortcut, as well as a short-term, stepping stone to your own business. Under this system you have access to a ready-made service, complete with image, logo, trade secrets, and regional or national advertising. You pay the parent company an upfront fee and ongoing royalties for the use of its name, specialized services, and assistance with marketing and management. In return you acquire a name and reputation that the public is already familiar and confident with. In other words, you become part of a proven, national or regional operation. Depending upon how well known and reputable a particular tax franchise is, your affiliation with it could be a definite boost to your career as a tax professional.

2) Conditions vary from one franchise to another, but very often the parent company provides ongoing specialized training and other forms of service and supplies. In fact, you may receive professional assistance to accompany all phases of operating the business, from location, to equipment, to promotions, and more.

3) There is also the possibility for advanced training and continued assistance from the parent company with you, all the while gaining personally from their experience and proven methods of handling a professional tax practice. The parent organization invested in you—you are now an extension of all that they represent—so they are interested in seeing to it that you function well and continue to grow. Therefore, they usually continue to offer you further assistance and advice. Of course, you have a contract with the franchiser for a certain amount of time, but all of this time and experience can be instrumental in preparing you—if you so desire—for a tax practice that will one day be completely yours.

## Disadvantages of a Franchise

1) In exchange for what the parent company has to offer, you do give up a considerable amount of independence. To maintain their image and reputation, most franchise enterprises must exert strict controls over their franchisees to which you must agree and submit if purchasing one. There will be areas where you will have very little personal say—fees, for example—and you will feel like someone else's employee rather than your own boss.

2) There is an initial franchise fee, which may be quite substantial, and in addition, you will have to pay the parent company either a fixed fee or a percentage of your profits, probably for as long as you are part of that franchise.

3) You are bound by the franchiser's contract, and it usually operates in his favor, so if you want to someday sell out of the business you cannot do so on your own. You must involve the parent company, abiding by its terms.

4) Furthermore, whatever faults lie in the system or procedures of a particular franchise—**you** must suffer those consequences. You are dependent upon them to follow through on their promises. If they exercise poor market judgments, you are—more or less—at their mercy. Therefore, you share the burden of a franchiser's faults. Obviously, with a well-established franchise, your risks in this respect are minimal: you can be fairly certain they know what they are doing, or they would no longer be in business.

## How to Evaluate a Franchise before Buying into One

Basically, the bottom line is this: whether or not to buy into a franchise depends primarily on your personality. If you are looking for an established business name and mode of operation, where most major decisions are made for you, then a franchise is definitely something to consider.

On the other hand, if you are the independent, self-starter type who does not feel comfortable marching to the beat of someone else's drum, you may be unhappy with the rules and restraints a franchise imposes.

Which option carries a greater risk: striking out on your own, or joining a franchise? Well, the answer to that depends on whom you talk to.

According to recently published Small Business Administration (SBA) statistics, franchised businesses have a four-year success rate of approximately 62 percent, while 68 percent of independent start-ups are still in business after four years. Franchise associations dispute these figures, citing Department of Commerce studies that put the four to five year franchise success rate at 85 to 90 percent.

### The Franchise

- Have a capable lawyer, preferably one experienced in negotiating franchise agreements go over every facet of the franchise contract for approval.
- Find out precisely under what conditions you can terminate the franchise contract and vice versa.

### The Franchisor

- Find out how many years this firm has been in business. Do objective research and get hold of reliable information regarding the firm.

- Does it have a reputation for fairness and success in how it handles both franchisees and its clientele?

- Have you seen any certified records and figures reflecting the success and trends of this particular company?

- Will the parent company assist you with location, training, public relations, capital, credit, and an ongoing support system?

**You: the Franchisee**

- Ask yourself: Are you willing and prepared to give up a measure of independence to conform to this firm's standards and requirements? Do you firmly believe—after examining the particular features of this franchise—that you can work in conjunction with its personnel and policies?

- Did you adequately survey the location you would be working in to know whether a franchised tax service has a market there to accommodate the prices you will have to charge? What other competition already exists in that area?

**Other Considerations to Bear in Mind**

- When looking into a franchise, proceed with caution and thoroughly examine the franchise under consideration. As with most every business, there are more reputable and less reputable firms to deal with. You don't want to sign yourself over to a firm you will soon regret working for. Today, franchise operations are partly regulated by the federal, and in some cases, even the state government. They also have a self-policing trade association. Furthermore, franchisers are required to file disclosure statements with the federal government, all of which makes it easier for a prospective franchisee to evaluate each franchise operation.

- One good way to check out a franchise is to talk with some existing franchisees. Ask them about different facets of their relationship: Has the franchiser done what he said he would do? Have the financial results been worthwhile? Does the franchiser continue to give advice and support? What—if any—are the problems? You will discover a lot of important information this way, and even if it means making several long distance trips, it will be well worth your time and expense.

- Compare the cost of the franchise you are examining with what it would take to begin a tax practice of your own, including facilities, supplies, promotional activities, and operating expenses. Ask yourself: Would I do better by investing the money in my own independent tax practice—perhaps even running the business out of my own home? This question of comparison is worthy of careful consideration. Remember: you already are a trained professional, and presumably, ready for business. You don't need the franchise for training purposes. Therefore, unless the company is well established and spends a lot on advertising or other forms of promotion to ensure you of a clientele, you may be better off investing your money to promote a practice where you will be your own boss.

- The best time, of course, to evaluate and get the true feel of a tax practice is during the height of the season. If a prospective franchiser has any offices in your area, pay him a visit around this time. You might even go and have a tax return prepared. Personally observe how they operate, strike up a conversation with clients in the waiting area as you wait your turn. Find out what brought them in and ask them how they view the service. Try, if you can, to strike up a conversation with the employee working on your return. You can pick up a lot of worthwhile information about a company's procedures and reputation this way.

## In Conclusion

At present, there are a growing number of tax service franchises in operation. These range from national organizations to small, regional franchise companies that currently have only a few offices, but are looking to expand with additional franchisees.

If you are seriously interested in a tax franchise, we simply urge you not to part with any money until you have thoroughly examined the franchiser and the franchise agreement, and you—together with your lawyer—are satisfied with what you see.

Make sure you understand all aspects and conditions of the contract: Is it for only a few years, after which you are at the mercy of the franchiser; or is it renewable at your option under terms fixed in the agreement? Are you obligated to do a minimum amount of business per year? Will you have an exclusive territory, and if so, how large is it?

If, after weighing and comparing all vital factors, examining the agreement, and having done the necessary research, you find that this is a viable option for you, then you are ready to proceed and take advantage of the positive attributes franchising has to offer.

Under the right conditions a tax franchise can be a promising venture that can lead to an even more promising future.

## Franchise Resources

As of this writing, there are several sizeable national income tax preparation franchises in existence. Call them if you're interested.

- H & R Block (approximately 14,000 offices)
  www.hrblock.com—800-472-5625

- Jackson Hewitt Tax Service (approximately 6,600 offices)
  www.jacksonhewitt.com—800-234-1040

- Liberty Tax Service (approximately 4,000 offices)
  www.libertytax.com—866-813-4871

There are also a number of regional and local franchise operations. Try the Yellow Pages from a few larger cities in your area, under "Income Tax," or call the International Franchise Association at 202-628-8000. Your local library may also have a copy of the Franchise Annual, which lists over 5,000 franchises plus other valuable information for would-be franchisees.

Bear in mind that with smaller franchises—and especially with recent start-ups—you have to be particularly cautious.

# Chapter 19

# How to Profitably Sell or Merge Your Practice

*If you want them to show you the money, you better show them the reason.*

*Be like the turtle...if it didn't stick its neck out, it wouldn't get anywhere at all.*

*Mergers and acquisitions are like second marriages: a triumph of hope over experience. In both cases, success depends on the quality and chemistry of the people involved.*
**Harvey Mackay**

Presumably, you are either just beginning your practice, or have an established practice and are looking for ways to further develop it. Nevertheless, a book of this sort would not be complete without a chapter on how to terminate a practice—if and when you desire to call it quits.

Alternatively, instead of selling, you may have reached a point in your practice where you are interested in forming a partnership by joining forces with another practitioner.

These are the two options we will examine more closely in this chapter.

## Reasons for Selling a Practice

The reasons for selling a practice vary, and this will have a definite bearing on the selling price you can expect. Among the more common reasons for selling a professional practice is the retirement or illness of the practitioner. Other reasons may include planned relocations, the owner's involvement in other business concerns, excessive job related stress, the business no longer appeals, family reasons, or the practice may have gotten too big for the owner to handle and he just doesn't want to deal with it any more. It is important, however, for you to be clear as to why you are selling your practice. It is also important to note that there are many valid reasons for selling a business, and that "losing money" does not have to be one of them.

In any case, every prospective buyer will want to know why you are selling; if it's because you are simply tired of the business then tell her that. Being honest and straightforward in this regard is the best and surest course to follow.

### Your Personal Involvement in the Sale

You should take the sale of your business personally, and not be a detached bystander to the procedure. After all, your practice is your personal achievement. You built it up, nurtured it, and devoted your energy to it, so you should be instrumental in the transfer as well. This is not to say that you should not employ professionals to help you, but they should help you to carry out **your goals and your objectives**—not theirs. You should regularly be in touch with those who are helping you, so they can be most effective in carrying out their tasks on your behalf. Remember: getting a good price will have a profound impact on your own financial future.

Although you should be actively involved in all aspects of the sale, you should also consider the following: naturally, you are emotionally involved and connected to your practice, but you cannot let your emotions and anxieties interfere with the sale of your practice. Don't let your feelings, as valid as they are, stand in your way. To achieve this you will have to mentally prepare yourself for the negotiation procedure. Be relaxed, be clear, and be calm. That way you will be negotiating from strength and not from weakness. Always think positively. This will also help you to negotiate successfully. Don't be critical by focusing on whatever problems you see in the practice; rather, view the situation as one of opportunity. If there is currently a problem or a setback, it's just temporary and solvable. In other words, your attitude should express the potential that is genuinely there. See the practice as an asset and not a liability. To a great extent negotiation is a tug of wills, and this kind of positive, confident outlook will help you immeasurably.

## The Role of the Business Broker

Since you likely will not sell a tax practice more than once in your life, it is not a skill you are likely to be proficient in. Therefore, you might consider placing the practice into the hands of an experienced broker: one who specializes in the sale of businesses. Buying and selling a business can be a rather technical and complex procedure, so hiring a qualified broker may end up saving you a lot of time, worry, and money as well.

A broker is employed by the seller and earns his commission once the business is sold. It is therefore in his own best interests to be instrumental in obtaining a buyer at a good price. If you are able to find a buyer yourself, and if the transaction is relatively simple, then a good lawyer may be all you need. But if the circumstances are such that the sale is not moving along, and it's taking up more time and energy than you can afford, you may want to enlist the services of a good broker.

**A good broker can be of help in a number of ways:**

- Since this is their business, they are likely to have a pool of potential buyers to draw upon.
- A broker can assist you in making decisions on vital factors, such as evaluating offers, pricing, and terms to consider in the contract.
- A broker can help screen potential buyers and save you time by filtering out insincere prospects, allowing you to focus on the sincere ones.
- A broker can serve as an intermediary, absorbing and diffusing some of the personal and emotional issues that may stand between a buyer and a seller. Thus he keeps extraneous material from interfering with the procedure, and thereby keeps the transaction moving along. With his assistance the deal is less likely to come undone.

Remember to interview several brokers so you can compare their personalities and their terms. Be sure the one you pick is capable of handling the sale of a practice such as yours. Also, ask for references from previous business clients who were satisfied with the way this broker handled their affairs.

As an added note, to hire a broker is an option you will have to weigh depending on your circumstance, but lawyers are absolutely indispensable when it comes to a business changing hands, so it is essential that you hire a lawyer familiar with the transfer of small business enterprises.

## Pricing Your Practice

One of the most difficult aspects to buying or selling a business, especially a "service enterprise" such as a tax practice, is to determine an equitable and realistic valuation.

Appraising a service business is always more complex than pricing a "product enterprise" where you have more in the way of fixed assets and inventories. This is because of all the intangibles involved. There are virtually dozens of factors to examine and consider, by buyer and seller alike, before arriving at a reasonable figure.

It would be most helpful for all concerned if you, as the seller, take the necessary time and effort to provide accurate figures, and even break them down so a buyer knows exactly what she is getting.

**For example, this would include:**

- **Asset value**—all the tangible assets belonging to the practice such as equipment, furniture, supplies, etc. In setting an asking price you should prepare an inventory and then establish a price for each item. Naturally, you will have to take into account such factors as age and depreciation.

- **Goodwill**—this term is used to describe a conglomerate of intangible features that nevertheless account for a substantial portion of the asking price. Not only is this a difficult feature to objectively measure or assign a dollar value to, but also an "earned feature" for it takes years to carefully develop and nurture. "Goodwill" encompasses such qualities as a good reputation, a convenient location; the steady, reliable rhythm of repeat clientele; a history of dependable service; a competent staff; name recognition, among others. In other words, "goodwill" refers to the quality service and good spirit of a smooth running and reliable office environment. On the one hand, this is a "priceless" feature: how do you assess it in terms of monetary value? On the other hand, how can you ignore it? This is essentially what the success of your practice is all about!

- Furthermore, every practice must be assessed individually. Like houses, no two are exactly alike. Each practice is accompanied by its own unique circumstances and its own particular strengths and weaknesses, so it must be evaluated on its own unique terms.

- Subtle yet vital factors such as "timing" also play a significant role, both in terms of the general economic climate of when you sell, and your own particular "frame of mind" when you sell. If the country is in the middle of a recession that will strongly influence the deal, and if you somehow find yourself in unusual circumstances you may be forced or eager to sell. That too will have an impact on the selling price.

These considerations are by no means exhaustive. There are more to account for, and some of them are also difficult to quantify, but somehow they must all enter into the overall equation. One thing, however, is certain: as with any other worthwhile endeavor, your chances at success increase with the amount of planning and preparation you put into the project. The more you can account for, quantify, and validate, the stronger your position is in terms of a successful sale.

**Selling Your Tax Practice: Getting Down to Basics**

To begin with, you must realize that in most instances selling a practice will involve time and energy on your part. It may take you away from some of your daily routines—both inside and outside of your practice. To make things easier, we will discuss the procedure by breaking it down into four basic stages. If you decide to employ a broker, he or she will attend to some of these details, or assist you with them.

1. **Preparing for the Sale**

    There are basically two components to this:

    - Outwardly—it means presenting your business in the best possible light;
    - Inwardly—it means preparing and arranging all the necessary paperwork and documentation.

    To those who visit and look around, your office and office operations should appear presentable in every respect: clean the carpets, paint an ugly wall, be sure everything is functioning properly; make improvements and corrections wherever you can.

    At the same time, be ready to document and present your financial operation in a way that makes it easy for prospective buyers to see what the practice consists of and is truly worth. You cannot expect anyone to buy a business without a thorough analysis of the past and present financial condition of the practice.

    Make sure all your business records are up to date. Have profit and loss statements, income, expenses, balance sheets, and other financial statements available for inspection, along with a copy of your lease. Any serious business buyer will absolutely want to see all the current books to evaluate the health of your business. All this will help the prospective buyer ascertain the value of your practice and facilitate any transaction.

    As a note of caution, during initial discussion of any detail or negotiations make sure that any prospective buyer who's serious about examining your business signs a nondisclosure agreement first. This agreement should be binding and restrict the party from disclosing, working with, or using any information that he may look at while examining your business. This should include proprietary information, client data and files, accounting records, and anything that your business relies on for its success. Too often an unscrupulous competitor may pretend to be a buyer just to see if your office has a vulnerable market to steal away. It happens.

It also helps at this stage to prepare a brief written history of your practice—a business profile or fact sheet—where you highlight positive features: location, traffic, lease conditions, types of clientele, rate of growth, etc.

Another point to consider during this phase, as you prepare for the sale try to be aware of and be sensitive to a prospective buyer's frame of mind. Here is someone who is probably looking for financial independence and a chance to grow. Your ability to understand the buyer's perspective and to show how your practice can fulfill those expectations will help bring you closer to signing on the bottom line.

2. **Locating Prospective Buyers**

   To help you find potential buyers, begin by making a list of possible prospects: people you know who might be interested in such a purchase themselves, or know of others who might be.

   Consider professional employees—past and present (or even someone you interviewed but did not hire). If these individuals are technically competent, trustworthy, and willing to stand on their own two feet, then why not contact them? In fact, they may already be familiar with your clientele and with your office routine, and are logical considerations for the position.

   Another likely source would be fellow practitioners who may be looking to move, expand their practice, or even open another office. If you drop a few hints that you are thinking of moving or retiring, and are looking to relinquish your practice, you can rest assured that word will get around fast.

   Your list can also extend to suppliers, friends, relatives, or business people in related fields of endeavor such as bankers, realtors, accountants, etc. You can also put classified ads into local and regional newspapers, trade journals, and other special interest publications.

   Once you start getting some feedback you face the task of having to screen your prospects. Early on, try to distinguish viable candidates from those who are simply unqualified or just wasting your time. You want to be able to quickly assess whether the prospect can A) afford the price, and B) competently service and manage the practice. Reasonable and serious prospects will respect and favorably respond to your being candid about this.

   As a seller you have every right to request financial and other information to establish whether a prospective buyer has sufficient capital, knowledge, and experience to make the business a success. It's time consuming, exhausting, and costly to enter negotiations with someone who is not in a position to follow through. Plus, you owe it to your clients to make sure you are putting them into the hands of a capable and competent successor. Therefore—unless you know the individual well—ask for business and personal references, and be sure to carefully check them out. It happens all too often that an unqualified buyer takes over a business and the consequences can be disastrous. If he runs the business into the ground, loses clients, and has to close down you may be left holding a worthless debt.

One final bit of advice in this section, try to limit the information you transmit to inquiries made over the phone. Calls may come in from prospective buyers, but do not divulge amounts, details, and other specific information over the phone. Insist on meeting with prospective buyers in person so you can assess them properly before sharing personal business information.

3. **Negotiating the Terms**

As a seller you will naturally want the highest price you can get, whereas the buyer will endeavor to spend as little as possible. Negotiation consists of the various stages of bargaining, trading, and compromise that take place between buyer and seller. You are both aiming to reach an agreement…you arrive at agreements through compromise…and compromise calls for a clear and level-headed approach to every element pertinent to the transaction.

It will help to realize that your negotiating power will be greatly enhanced by how well you know your own financials as well as the buyer's financial position. Be aware of the various bargaining variables that will enter into the discussion. Be precise about where you can afford to be flexible, where you cannot afford to be flexible and just how flexible you can be. In fact, write all of this down for yourself, so you have it clearly stated. Once you know your limits—where you can and cannot give in—you will know precisely how and where you can maneuver. That knowledge and clarity is powerful at the negotiating table, as opposed to going in blind, stumped, unsure, unprepared, or being caught off guard.

As negotiations continue do not rely on your memory or on someone else's to recall important matters and decisions. Keep records and take notes of meetings as well as telephone conversations, then confirm and commit important, agreed upon points to writing. Next, let an attorney draft these matters into a legal format.

It may also be worthwhile at times to have an impartial mediator take part in the negotiation procedure. It may be a small price to pay if the outcome is a mutually favorable and irrefutable transaction. If both parties agree to a mediator, try to find someone with broad business experience, preferably one who has previously assisted in business transfers.

### Other Points to Bear in Mind during Negotiations

- How and when the practice will be paid for must also be resolved at an early point in the procedure. Terms must be clearly defined in the contract, and penalties established in the event of default. As a seller you should take every reasonable precaution to protect yourself and bargain for a safe contract.

- Try to get as much cash "up front" as possible. If you can get the buyer to pay the whole amount in advance, so much the better, even if it means having to go down somewhat on the price. You are more likely, though, to receive one third to half down, with the balance due over a period of one or two years. But by no means should you enter into an arrangement whereby the entire purchase price is to be paid out of receipts from the practice. This gives the buyer little or no incentive to carry on the business properly, and as a result you may find yourself with no money and no business. If you have a prospective buyer who sounds good but has no money, tell him to get a bank loan, take a mortgage out on his house, borrow money from relatives, or find another method of raising the down payment. Chances are, if he can't come up with this minimal amount, he will not do well in the business either.

- Very often, contracts make provisions for reductions in the purchase price for fees lost through client drop-offs during the first year or two. Naturally, as the seller, you will try to resist such a clause. You can point out to the buyer that just as he will most likely reap the benefits of added business from some of your clients, he will have to assume the risk of others leaving. In any event, try not to make the drop off contingency extend more than one season. Any clients that leave after the first year presumably do so because of their dissatisfaction with the new service provider, and for this you should not be penalized.

- Be prepared to give the buyer substantial help in order to effectuate a smooth transfer of clients. This alone can increase the value of your practice. If time permits, prepare a fact sheet on each of your better clients, giving essential background information, history, personal idiosyncrasies, etc. Showing a prospective purchaser the efforts you have made, and will make, to help him through this vital period of transition and adjustment will facilitate a quicker and more advantageous sale at negotiation time.

4. **Closing the Sale**

Each and every tax practice is an individual enterprise, and there will be a variety of conditions that will uniquely affect the outcome of your transaction. Therefore, a contract that might be satisfactory in one circumstance will not necessarily fit another. The final contract, when it is drawn up, must reflect and protect the special interests and concerns of the buyer and seller, and must cover a wide range of contingencies and possible problems that bear upon this particular transaction.

Only a skilled and competent attorney can and should draw up this precise sort of document. Of course, the question always arises as to whose lawyer is going to do this work and how will it be paid for. If both parties agree, you can try to find an impartial attorney who can capably serve both buyer and seller alike, and then split that fee.

At the closing the sale is completed, contracts are signed, ownership is transferred, and preparations are made to transfer the practice to the new owner. The buyer now stands on the threshold of a new enterprise, while the seller will either embark upon his own new endeavor or perhaps enter a more leisurely stage in life. In any event, the most successful transactions are those where continued cooperation and communication exist between buyer and seller, especially in the first few months after the sale. The buyer should feel that his inquiries are welcome and that advice and assistance will be forthcoming; and the seller, by being available to help and advise, stands to protect the future payments due to him under the terms of the contract. This sort of cooperation is mutually advantageous.

## Merging or Restructuring

Most tax practices start as sole ownerships—whether as proprietorships or single owner corporations—and remain that way until the business grows enough to warrant transforming into a partnership or multiple owner corporation.

### The Legal Entity

Whatever legal form of ownership you operate under (sole proprietorship, partnership, S Corp., C Corp., PC, or LLC), you should realize that each entity has its own distinct drawbacks and advantages, tax-wise and business-wise. Therefore, before you switch from one form to another make sure you consider all the pros and cons. The key here is to select the form of ownership (seek professional advice, if necessary) that best meets your specific individual needs.

But legalities notwithstanding, there are basically only two operating structures:

- **Sole ownership** and
- **Multiple** or **shared ownership.**

### Sole Ownership

The sole ownership is the most common way of starting out in business. As a sole owner you are totally responsible for your own tax practice. You make all decisions, and you answer only to yourself. You open the office in the morning and lock up at night, you set the policies, you hire and fire, and you keep all the records. A sole ownership offers you the greatest psychological freedom and reward, but the entire burden rests on your shoulders as well.

## Multiple Ownerships

The traditional multiple ownership entity in a professional service business is a **partnership**, though many now also use any of the forms mentioned above. We will simply employ the "partnership" designation in the discussion that follows.

A partnership is an association of two or more people who, together, own and operate a business. There are basically two ways of forming a professional partnership:

   **a)** By merging with another independent practitioner; in other words—combining two individual practices, or

   **b)** By taking an employee or other suitable individual into your business, and thereby converting your practice into a partnership.

The idea of having a partner in your business can be very appealing. It means having someone to work with, rely upon, and share ideas with. But before you proceed with such an arrangement you should be aware of all the foreseeable advantages and disadvantages, and then—after careful consideration—you will be in a position to make a more informed decision.

Operating a professional practice in partnership form certainly has its advantages, as evidenced by the fact that so many accounting, legal, medical, and other professional services operate in this mode. One primary advantage is that it avoids the dangers inherent in a one-person operation. An organization run by two or more individuals can generally cope with a brief or even prolonged absence by one of the principals—due to vacations, illness, physical infirmity, or death. The latter contingency, in particular, should not be overlooked. Where a sole practitioner is suddenly incapacitated or dies, his family generally has no choice but to dispose of the business immediately—at a price that usually reflects a state of desperation. Otherwise, the practice will soon be worth nothing. In a partnership, however, arrangements can be made to have the surviving partner take over, based on predetermined conditions.

A partnership also brings together the talents and specialties of each individual partner, which gives the overall practice greater strength and diversity. One partner may be more of an introvert, the other outgoing; one partner may be good at marketing and dealing with people, while the other is better at paperwork and organizing. Together they can divide the work according to their skills, talents, preferences and inclinations, thus creating a more effective, well-balanced practice.

Consider, too, the reduction in overhead: one office instead of two, and the possible reduction of outside help. Also, if you are growth-oriented, it is usually easier to attract top quality assistants to a partnership.

Another advantage is that, as a partnership, you will probably attract a greater variety of clients. Some may relate better with your partner, while others will relate better with you. That's the up side. But before you rush headlong into a partnership agreement, you should become aware of the disadvantages as well.

First, if you are accustomed to being fully independent or if that's your nature, you may recoil at the built-in restraints of a partnership. You will not be able to run or do everything your way. You now have another person to answer to—for everything. More importantly, there may be differences in temperament, personality, philosophy, styles and habits that may, over time, prove to be irreconcilable. For instance, if your goal is to develop a low volume but high quality tax practice based on personal service to your clients, while your prospective partner has visions of a mass volume "assembly-line" approach to dealing with clients then you may be heading for real trouble. Your clients, in turn, may be apprehensive about your service losing its personal touch. It doesn't matter whether these fears are real or imagined, either way they can harm your business.

There is also the danger that small disagreements between partners may escalate into a major feud, and even if they do not, the ongoing presence of a negative undercurrent can undermine the genuine effectiveness of your partnership and of your practice.

Nevertheless, if after carefully weighing the pros and cons, you feel you have the right person with whom to create an effective partnership, then by all means go ahead.

As you proceed to actualize the partnership, it is important to hire a good attorney—preferably one experienced in professional partnership contracts. Many potentially aggravating "trouble spots" can be avoided by drawing up a detailed agreement that spells out clearly the rights, duties, and privileges of each partner, and leaves as little as possible to misinterpretation. More importantly, be sure provisions are made for an equitable termination of the partnership, if for any reason it doesn't work out. We also recommend that your agreement stipulate that any dispute be resolved through binding arbitration. We don't mean to appear pessimistic, but this may one day save you an absolute fortune in legal fees and court costs.

## Financial Arrangements in Partnership Agreements

One of the more critical clauses in a partnership agreement is the interest or equity assigned to each partner. In the case of a merger of two individual practitioners, both having practices of approximately equal size, then presumably, both partners would receive the same interest in the partnership. But if one practice is larger, more lucrative, or otherwise more desirable than the other, then that partner is normally entitled to fair compensation for his extra contribution. The same holds true where one partner contributes considerably more in physical facilities and supplies.

An alternate arrangement would be for one partner to make a cash settlement to the other for the agreed-upon value of this extra contribution, and then both may proceed as equal partners. To estimate the comparative value of each partner's contribution, you can apply the criteria we discussed for establishing the sale price of a practice. In other words, figure out a fair selling price for each practice, and then adjust the partnership equity accordingly.

Not to be overlooked in any such agreement are items such as salary or drawing arrangements. Will both partners draw equal pay? Will one devote more time to the practice than the other? Are there any other valid reasons that justify different salaries for each partner? How is outside income to be handled? What about expense reimbursement? All such questions should be brought to the table and settled beforehand, or they may come back to haunt both partners later.

Another essential part of the agreement (and we briefly mentioned this) is an equitable provision for the remaining partner's acquisition of the practice in the event of one partner's death or incapacitation. Here, too, it is important to establish—before entering into a partnership—a method for evaluating the total worth of a business, such as 125 percent of the previous year's gross fees. Assume, for instance, that at the time of one partner's death, gross fees of a two-man partnership amount to $120,000. The total assigned value of the partnership would then be $150,000 to $180,000, and each partner's share (assuming a 50/50 arrangement) would come to $75,000 to $90,000.

Naturally, provision should also be made as to how, and under what terms, this price is to be paid by the partner taking over the business. A common arrangement is to take out a life insurance policy, with a face value equal to the approximate purchase price, on the life of both partners (or often the senior partner), with the proceeds earmarked for purchase of the deceased partner's equity.

In any event, no matter what the arrangements are, they should be agreed upon beforehand, and spelled out clearly in the partnership contract.

### Taking an Employee as a Partner

It often occurs that an employee performs so loyally and so well that the employer offers him a chance to join as a partner; or a practitioner who would like to retire may find the most logical choice for a successor to be one of his own staff members. This makes good sense, for here is someone familiar with the clients as well as with the entire office procedure.

The steps for evaluating a practice have already been outlined. However, one problem often encountered in negotiating a buy-in agreement—as this would entail—are the terms of payment. One common method is to let the new partner acquire the interest in the partnership, and pay for it, in agreed-upon stages. In other words, he may purchase 10 percent to 25 percent in the first year, another 10 percent to 25 percent the following year, and so on, until he has achieved full partnership status. This type of arrangement also makes it easier to dissolve the partnership early on if it does not work out.

Here too, as we pointed out before, it is important that the incoming partner invest some cash, so he will have a decided stake in the business, and the necessary incentive to put his best into it.

One thing, however, to bear in mind: good employees do not necessarily make good partners. Just make sure you have a good escape clause, and use it at the first sign of serious trouble.

## Dissolving a Partnership

Regardless of how well matched partners appear to be, some partnerships—like some marriages—simply don't work out. The sooner that fact is realized, the better.

If the merger of two or more individual practices initially formed the partnership, the accepted method of dissolving it is to have each partner take with him all the clients he brought in. New clients obtained by the partnership are generally divided equally among all partners on the basis of gross fees. In some cases, however, each new client is assigned to the particular partner who either acquired him, or worked with him most, if not all of the time.

If the partnership was formed through a buy-in arrangement with an employee, or other individual who did not have an established practice, you have two choices. If you brought the new individual in with a view toward later retirement, you can opt for early retirement and give him an opportunity to buy the entire practice from you. If you are not ready to retire, or the employee does not have the means to acquire the practice (or you feel he can't handle it), then you will simply have to refund his investment.

It cannot be stressed often enough that all these contingencies should be spelled out clearly in the original partnership agreement.

## Choosing Business Partners: A Few Tips

1) Generally speaking, look for a partner who offers a talent, skill, strength, or expertise that you are lacking. Don't just duplicate common strengths unless the one goal you share is to simply sustain a greater workload. Make sure that you and your prospective partner share similar principles and ideas about business goals and methods of how a business should be run. Furthermore, investigate the work habits of the person under consideration. Openly discuss and define what you think your respective roles should be. Never accept what others or what a prospective partner says at face value.

2) Be wary of an authoritarian figure, someone who is only happy when he "runs the show." What you really need in a partnership is someone who is tolerant, trustworthy, compatible, respects others, and appreciates the benefits of teamwork.

3) Be cautious of prospective partners who have a lifestyle radically different from yours, whose habits may be excessive or extreme, are big spenders, or whose value system is not compatible with yours.

4) Do not pick a partner for monetary reasons alone, i.e. because you are financially desperate and he can improve your situation with his financial input. After the money is gone, you may be stuck with a partner you can't live with. Only pick a partner for the right reasons.

5) Be especially careful before choosing family and friends as business partners. If it works out it can be an excellent arrangement. But if not, you may be faced with the unpleasant choice between destroying a relationship and hurting your business. In fact, the same holds true when considering a prospective employee. The old saying, "Never hire anyone you can't fire," is still valid, as many have learned from bitter experience.

# Chapter 20

# Niche Markets and Value-Added Services

*Luck is what happens when preparation meets opportunity.*
**Darrell Royal**

*You have brains in your head. You have feet in your shoes. You can steer*

*Yourself in any direction you choose.*
**Dr. Seuss**

When you consider the ever-changing economic environment along with the explosive competition in the tax and accounting professions, it becomes apparent that new marketing strategies are in order. To grow within this "new economic reality" many service providers try to meet the needs of specific target markets or offer nontraditional services to current and prospective clients.

A number of such "hot" niche markets and specialty services were already discussed, but following are some additional ones worthy of further consideration.

You'll also find more elaborate information and resources in your local library, larger bookstores, and various current accounting publications. If you're Internet connected, try browsing the various search engines for more specific, additional information.

## Develop a Consulting Niche for Your Physician Clients

By setting up practice management systems for your physician clients, your own practice will grow.

Indications are that most physicians are in need of up-to-date business advice now more than ever before, and they look first to their accountants to provide it. Those professionals that do offer such specialized services to physician clients have uncovered a wealth of lucrative opportunities. As one leading accountant puts it:

> *"If you do more for your client, it's less likely that he'll ever replace you. And if you're doing things that are different than what most do, he's got no reason to change."*

Many physicians and medical group practices are operating under financial pressures unheard of just a few years ago. Their need to relieve some of that pressure may open up professional opportunities for you. More specifically, by understanding what software systems are available to help physicians manage their practices better, and by knowing how these work, you can develop professionally, into new areas and dramatically increase your income.

Physician practice management software systems give a doctor's office or medical group the ability to administer all sorts of vital office functions, especially in the area of generating bills and keeping track financially after a patient visit. In the health care industry billing can be quite complex, involving different payers from patient, to government, to insurance agencies, and at times, even lawyers. Each bill or claim will be in a different paper or electronic format.

For example, after a single patient visit, the doctor may need to send a bill to the patient, prepare appropriate claim forms for Medicare, and then wait for results to see what claims must be sent to other insurers for supplemental coverage. A single error can result in all sorts of resubmissions and claim adjustments. It can take months before a doctor receives payment.

Effective practice management systems can go a long way towards solving various problems that arise and making sure that payments are made within a normal time frame. In fact, the benefits of using the Internet and electronic claims submission are many: claims get to payers more quickly, and many payers reimburse electronically submitted claims more rapidly than paper claims.

The prognosis is that the picture will get even more complex. With today's reimbursement and managed care concerns about what new requirements doctors will have to comply with in order to be paid consultants say that practice management systems are becoming a necessity, at least to help clean up billing, reduce accounts receivable days outstanding and improve cash flow.

Physician practice management systems can also get quite sophisticated, so you can produce highly detailed business and financial reports that you can use to analyze your clients' practices for developing business or compensation plans. Most systems track costs, charges, and actual reimbursements generated by each physician in the practice, so it's easy to identify who the top income producers are, or who is getting stuck with all the managed care cases.

## Taking a Closer Look at Business Valuations

Business valuations can provide good fees and serve as great business builders. Clients expect to pay a substantial fee for valuations, and if they're satisfied, will recommend you to others who require a similar service. In this regard bankers, lawyers, business brokers, arbitrators, insurance brokers—if properly cultivated—can become an excellent, ongoing source for referrals. Some valuation engagements may even turn into regular year round clients.

Many different situations call for valuations, and each has its own inherent factors from which the valuator makes certain presumptions. There are presumptions that arise from legal precedents or regulations and rulings, while others result from business or marketplace practices. Therefore, depending upon the facts and assumptions that accompany a specific situation, the valuation arrived at for the very same item can be different.

### Purchase or Sale Value

One of the most common reasons for determining the value of a business is for the express purpose of the sale or purchase of that business. Let us presume that neither side to the transaction is under any pressure to buy or sell with this type of valuation. That being the case, other items to consider include the following:

- The value of the business as an ongoing concern;
- The risks relating to the continuity of the business;
- The historical earnings of the business;
- An analysis of any uncertainties involved in the business.

The projected future income is also a factor in a valuation for the purpose of sale or purchase.

### Valuation to Obtain Financing

The lending party's valuation presumes a certain necessary level of cash flow to meet the bank's interest and principal payments, as well as the liquidation value of collateral, in case of a foreclosure. These may be different presumptions than those made for a purchase or sale value. So once again, the value finally arrived at may be different.

### Valuations for Tax Purposes

Valuations for tax purposes are often the area of concern for IRS rulings. Inheritance tax valuations may presume the loss of what may have been a key employee, and perhaps even the liquidation of the business to pay the inheritance taxes.

Gift tax valuations may presume a minority interest discount or lack of marketability discount. Naturally, since the purpose of gift tax valuations is to objectively minimize tax payments, these discounts are generally provided for.

### Valuations between Partners and Shareholders

Valuations between partners and shareholders also carry different presumptions. If the purpose of a buy/ sell agreement is to penalize a shareholder for terminating ownership or employment, the valuation method might not be reflective of fair market value.

If a buy / sell agreement is funded with the proceeds from life insurance, the controlling presumption is often the estate planning needs of the owner, rather than the true value of the company.

### Finding the Right Value for Your Purposes

It must be clearly understood that there is no one value for a business, and what may be the right value for one purpose will not work in a different situation. A valuator analyzes these vital differences and understands clearly the presumptions inherent to each type of valuation. They can select and then implement a method to determine the proper value for the purpose at hand.

A good valuator will work closely with the client to provide the business valuation that best suits the particular situation.

## Look into SOHO: the Small Office / Home Office Market

Computer technology, as we all know, keeps influencing the way we live and changing the way we do things—in almost every area of our lives. For example, just look at the tremendous increase in home-based businesses. Now, more than ever before, people are able to simply stay home and execute all manner of transactions from the convenience of a home-based office business. This trend is continually on the rise, and there is virtually no end in sight. Just as you can shop and order merchandise from the comfort of your easy chair, you can do most, if not all, of your work from there as well.

Many of these millions of home-based businesses are run by individuals who find themselves in the awkward position of having to manage all aspects of their business development. This exerts added pressures and concerns that could be alleviated if others could provide them with affordable services, support, and information beneficial to their business.

And this is where you come in.

As a tax professional you can offer insight and information in a number of vital ways. You know how important proper accounting procedures are to a developing business, so you can help a home-based business "straighten up and fly right." Plus, this is virtually an untapped market! A majority of financial service providers totally overlook it because in many ways it's an invisible marketplace neatly tucked away into neighborhood homes. And, many service providers simply do not want to be bothered by "clients that size." But don't overlook this area of vast potential!

This is a new, rapidly developing market niche with new SOHO businesses opening all the time. And besides accounting and tax matters, many of the SOHO clients stand to benefit from assistance in marketing, management, handling local regulations and related financial concerns and any constructive advice, suggestions, and strategies you have to offer would be greatly appreciated. Here is an area where you can step in at the ground level, and watch your own business grow as your SOHO clients grow as well.

Consider print ads, cold calling, or a direct mail campaign whose sole aim and message addresses the needs of the SOHO market. You may have just struck gold!

## Client Credit Concerns can Spell Extra Business for You!

For better or worse, we are increasingly becoming a cashless society, depending more and more upon the use of sound credit. But as we all know, there are two sides to every story: In addition to the opportunities and privileges credit provides, there is a downside as well. With credit, you can enjoy your purchase while you are paying for it, but there are strings attached. There is no such thing as a "free ride," and what is borrowed must be paid back. There are a substantial number of people who unfortunately fall into a credit trap and create a whirlpool of debt for themselves from which they cannot easily escape. They need sound financial advice and guidance to not only help them climb out of debt but to improve their credit rating so that they can proceed to live financially sound lives.

With a good credit rating, individuals, families, and businesses can develop and advance both personally and professionally to purchase merchandise for a home or business; to purchase or lease a home, or some other form of real estate; or to acquire an education or specific training for employment. It's just that such steps need to be taken with care and deliberation. With regard to any of these considerations, you have to be able to figure out how much it will cost and whether you can afford it.

With some basic knowledge and information supplementing what you already know, you can provide numerous financial services for clients with regard to a variety of credit concerns. On the one hand, your financial foresight and insight can ward off poor credit choices that clients may be all too willing to make. Once a client falls into debt that is too difficult to get out of, he or she may be unaware of what options are available to alleviate their situation. Here again, your expertise with regard to the law, to the workings of credit bureaus, disputes, and client rights, all of this can help resolve the financial distress people frequently find themselves in today.

## Seniors: A Lucrative and Growing Market

More and more accountants and tax practitioners have discovered that senior citizens comprise a vast, nearly untapped segment of the population that could substantially benefit from their services.

As a class, senior citizens are the most affluent population group, with more discretionary income at their disposal than most Americans. They have special needs that you, as a trusted financial adviser, can easily meet.

The type of specifically tailored professional assistance and advice older Americans are in need of can be broken down as follows:

**Long-Term Planning:** It appears that for the majority of individuals, the point in their lives when they begin to be concerned about, and plan for, their retirement years, is somewhere around age 50 to 55. It is then that they generally begin to seriously look into their post-retirement financial health. And it is fortunate that they do because with retirement a number of years down the road, the average individual still has options and choices to help ensure more comfortable, less traumatic, retirement years.

**Among these considerations are the following:**

- Maximizing social security benefits
- Long-term care insurance
- Other long-term care provisions
- Life insurance and annuity plans
- Maximizing company or private pension benefits
- Possible changes in investment strategy
- Estate planning
- Planning for business succession.

As a group, these individuals are fairly well off, financially. Their children are grown and mostly self-supporting. Their homes and other investments have appreciated in value over the years and their mortgages are paid off.

**Pre-Retirement Planning:** Around age 60, as the seniors near actual retirement, important decisions have to be made and some professional guidance is often vital. Clients will need advice on questions such as:

- Whether to apply for reduced, early social security benefits
- How, and to what extent, they can remain active in their business without losing social security benefits
- How to maintain adequate life and health insurance
- How to choose the best payout options for distributions from retirement and profit-sharing plans
- How to invest plan distributions
- How to liquidate a business.

**Post-Retirement Planning:** At this stage clients are concerned with the various issues and problems affecting the elderly. They may be considering selling their homes and moving to retirement communities, condominiums, rented apartments, or even joining their children. Proper tax planning here is a must.

**Other situations that make the services of a tax or financial professional imperative or, at least, desirable are:**

- Loss of a spouse,
- Remarriage, or contemplation of remarriage,
- Qualifying for long-term care benefits, or
- Part-time employment or self-employment.

As clients get older, they may also be in need of help with insurance claims, general management of their financial affairs (e.g. paying bills, balancing bank accounts, keeping track of investments, etc.), applying for senior citizen real estate tax breaks, and numerous other everyday chores that have become too burdensome for them to handle.

It is important to target not only individuals in the above age groups but their children as well. In fact, it is often the children who convince their parents to place these matters into professional hands, if only to free themselves from doing it.

Keep in mind that older people are generally more conservative, and expect you to spend some time talking to them. In other words, they appreciate the personal touch rather than the cold efficiency so many professionals pride themselves on, and they're willing to pay for it (within reason, of course). It is important that you instill this awareness in everyone in your firm who comes into contact with these clients—including your secretaries and receptionists.

Many practitioners who cater to this clientele make house calls. Besides the great convenience this represents to the older clients, your willingness to visit them at home signifies your commitment to rendering a truly personal service.

One final caveat: Some of the areas mentioned above, such as estate tax planning (especially for wealthier clients) require specialized professional expertise that you can't expect to acquire by reading one or two books. Others are legally in the lawyer's domain. What you need is sufficient knowledge and familiarity with the subject to be able to make appropriate suggestions and intelligently discuss the various options and strategies so the client can decide whether to seek further professional help.

## Medical Claims Processing: Is it For Real?

You've seen the ads: "Make easy money at home helping doctors file insurance claims!" Or: "Unlimited earnings potential!" "It's today's hottest income opportunity!"

Basically, medical claims processing involves computerized preparation and filing of insurance (including Medicare) claims for doctors, dentists, hospitals, and other healthcare providers. It requires a thorough knowledge of health insurance policies and coverage, claims procedures and medical coding. But specialized software is available to automate most tasks.

On the surface this service seems to be a natural for accountants and tax practitioners who are looking for additional earnings possibilities. And, in fact, it could be if your current client base includes doctors and/or other medical providers. In other words: if you already have ongoing business relationships in the medical field, and you are equipped to provide the services described, you have a good chance of landing some accounts. Once you're an active player in the field, referrals and recommendations should enable you to build a viable business.

On the other hand, if you have no contacts in the industry we suggest that you take the hype with a grain of salt. This market is very competitive and not easy to enter for a newcomer, no matter what the ads promise you. Study the sales literature with a critical eye, ask hard questions, and check with previous trainees or customers about their experiences.

If you decide to go ahead, you have two choices:

1) Sign up for a complete package deal, covering training, software, marketing assistance and continued handholding. The program may or may not be in the form of a franchise and will set you back anywhere from $1,000 to $2,000 to as much as $10,000, or more.

2) Do-it-yourself by investing in a few books, attending a training course or seminar and purchasing the appropriate software. You're on your own, but you'll save up to 90 percent of the cost. If you choose this option, you probably ought to ease into the field gradually, not taking in more than one or two clients at the outset and then expand as you develop more expertise.

Our suggestion: Send away for literature from the "package deal" providers; also scan one or two good books to get a good "feel" for this area, and then make your decision.

## Life Insurance Consulting

Many—if not most—clients are sophisticated enough to realize that life insurance agents must keep on selling new policies to survive. There's little incentive for them to spend time reviewing a client's current insurance portfolio, other than as a springboard for scaling up to a more expensive, i.e. higher commission policy, or to convince the insured to buy additional coverage.

Yet, it's clear that changes in the insured's circumstances, changes in the life insurance industry, as well as changes in the overall economy, demand continued vigilance, plus periodic in depth reviews.

Areas that should be checked more or less frequently include:

- Is the insurance adequate for the insured's needs (considering ability to pay)?
- If not, which of the numerous available options should be suggested?
- Are there policies that should be canceled, cashed out, or converted?
- Should available cash values be tapped as a source of business or personal financing?
- Are all current insurance providers financially sound? (check rating services)
- How is the economic performance of this client's whole or universal life policies? Is it up to par compared with that of other policies or companies?

This provides an excellent, extra work, extra fee, opportunity for those accountants and tax professionals willing to put in the necessary time and effort to acquire some expertise in this field. Your clients will appreciate the fact that as a fee only, non-commission based advisor you can be completely objective in evaluating and recommending insurance products suited to their needs and objectives. And as their present financial and tax consultant you are in an ideal position to market this service to them.

## Helping a Small Business Stay Afloat—After a Disaster

Small businesses often suffer the most when disaster strikes. In many cases they are completely wiped out. It could be a natural catastrophe such as a flood, earthquake, or hurricane; or other sort of calamity such as fires, riots, or bombings. Whatever the disaster, small businesses are particularly vulnerable because of lack of preparation and a lack of insurance—which is very expensive for them. In fact, statistics indicate that many, if not most small businesses, are likely to close permanently: either because of damage to inventory; loss of files, furnishings and records; lack of insurance, and loss of customers. But it doesn't have to be this way!

Catastrophe—when it strikes—can be terrifying…physically, psychologically, and emotionally. But small business owners can take heart in knowing that recovery is possible, especially with the resources and services you can offer.

Unfortunately, most small business owners are simply not prepared to handle the various disasters mentioned above. Moreover, most maintain the mindset that this sort of thing "will never happen to them." But the truth is that catastrophe, in one form or another, can strike any business. Once it occurs, you can step in to mitigate the damage and speed the recovery process so that this enterprise will not only survive, but will be up and running again—as quickly as possible.

Remember, this is a two-sided coin: Most small businesses are unprepared to cope with the sweeping effects of disaster, and are unaware of the full range of resources available to them to assist in recovery. This is where you can be of immense help—as a consultant, advisor, and liaison to those many services and resources.

## Getting Your Client the Loan He Wants

The trend is undeniable. Banks are consolidating more and more all the time. In the coming years mergers and acquisitions are expected to consume thousands of smaller banks all across America. The implications of course, especially for the small business entrepreneur, are numerous.

Some experts claim small businesses will suffer as a consequence. As lending decisions become more centralized, the argument goes, there will be less room to consider the special circumstances surrounding every individual applicant. Other experts claim that overall administrative costs will decline, making small loans more affordable to big banks. Judging by current statistics, it would seem that banks are in fact turning to small businesses in an effort to develop a new and broader client base.

But however you look at it the times are changing, and the strategies for acquiring that much needed loan are changing too. Here are some points to consider that may finally help you get your client the loan he is after:

- **Steer clear of large-scale ad campaigns launched by banks and other lenders.** Instead, go to the business people of your community and find out directly from small business owners, from trade or business associations, from the Small Business Development Center in your area which banks are committed to lending to fledgling or developing entrepreneurial ventures.

- **How's your client's credit track record?** Your client's personal credit history, as well as that of her company, is more important now than ever before. Most banks take a good hard look at this data when making their determination. Oftentimes, the person, and his or her business, is assessed as a single entity. The information in this area can make or break a loan.

- **Come with a plan:** Lending officers simply want to know how borrowers plan on repaying their money. Therefore, a small business owner should be able to indicate what he wants, describe in quantifiable terms what it will do for his business, and show how he plans to repay the loan. Lenders also like to see how long you've been in business: they take into account positive cash flow and any evidence of managerial expertise.

- **Remember to negotiate:** From the lender's perspective, a small business loan is simply one of many possible investments. Be prepared to make your presentation as attractive as possible with various negotiating terms and options. Whatever the bank agrees to on your client's behalf, put it in writing.

- **Don't forget the human factor:** On the surface, lending may appear to be about nothing more than facts and figures, but the "human factor" cannot be denied. Try to develop good relationships with your bankers—long before you ask for a loan. Be sure to maintain contact with bankers at various functions, gatherings, meetings, and seminars. Keep them posted of your practice and how it is doing. That way, when you come for a loan you won't arrive as if in a vacuum. Instead, you will have developed a history with the bank.

If you find that one or more banks turn you down, don't give up. Keep on applying. Also, make a point of going to your local Small Business Association regional office. Ask for a loan guarantee, or information about any new or up-and-coming programs that may be of help.

Exploring the area of "niche markets" is most worthwhile, and the right niche market for you may arise quite naturally as a result of your own interests or acquired experiences.

When you realize that there is a specific area which you are drawn to, or one that has somehow been drawn to you then endeavor to learn all you can about that target market. You can learn on the job or in your spare time, but try to learn as much as you can. Become an expert in that field. Then devise a plan to mine that particular field, and be patient. Give it time. In almost all cases, it may take 1 to 5 years to develop a successful niche. If you closely examine any "overnight success" you will most likely find that it was preceded by years of planning, training, and hard work.

# Chapter 21

# Sample Portfolio Letter

*Success is a journey, not a destiny. It should be enjoyed throughout the trip, not endured until the final reward.*
**Art Linkletter**

*Three things are needed for success: a backbone, a wishbone, and a funny bone.*
**Anonymous**

One proven strategy for getting new clients—and keeping old ones—is to develop a series of short, friendly letters. These are great business builders because they combine the friendliness of a warm personal letter with a brief description of the services you have to offer. Plus, they can be designed to address a variety of specific professions, situations and personalized circumstances.

Here are a number of suggested sample letters that you can use as they are, or tailor to suit your own specific needs. Hopefully, they will work for you as well as they have worked for many other professionals.

**Letter Welcoming a New Client:**

> Dear Donald,
>
> I just want to let you know how much we at J & J Tax Consultants appreciate your business, and this opportunity to be of service to you. I hope this will be the beginning of a long and mutually beneficial relationship.
>
> If there is anything I can do for you, please do not hesitate to call.
>
> Sincerely,
> Jay Johnson

## Post-Season Thank you Letter to Last Season's Clients:

> *Dear _____,*
>
> *Now that the rush for filing income tax is over for the year, I can take the time to tell you how much I appreciated the opportunity to be of service to you.*
>
> *A number of my clients continue to consult with me on special tax matters throughout the year, so I make it a practice to keep my files as up-to-date as possible. Once I become familiar with a client's personal or business tax concerns, I am in a position to offer my professional advice and assistance on an on-going basis.*
>
> *I mention this so that you will feel free to contact me at any time for any help you may need.*
>
> *Again, thank you for calling upon my services. And by the way, if I come across any tax news of concern to you expect to hear from me.*
>
> *Looking forward to serving you again next year.*
>
> *Sincerely,*
> *Jay Johnson*

## Thank You Letter to a New Client:

*Dear _____,*

*In the rush of daily living, we often overlook some of life's most important considerations... such as thanking a client.*

*Therefore, I would just like to stop for a moment and express my appreciation to you for giving us the opportunity to prepare your tax return this year. I hope that we provided you with the very best service possible.*

*Although the actual tax preparation takes place during the "tax season," I am often in a position to help clients with tax issues or tax planning throughout the year. There may even be changes in your tax status that you may want to discuss with me.*

*For these, and any other tax questions you might have, I extend an invitation to you to please call me at any time during the year.*

*Again, thank you for allowing me to be of service to you.*

*Sincerely,*
*Jay Johnson*

## Thank You for the Referral:

> Dear _____,
>
> Now that the rush for filing income tax is over for the year, I can stop and tell you how much I appreciated the opportunity to be of service to you.
>
> I also want to sincerely thank you for your kindness in recommending Mr. _____ to me. I hope he was pleased with my service, and that I may consider him as another satisfied client.
>
> A number of clients continue to consult with me on special tax matters throughout the year, so I make it a practice to keep my files as up-to-date as possible. Once I become familiar with a client's personal or business tax concerns, I am in a position to offer my professional advice and assistance on an on-going basis. I mention this so that you will feel free to contact me at any time for any financial assistance you may need.
>
> Once again, I thank you for calling upon me and for recommending my service to others. In the meantime, if any tax news of concern to you comes my way expect to hear from me.
>
> Looking forward to the opportunity of servicing you again next year.
>
> Sincerely,
> Jay Johnson

## Prospecting Letter for New Clients:

- Are you paying the lowest possible income tax?
- Are you aware of how the new tax laws affect your income?
- Do you know that a professional tax consultant can be of help to you?

> *Dear Friend:*
>
> *It is to your advantage to have your tax return prepared by someone who is professionally trained and qualified for this very purpose.*
>
> *With new rules and regulations further complicating tax preparation every year, you owe it to yourself to have your taxes prepared by a trained, competent, and trustworthy tax specialist.*
>
> *To discover what a good tax consultant can do for you, make an appointment by calling 123-4567. Daytime hours are Monday—Friday 9 a.m.—5 p.m., and for your convenience, evening hours, Sunday—Thursday, 7- 9 p.m.*
>
> *It is also to your advantage to make an appointment as early in the season as you can.*
>
> *It will be my distinct pleasure to be of service to you.*
>
> *Sincerely,*
> *Jay Johnson*

## Prospecting Letter to Newlyweds:

Dear _____,

Congratulations on your recent marriage. May it bring life-long happiness to you both.

I am sure you are well aware that marriage also brings with it added responsibilities—even a change in tax status—and this is where I can be of help to you.

Allow me to explain...

I'm sure you would just as soon not think about it right now, but the new tax season is almost here, and as a tax professional, I make it my business to financially help clients in whatever way I can, so that filing taxes should be as painless and as beneficial a procedure as possible.

There are always new tax laws "in the works" and for many this can even mean "lower taxes." It's my job to be aware of such legislation and make sure that my clients, each year, pay the lowest tax possible.

Your marriage, your new status, together with other financial considerations, might just amount to a refund for you—instead of further tax expense. This is the way it turned out for many of my clients last year, and I would be happy to try and do the same for you.

However, this does entail some advance preparation on your part: collecting facts, figures, bills, checks, and other documents to represent a more complete picture of your tax deductions and liabilities. The more careful you are about keeping records, the greater the possibility of tax savings.

If you are at all interested in pursuing the matter further, you are welcome to contact me at your earliest convenience.

One thing is certain: you can count on me to see that you get full advantage of any legal provisions—old and new—for which you qualify.

Hoping to be of service to you, and "Congratulations" once again!

Sincerely,
Jay Johnson

## Prospecting Letter To Those Who Prepare Their Own Returns:

*"I usually prepare my own tax return..."*

> *Dear Friend;*
>
> *Many clients enter my office and with exasperation report: "Until now I've prepared my own tax return, but it just doesn't pay!"*
>
> *With new and more complex tax legislation appearing each year, tax returns become more difficult to prepare. That is why more men and women are discovering that it just makes "good business sense" to have a professionally trained Tax Specialist handle this most vital part of their financial lives.*
>
> *A tax return—incorrectly prepared—may amount to overpayment, embarrassment, and frequently an audit. A tax return prepared by a qualified, reliable Tax Professional spells peace of mind and the assurance that you will pay no more than you legally owe.*
>
> *One last point: it's to your advantage to make an appointment with us at your earliest convenience (before the seasonal rush), so we can give your financial matters the time and attention they truly deserve.*
>
> *Sincerely yours,*
> *Jay Johnson*

**Prospecting Letter to New Business Owners:**

> Dear _____,
>
> Best wishes for continuous success in your new business! There is plenty of room in this community for well-managed, progressive endeavors such as yours, and I am certain that your future will be financially bright.
>
> At the same time, I am sure you are aware that "taxes" are a source of concern for any new business venture. The question is: Will you get the benefit of every tax saving provision you are entitled to? This is where I can be of help: At J & J Tax Consultants we make it our business to see that you do get every benefit that is coming to you.
>
> Tax law is constantly and rapidly changing, and some of it can result in lower taxes for you and your business. This means that whoever helps with your next return should be on top of such matters in order to protect you from paying more than you should, and hopefully enable you to pay even less than you did last year.
>
> As a trained, professional Tax Consultant, and as a long-time resident in our community, I stand ready and able to provide each of my clients with the best possible year-round tax service.
>
> Please feel free to call if I can be of assistance to you, and once again, all the best in your new endeavor.
>
> Sincerely yours,
> Jay Johnson

**Prospecting Letter to New Residents #1:**

> *Dear _____,*
>
> *We would like to take this opportunity to formally "Welcome" you and your family to Pleasant Valley. It's a wonderful community—warm, hospitable, and full of opportunities. I know, because I've lived and worked here for over 25 years.*
>
> *That's right: I am a certified financial consultant, and for a quarter of a century I have proudly served many of the businesses in Pleasant Valley. I specialize in tax and estate planning. Many of my clients have found that their taxes have dropped dramatically with my tax planning strategies. My expertise can also help you keep more of your money, in your pocket, and I would like to be of service to you.*
>
> *My initial consultation is absolutely free. If you give me just 30 minutes, I will give you a new way of thinking about your taxes.*
>
> *I welcome you once again and look forward to meeting with you in person.*
>
> *Sincerely,*
> *Jack Smith*

## Prospecting Letter to New Residents #2:

*Dear _____,*

*Welcome to Centerville!*

*I know you will greatly enjoy living here. This is a town that has a lot to offer you and your family. In fact, if you have any questions about the community I would be glad to try and answer them. You might even say answering questions is an important part of my business. I am a professional tax consultant and my work entails helping friends and neighbors prepare their income tax returns, properly and to their best advantage.*

*You may not be looking forward to tax-time, but like anyone else, I am sure you would like "filing taxes" to be as painless and advantageous a procedure as possible. As a taxpayer you have a right to know:*

*"Am I benefiting from every tax-saving provision available to me?"*

*Tax legislation is constantly in flux. There are changes being proposed right now that could mean lower income taxes for you—if only you knew about them. This means that whoever helps you with your next return should be on top of these matters in order to protect you from paying more than you have to, and to hopefully pay even less than you did last year.*

*I am a trained, professional tax practitioner and a permanent resident in our community ready and able to be of service to you.*

*If I can be of any further assistance, please feel free to call. And once again, welcome to Centerville!*

*Sincerely,*
*Jay Johnson*

**Prospecting Letter to New Parents:**

> Dear _____,
>
> Congratulations on the birth of your son/daughter. My very best wishes to you and your family for a healthy and happy future.
>
> You are probably aware of the fact that an addition to your family means a change in tax status as well. As a trained tax professional this is an area in which I can hopefully be of service to you.
>
> Tax legislation is constantly in flux, and there are a number of changes "in the works" right now that could mean lower taxes for you this year. It is my job to make sure that my clients do not pay any more than they have to, and hopefully pay even less than they paid last year. Nothing would make me happier than to be able to do the same for you.
>
> However, this does involve some advanced preparation on your part: collecting facts, figures, bills, checks, and other documents that represent a more complete picture of your tax deductions and liabilities. The better you are at record keeping, the greater the possibility for substantial tax savings.
>
> If this is something you would like to discuss further please feel free to call me at your earliest convenience. You can count on me to see that you get the full advantage of any tax-saving provisions for which you qualify.
>
> Hoping to be of service to you at tax-time, or whenever you may need my professional advice or assistance.
>
> Congratulations, once again!
>
> Sincerely yours,
> Jay Johnson

**Letter Offering a Payroll Tax Service:**

> *Dear _____,*
>
> *As a successful business owner you are certainly aware that in today's competitive market continued business growth calls for the full and undivided attention of owners and managers to the affairs of their business.*
>
> *For this reason you will be pleased to learn that our convenient payroll and tax service can relieve you of the time you spend in daily payroll work, preparing the various payroll, income, and other tax returns.*
>
> *But what we offer is far more than a time saving device. As specialists in the field we can provide you with other valuable services as well. Tax work is no longer a matter of filling out forms and keeping accurate records. Tax law is rapidly and constantly changing, and tax work extends to the delicate craft of analyzing and devising various tax planning and tax saving methods that would prove beneficial to you.*
>
> *It just makes good business sense for you to spend your time doing what you know best—building your business—while we perform in the way we know best—providing you with a fully reliable and competent tax and payroll service.*
>
> *I invite you to call on me at your earliest convenience to discuss the matter further. Of course, there is no obligation on your part.*
>
> *I look forward to being of service to you.*
>
> *Sincerely,*
> *Jay Johnson*

**Pre-Season Letter to Previous Clients:**

Dear Client:

In order to serve you better and to give us ample time to properly prepare your income tax return we would like to schedule a meeting with you.

We have tentatively scheduled the following date for you:

Date: _____

Time: _____

However:

1. If this is not convenient, please let us know by using the return notation slip below, or call us at _____.

2. If you prefer to review your tax situation before the time set, please check with us. We can arrange a time at your convenience.

3. Please bring your tax form packets with you.

4. Save this slip and please mark the date on your calendar. During the first months of the year we usually do not have a chance to send follow-up reminders.

-----------------------------------------------------------------------------

Please return this slip in the enclosed envelope.

[ ] I will be able to see you at the time and date you have specified.

[ ] Please change my appointment time to: _____.

Your Name _____

Phone: Daytime _____ Evenings _____

Comments _____

_____

_____

**Letter Welcoming a New Client #1:**

> *Dear Mr. Clayton,*
>
> *We are pleased to welcome you as a new client and want to take this opportunity to thank you for your selection of J & J Tax Consultants to handle all of your annual tax needs.*
>
> *You have chosen a firm that is committed to providing you with excellent service and superior professional advice. We hope to work closely with you to ensure that you will receive the best guidance on all tax matters.*
>
> *Should you have any questions on any or all of our tax services please do not hesitate to call.*
>
> *Again, welcome to J & J Tax Consultants.*
>
> *Sincerely,*
> *Jay Johnson*

**Letter Welcoming a New Client #2:**

> Dear Mr. Sutton,
>
> We just wanted to take time to say "thank you" for selecting J & J Tax as your tax-consulting firm. This note is written to let you know how high a value we place on this relationship.
>
> We will do our best to provide you with the finest professional tax service possible. If you like our service and the way we do business we hope you will recommend us to your friends and associates.
>
> Please call upon us with any questions you may have. We want you to feel that J & J Tax is always responsive and eager to give you the best service in the field of taxes.
>
> Very truly yours,
> Jay Johnson

**Letter Announcing the Formation of a New Practice:**

> Dear _____,
>
> In June I left my position as Tax Manager at Adams & Associates to establish my own accounting and tax practice. I would like to take this opportunity to pass along to you my card, and to tell you a little about my business.
>
> My practice will deal primarily with individuals and small businesses and my services will focus on the following:
>
> - Individual and business income taxes
> - Payroll taxes
> - Tax planning
> - Installation of accounting and bookkeeping systems
> - General business consulting
>
> If you would like to get together and find out more about how I can be of service to you, please feel free to call.
>
> Sincerely,
> Jay Johnson

**Acknowledging a Referral:**

> Dear Dorothy,
>
> Thank you for referring me to Dr. Paul Snyder. I called Dr. Snyder last week and we met Friday morning.
>
> You were right in your assessment of Dr. Snyder's tax situation, and I am sure that we will be able to help him better plan for his financial future.
>
> Dr. Snyder also told me how positive you were about my services. That endorsement from you really "paved the way" for our meeting.
>
> So thank you again for your referral and your kind words.
>
> Sincerely,
> Jay Johnson

## Appreciation for Ongoing Support:

*Dear Allan,*

*All the trite expressions appear to be true, and "time really does seem to be flying by." It's hard to believe that you have been a client of ours for 10 consecutive years now.*

*Here at J & J Tax we are proud of the way our service has developed over the years, and much of our success is due to the support of loyal clients like yourself, who have consistently come back to us with your tax questions and concerns.*

*We plan to continue providing you with the sort of tax service that has satisfied you in the past.*

*We look forward to a prosperous future together. Thank you again for your continuous support over the years.*

*Most respectfully yours,*
*Jay Johnson*

Like it or not, few people today have time for long, leisurely letters, so as a rule, try to be concise and get right to the point. Moreover, today you may find yourself sending many of these correspondences via fax or e-mail. But however you relay them to your client, here are a few tips to keep in mind:

- Be sure you have your client's name and title correctly listed, and write directly to your client.
- Write in short sentences and use words that are clearly understood, not obscure and cumbersome terms.
- Try to couch your verbs in the active rather than the passive voice.
- Get rid of useless words or sentences that clutter your writing and have nothing to do with the point of your letter.

With these few guidelines in mind, you will be that much closer to getting the results you are after.

# Chapter 22

# Special Practice Builder Reports

*Opportunity is missed by most people because it is dressed in overalls and looks like work.*
**Thomas Alva Edison**

*The reason most people do not succeed is that they will not do the things that successful people must do. The successful scientist must follow a formula. The successful cook follows a recipe. It is not important that you merely want to succeed, unless you want to badly enough that you are willing to do certain things.*
**Author Unknown**

As a final chapter to this volume we are reprinting several "Special Reports" we send to our graduates. These reports summarize basic ideas, suggestions, and hints that can boost your level of success when opening and operating a tax practice.

Although some of these concepts and strategies were discussed in previous chapters, the reports are helpful for the additional tips and techniques they convey, and for providing a quick, convenient review of some of the key points discussed in greater detail in this volume.

## Report #1: Professional Ways to Advertise Your Service

The tax profession, in supplying a service, is unlike a "product oriented" enterprise. When you provide a service—as a doctor or lawyer does—you tend to deal with a more confidential and sensitive area in a person's life. Personal finances also fall into a category of information regarded as "strictly private," placing you, as a tax professional, in a privileged position of trust. Public attitudes toward you, therefore, require that you conduct yourself and your practice in a conservative manner—that you stay within the traditional bounds of propriety and follow an accepted code of professional ethics. This attitude also applies to the methods you use to promote your service.

At first glance, it might appear that such an outlook would restrict the manner in which you promote yourself, but this is not the case. There is more than ample room for effective, creative, business-building endeavors as well as promotional activities. Just keep in mind that aside from any and all advertising efforts your professional reputation really hinges on your ability to provide a competent, qualified, friendly and reliable service. Whatever else you do, don't lose sight of this!

When you do a good, conscientious job for a client, you sow seeds that will bear fruit in new clients coming to you by recommendation. Word-of-mouth advertising alone accounts for the extraordinary success of many tax practitioners. But to develop your business exclusively by this means, though virtually certain, would take time. Here then, are some simple, time-tested ways to jump-start and accelerate the process of growth and increased profits:

**Personal Exposure:** Make it a point to join local business, social, and church organizations. Always carry business cards with you. In an unobtrusive way, take advantage of conversational opportunities to inform people of what you do. This will bring you in contact with prospective clients. Relatives, friends, and business associates will also be willing to help spread the word.

**Business Exposure:** The following strategies represent a complete advertising and promotion campaign. Take your pick: use them all, or just those that best fit your circumstance.

1) If you live in a private home, put up a TAX CONSULTANT sign with your name and phone number so passers-by can see it. Make it attractive yet dignified. If you have an apartment, include TAX CONSULTANT on your nameplate on the building directory.

2) Whether your office is at home or outside your home, make it comfortable but businesslike, with tax and other reference works, your framed NTTS diploma and other noteworthy certificates in plain sight. A client's first impression of

you is important, so do whatever you can to create the proper image of a professional who knows his business.

3) Have self-adhesive stickers made showing your name, business, address, telephone and fax number, and website or e-mail address. Stick one on each duplicate copy of a return you give to a client for his personal records. Repeat business is what you want, and the sticker serves as a convenient reminder.

4) Develop a series of short, friendly letters to utilize as business-building opportunities present themselves:

   a) To New Residents—a letter of welcome and an offer of professional tax advice if and when the need arises.

   b) To Newlyweds—a letter of congratulations and offer to help with tax issues that come about with their new change in tax status.

   c) To New Parents—a letter of congratulations along with your hope to be of assistance as they take a new look at their income taxes.

   d) To New Businesses—a letter offering your best wishes for success, and information about your qualifications to service their various tax questions and concerns.

   e) To select prospects—a letter emphasizing the friendly, trustworthy, and personalized aspects of your tax service, as opposed to the trend toward mass, routine, impersonal service. Close your letter with the thought that you welcome the opportunity to be of help in this regard.

5) List your service in the business section of your local directory, and in the Yellow Pages under "Tax Return Preparation."

6) Contact your local newspaper editor about supplying material for a column on TAX FACTS AND TIPS with your name as the contributor. You don't have to be an accomplished writer, and there is usually someone on the staff to rewrite the material in a manner suitable to the paper.

7) Place a classified or small display ad in your local paper. Limit your message to a simple announcement, such as **"PROFESSIONAL TAX CONSULTING SERVICE**, Personal and Business Income Taxes, Payroll Taxes, and Tax Planning." Follow with your name, address and phone number. Do this on a regular basis during the tax season; on an occasional basis between seasons.

8) If you have extra time, consider offering your services to help out accountants, tax attorneys, and other tax specialists during the busy season. Some of our new graduates add several thousand dollars this way to income earned from their own practice.

There are other ways for a Tax Consultant to advertise his service in good taste, but as with all your efforts, you will have to determine whether the results are worth the time and energy you are investing in any particular form or venue. Whatever method you use, be sure to keep one thought in mind: it must reflect and be consistent with the dignity and professional ethics expected of those who serve the needs of taxpayers.

## Report #2: How to Cope With Chain Store Competition

Here is a copy of a letter we received which we would like to share with you:

> *"I have a disturbing problem which I would like to discuss with you.*
>
> *The past three tax seasons I have operated a part time tax service from my home. My clients have steadily increased and prospects for a continuing, growing business seemed good.*
>
> *However, I am greatly disturbed this year because rumor has it that a nationally advertised tax service will soon open a branch office in my town. Once this happens, I fear that I will lose all or most of my clients. Is there anything I can do to compete with this type of service?"*

Since this is a concern that frequently arises, we will devote this report to a discussion of how to deal with this type of competition in the marketplace.

When faced by a large multi-office competitor, the independent tax practitioner must carefully analyze his own, as well as his competitor's, strengths and weaknesses. Then, instead of panicking, he can decide on how to effectively challenge the competition.

For example, the "chain store tax service" usually features or advertises "quick, while-you-wait service," "low fees," and a mass production type of operating procedure. Sometimes they also guarantee to pay any interest and penalties (but not additional tax) arising out of errors made by them in preparing a return. To procure clients they undertake considerable local and national advertising campaigns. And in order to service a large number of anticipated clients, they will quickly train numerous assistants and clerical help. After the season, they generally close up shop, leaving no more than a "caretaker" staff where someone connected with the organization can be reached. In larger cities where they have a number of locations, they'll keep some facilities open year-round and close the rest.

With minor variations, this basically describes the kind of tax service offered by the typical chain organization.

In contrast to this, the independent tax professional—like the author of the letters quoted in the previous chapter—offers his clients concerned, personal attention; expert, unhurried, tax advice; and skilled tax return preparation in a professional setting as well as year-round accessibility to answer questions and provide guidance in all tax related matters. Frequently, he will even come to the client's home or place of business. Even if he operates his office primarily during the tax season, he is a full time member of his community and is still available year-round for consultation or for assistance if a client's return is audited or questioned.

The differences in type of service, quality and reliability of service are substantial. So where do you go from here?

First, we suggest that you do not attempt to "out advertise" the competition.

No matter what your advertising budget is, these organizations pour exorbitant amounts of money into sustained advertising campaigns, which is considerably more than the average independent tax professional can afford to do.

We also do not think it wise, or a good business practice, to cut your fees to engage in any sort of "price war." Incidentally, it is important to note that in most cases the taxpayer whose return is prepared by a so-called "cut-rate" chain tax service does not pay the low advertised price, but rather a considerably higher amount. In fact, one "Business Week" survey discovered that the average fee received by one large tax service was double their popularly advertised price.

After eliminating the areas where you cannot successfully compete (such as advertising), let us concentrate on your strong points, and those areas where you have decisive advantages over the competition, and these are:

- Providing a sustained, quality professional service
- Ongoing, sincere, personalized attention
- Continuing support and loyalty to clients
- Perhaps of greatest importance, you serve a concerned, mature clientele

In other words, you are there for people who seek quality in those that provide their lives with vital services.

We are well aware of those—and there are many such individuals—who react only to "price," and to whom quality service means little, if anything. But we are also aware of another group who both need and appreciate high-quality service, be it in the field of taxes or in any other area. It is this second group of clients and prospective clients that can help you build a successful, rewarding, and highly satisfying tax practice.

Bear in mind, too, that the first group generally consists of lower income taxpayers who pose few tax problems and provide little opportunity for tax savings (and lucrative fees). Whereas the second group usually consists of men and women who are better educated, earn larger incomes, may be in business for themselves or have others in their employ. Consequently, they require more knowledgeable (and more profitable) tax preparation and advice. In essence, then, it pays to focus your attention on this group of taxpayers. This is the group least likely to be lured away by mass-production, assembly-line tax services.

Moreover, many independent tax professionals do find that they are able to attract and retain a sizable following among low-income, simple-return, taxpayers—even in the face of stiff competition from the large tax-service organizations. The reason for this is quite simple: in this age of ever increasing mechanization and computerization, people yearn to be recognized and treated with concern and as distinct individuals, rather than just another number on a screen. They appreciate and remember the gestures and interactions that accompany a fully personalized service: a face-to-face meeting, a sincere smile, a personal telephone call, a friendly word and a friendly letter, a relationship that grows and develops from year to year.

To many, this is worth far more than any savings one may or may not get at the assembly line tax services where the client is just "another face in the crowd" who must proceed "express lane" style, so that as many clients as possible may be serviced, and the one who assists you—the client—may never see or service you again.

Therefore, the wise practitioner who understands these differences and capitalizes upon them has little to fear when it comes to being pushed out of business by the giant tax-service organizations. On the contrary, by providing a fully personalized, quality service, you can look forward to steadily increasing recognition, advancement, and income growth—sparked, to a large extent, by a growing number of loyal, satisfied clients.

## Report #3: Should you "Guarantee" your Income Tax Returns?

Our advice is often sought as to whether or not it is advisable for practitioners to include a "guarantee" with the income tax returns they prepare. Some of the larger tax services, you may be aware, advertise that all their returns are "guaranteed."

Before answering this question, let us first examine what is meant by the "guarantee." Under the terms of a typical guarantee, the tax service undertakes to reimburse the client for any additional interest or penalty incurred as a result of their error or negligence. Note that the service does not undertake to pay any tax deficiency that may be levied against the client, nor does the guarantee provide that the tax service will represent the client (with or without fee) before the IRS and argue his case in the event of an audit.

Also note that the guarantee is strictly limited to interest and penalties incurred as a result of the tax services or tax consultant's error or negligence. Thus, if the error or penalty results from the client's failure to disclose information or from his inability to substantiate deductions claimed on the return, the tax preparer is absolved of any responsibility.

Instances where penalties are levied against a taxpayer because of the tax consultant's error or negligence are extremely rare (except in the case of a tax consultant who is obviously fraudulent), and interest payable for the same reason—while perhaps more frequent—is usually a negligible amount. One may therefore wonder if this so-called "guarantee" is not much more than an advertising ploy. It does not seem to carry much practical value to the client, nor does it carry much risk to the practitioner.

For this reason, if you are in competition with tax services offering this type of guarantee, and if clients ask you about it, we see no reason why you should not offer the same to your clients (orally or in writing).

There is another sort of guarantee some practitioners give, under which they promise to represent the client without charge before the IRS in the event of an audit. Note: they will not pay any additional taxes; they merely offer their service free of charge.

This type of guarantee simply boils down to a matter of dollars and cents as far as the practitioner is concerned. If you have an established practice, you can be reasonably certain that a number of your returns will be audited: the question is merely how many, and how much work on your part the audits will entail. The guarantee, then, is bound to cost you a certain amount of time, plus a loss of fees you otherwise would collect for representing these clients. You must then balance this cost against the benefit you derive from it, that is, the amount of additional business it brings you.

In our opinion, the benefits are not worth the cost. In fact, we feel this type of guarantee works to the disadvantage of the client as well, because it puts a certain amount of pressure on the practitioner to always "play it safe" by resolving all questionable income and deduction items in the government's favor, rather than in the client's. This is generally not in the client's best interest, for though it may be advisable to avoid controversy on minor items, there are many times when the amount of money involved justifies taking a chance on an audit (or even incurring a certain audit), if you feel you stand a reasonable chance of substantiating your position.

If all or most of your competitors do guarantee no-charge audit representation, you have two choices:

1) To go along with the trend, or
2) To set yourself apart from the competition by refusing to engage in a practice that is not necessarily in the client's best interest.

You can be sure that the majority of clients and prospective clients—especially the more intelligent, more desirable kind—will understand and accept a clear, sincere, explanation of your policy in this regard.

## Report #4: How to Develop Your Tax Business during the Off Season

For many practitioners the season begins early- to mid-January and ends April 15th or shortly thereafter. Here then is an innovative, effective way to extend the tax season into the rest of the year. Reports indicate that this plan is not only lucrative, but more importantly, an excellent source for new clients.

The idea is quite simple: In the tax season—especially during those last few hectic weeks—many taxpayers have their returns prepared by run-of-the-mill tax preparers who are either not fully qualified, or do not take the time to do the professional job a tax return deserves. When examining a new client's previous year's returns, you have probably often found errors, inaccuracies, over-looked deductions, or other missed tax saving opportunities. In fact, some tax specialists routinely examine previous tax returns of new clients with a view towards filing amended returns and obtaining refunds for them. During the busy season, however, the average practitioner has his hands full keeping up with current returns and does not have the time or patience to delve into tax affairs of previous years.

One logical solution would be to suggest to new clients, at the time of the initial interview, the possibility of re-examining previous returns, and then set up an appointment for after the tax season to pursue the matter. Then send the client a reminder a week or two before the scheduled appointment.

You will also find it worthwhile to review the files of those taxpayers who had complicated returns, usually those who enjoy a higher income. By spending some time with each of these returns you should be able to find possibilities and opportunities for instituting tax saving devices for the future: perhaps some kind of trust fund for charity purposes; or changing the business arrangement from an unincorporated business to a corporation, or to a family partnership; or transferring some property from parent to child. There are many opportunities you probably could not consider during the tax season. But now, by spending several quiet evenings with these returns, you could probably develop a whole line of worthwhile suggestions. What could be more pleasing to a taxpayer than to receive a note from his Tax Consultant offering advice on how to save money on last year's return, or profit from new tax angles in the coming year.

Now suppose you carry this idea one step further, and send a letter to selected (non-client) taxpayers in your area offering to thoroughly review last year's return at no charge. If your examination turns up any areas for refund or tax saving opportunities,

# Chapter 22: Special Practice Builder Reports

you will so advise the client and—if he chooses to do so—you will file an amended return. Needless to say, any client for whom it pays to file an amended return will not only be happy to pay your fee, but will become your client as well. Moreover, many clients (even if the tax savings you uncover do not warrant an amended return) will be impressed by your expertise and will give their business to you.

If any of this sounds unusual to you at first, rest assured that it has been done, and is being done by a growing number of tax professionals, with results beyond their expectations. They report, on average, that one out of every three or four returns examined reveal substantial errors or omissions.

Now what happens if instead of discovering an overpayment you find that the taxpayer underpaid his tax, either through claiming non-allowable deductions, or making an error on the tax computation? Surprisingly, many clients are grateful for this information, which may avert an IRS deficiency notice or even an audit. However, if the client refuses to take action to rectify the under-payment, you of course, are under no further obligation.

We advise you to give this matter serious consideration. As you proceed with your work, you may come up with some innovative, business-building strategies of your own. We encourage you to try them out; you may be pleasantly surprised by the results.

One graduate recently sent us a sample of a short, simple ad he routinely runs in local church bulletins, as well as house, trade, and organizational journals. In spite of the limited circulation of these publications, he reports excellent results and finds that the work coming in fills up much of his time between the busier tax seasons.

The ad he submits reads as follows:

*Did you take full advantage of all your allowable tax deductions and tax-saving possibilities?*

*An amended INCOME TAX RETURN FOR 20__ may yield a substantial refund now!*

*Call 123-4567 for a free consultation.*

Incidentally, after taking our advice and preparing a number of such amended returns, why not write a short article citing case histories (omitting names of course) detailing the errors or omissions you found, and what you did about them, citing the amount of taxes saved or refunds obtained. You can use it as a mailing piece and/or a newspaper column. It will make for interesting reading, and should help bring in new business as well.

**Remember:** many tax professionals discover—by implementing a few innovative strategies—that their service to clients after the tax season can oftentimes be as profitable as in-season tax preparation, if not more so.

## Report #5: More Post-Season, Business-Building Ideas

A problem that virtually every professional or business-minded person faces, and bemoans, is the lack of "time to think." Because of the daily rush and pressures, little time, if any, is spent on "thinking and planning."

However, with the April 15th deadline safely behind you, and extensions taken care of, why not spend some time in creative thought on how you can increase your client base as well as on how to develop new avenues of service to present clients. If you adopt one or two of the strategies we discuss below, you will be taking a tangible step toward building a more successful tax practice.

### Do Something Extra to Keep—and Win—Clients

The late Orville Reed, a famous direct-mail expert, once told of a car dealer who built up an unusually big business and attributed a great deal of his success to one simple strategy. A few weeks after a customer traded in his old car for a new one, he mailed him a sizeable check with a letter saying that he was able to sell the old car at a higher price than he thought. He felt it was only right to share this unexpected, but welcome sum of money with the previous owner.

Such a letter not only creates goodwill but the customer will undoubtedly tell his friends about this and the dealer will go on to get precious, free, word- of-mouth advertising. We advise you to give this matter serious consideration. As you proceed with your work, you may come up with some innovative, business-building strategies of your own. We encourage you to try them out; you may be pleasantly surprised with the results.

The idea here is a potent one; more importantly, it's adaptable to many situations, because everyone likes to be acknowledged and receive an unexpected bonus.

**For example:**

- Look over last year's client list: it may occur to you that Mr. Smith's son just became engaged. Write a short note to congratulate the parents and mention the fact that Junior's up-and-coming marriage may carry some unexpected tax consequences, and that you could be of help. Then invite the parents in to discuss the matter. Such a response on your part will help Mr. Smith become a lifelong client of yours and a staunch advocate of your services.

- Mr. Jones is building an extension to his home, creating a home office, or investing a considerable amount in landscaping. A brief reminder that keeping accurate records of his expenses will save him both taxes and headaches in the future will convince Mr. Jones that you are not just a "tax preparer" but a genuine professional who takes a personal interest in his clients.

- Last year you told Mrs. Thomas that she has much to gain by keeping detailed records relating to her part-time home business. But since we all tend to forget, it may be wise to check in with Mrs. Thomas, by letter or by phone, to see if she is following your advice and thus gaining the full benefit of your services.

Beyond a doubt, if you would spend a few minutes thinking about each client and each client's circumstance, you would come up with your own list of valuable, personalized, business-building ideas—all motivated by the goodwill you wish to extend to your clients. Remember: even your best, most conscientious service during the tax season may oftentimes be taken for granted, but the professional who takes the time and trouble to think about a client and his tax problems after the tax season, will make a most favorable and long-lasting impression.

**Thinking Ahead**

The previous discussion dealt with improving the "quality" of your service. But what about the many promotional ideas you may think of during the tax season when you have no time to do anything about them?

During the busy season, you are bound out of necessity to a strict regimen which does not allow you to think far beyond your current commitments. But the months after the tax rush provide you with an excellent opportunity to evaluate the season's results: how many taxpayers did you service, what was your amount of income per time invested, what did your advertising dollar yield?

Also consider the effect of local competition on your business: Where is the market going? Would it be to your advantage to join forces with others, or branch out by yourself? Did you lose any clients? If you did, then why? Did you take on new clients? If you did, then how? Now is the time to practically and creatively consider these and other important matters.

Getting lists of new prospects, preparing mailings, making contacts with groups of prospective clients, seeking and obtaining publicity, these, and many other ideas, could and should be worked out now, when you have the time and peace of mind to devote to such concerns.

How about training an assistant in simple office and tax procedures? Are you considering a more suitable location for your tax practice? This sort of speculation, once begun, may direct you to a greater and more lucrative practice in the months and years ahead.

Remember: once January and February roll around, you won't have the time to consider the changes you need to make in order to grow; for again, you'll be consumed with the business at hand. Now is the time—between one tax season and the next—to assess and plan for future growth.

### Thank You Letters

Once the busy season is behind you, why not send a short, friendly, personalized letter of thanks to every client? Since client referrals are the life-blood of most every professional service, what could be more appropriate than to send a special thank you note to each and every client who referred a friend or acquaintance to you? This thoughtful gesture will pay dividends in goodwill, and will further increase referrals in the years to come.

## Report #6: Achieving Success

It is interesting to note that although most graduates of our training program begin their practices with the same basic knowledge, the results—over the years—show that some will attain the ultimate in business success while others will attain a modicum of success. This idea holds true for most situations in life: the most successful person does not achieve this state due to superior knowledge, unusual breaks, special contacts, or a streak of good luck, but rather, as a result of two factors, the genuine keys to success:

1) **Direction:** Know where you are going.
2) **Determination:** Make up your mind to get there.

This brings to mind one popular saying: success is 1 percent inspiration and 99 percent perspiration.

You have undoubtedly read biographies of successful people. In reading these, take note of the real turning point in a person's life: it comes following a clear awareness of one's precise ambition and direction in life. Whether it was laying the first trans-Atlantic cable, building the longest suspension bridge, sending a man to the moon, creating an even smaller computer chip, or heading a multi-billion dollar corporation—whatever the field of endeavor—the steady climb to success begins once you establish a clear cut goal.

Once you are determined to succeed in a specific area, the next step is one of perseverance: to maintain the drive and motivation to achieve that goal—in spite of obstacles along the way. As another saying has it: a successful person may fall seven times, but gets up eight.

**How can we practically apply these principles in building a successful tax practice?**

First, when we speak of a "successful tax practice," it is important to remember that the word success has different meanings to different people. For example, we once received a letter from a graduate in California. He wrote that over the past three years he was able to open three offices. He now employs ten secretaries and three tax practitioners, and hopes to succeed in becoming the "largest tax consulting firm in the West." On the other hand, we hear from former students who annually prepare anywhere from 25 to 50 returns and report "they have attained success" and are "perfectly happy."

So the first thing to do is to define for yourself exactly what you mean by success. The person who envisions opening a new office in the most prestigious part of town is thinking even now, in different terms than the one whose concept of success is limited to preparing 50 to 100 returns each season. But once your sights are clearly set, try to conduct your practice and your dealings with clients in the same way as if you had already achieved the success you envision. For example, a successful professional exhibits a certain confidence and respect toward what he does. Try to develop that confidence and respect. There is a certain amount of joy, pleasure, and satisfaction every successful professional derives from his work. Try to convey this sense of joy, pleasure, and satisfaction to your clients as well. There is a genuine enthusiasm with which a professional approaches and handles an unusual tax problem. Try to develop this enthusiasm within yourself, and let it be contagious, so it influences—in a positive manner—everyone around you.

You will find that as soon as you have firmly and sincerely set your goal, it will influence your thinking from that moment on. For example, years ago, one of our successful graduates devised an effective tactic that still works wonders. It may be helpful to you as well.

In the first week of January he writes down every method he can think of to reach as many people as possible. He not only lists general areas such as co-workers, PTA, friends and relatives, but he works out practical methods of informing entire groups of prospective clients. For instance, he belongs to a men's club that has over 100 members. He makes an effort to talk to each of the members at least once or twice between January and March. Every year he also asks the president of the club that he be given a few minutes to address one of the meetings on a current tax concern. He employs the same method with the gardening, church, and various sports groups in which he is also active. Then he tallies the total number of new clients he estimates he will be able to obtain through this method. Surprisingly—or perhaps not surprisingly—his estimates over the years have been remarkably accurate.

This particular graduate discovered that this strategy works well for him. If you, in turn, examine your own circumstance and client base, and then think creatively, you may come upon unique strategies that will work particularly well for you.

## Report #7: Reviewing the Importance of Client Service

There is always a temptation to "look beyond" in the pursuit of new clients and bigger accounts, and to somehow ignore or overlook the importance of existing clients. This is a big mistake: because once you have a client, you have set the stage for a relationship that—if properly cared for—can be mutually beneficial for many years to come.

In the business world there has evolved an unwritten rule known as "the 80/20 rule" (remember the Pareto Rule we discussed earlier in this book?). This rule states that 80 percent of your business comes from 20 percent of your clients. The key to a bigger and better business is through your existing client base. If they are satisfied they will come back to you, and their word-of-mouth recommendations will bring you new clients as well. The key to success in this regard is: quality client service.

Of course, quality service can mean many different things and can be expressed in many different ways. It may begin with a sincere and friendly smile, but it certainly doesn't stop there. Here are some important points to keep in mind when extending quality service to your clients:

- **Be a good listener:** This may seem simple and obvious, but it is not. Good listening is a valuable skill and you have to be attentive to it. Everyone wants to be listened to, but few have the genuine patience and skill to listen properly. For example, when listening to a client, do not interrupt. Let your client finish before you start—even if you disagree with what he or she is saying. Also, give your client your full attention: don't fiddle with a pencil or flip through papers, don't look at your watch, don't eat or drink—simply focus on what is being said. Moreover, encourage your client with gestures or words…face your client, nod your head, say "yes" or "I see." Afterwards, you may even briefly reiterate what has been said, so the client knows he or she has been properly understood. This kind of "quality listening" will encourage clients to come to you, to confide in you, and thus enable you to make better and informed decisions on their behalf. After all: this is one of those precious areas where you can easily excel over the firms that are so many times your size!

- **Put good principles into practice:** It's not enough to hang a fancy plaque of "quality service rules" on the wall behind you for all to see. You have to put those principles into practice in everything you do and say. A client wants to be treated as an individual and wants to be referred to by name. A client expects certain qualities from you: He or she wants you to be attentive, dependable, prompt, and competent. Now that you know this, you have to be sure you conduct yourself in this manner.

- **Communicate effectively:** When you communicate with clients be clear, concise, and polite. If you have to repeat yourself or explain something more than once, be patient and courteous, never condescending: what may seem obvious and a matter of common sense from your perspective may be something entirely new to your client. At the same time, there are certain phrases clients love to hear: they are friendly, reassuring confidence builders. Here are a few examples:

    a) *"How can I help you?"* This is a positive and welcome way to open a dialogue between you and a client. A client has something to say and here is an opportunity to open up and explain in detail what he or she needs. With these, or similar words, there is no guessing or awkwardly waiting for your client to begin. Rather, you are inviting the discussion that will ensue.

    b) *"I can help you with that¼"* A client who comes to you is looking for a solution to his tax issues and concerns. When you respond in such a manner, you put your client at ease and instill confidence.

    c) *"I don't know but I'll find out¼"* If a question or concern requires further research, then admit that you don't know the answer at the moment, but that you will get back to your client as soon as you do have an answer. An honest reply such as this also instills confidence, credibility, and enhances your integrity. On the other hand, if you "hem and haw" and try to fake an answer, your client will very likely sense this and you will thus undermine your own credibility.

    d) *"I appreciate your business…thank you."* Genuine appreciation, actually expressed, can go a long way to creating the kind of bond that encourages a client to return, time and again (as well as tell others of your quality service). You can express your gratitude in person, over the phone, in a friendly note, letter, or e-mail, the important part is that you actually communicate your sense of appreciation.

- **Stay in touch:** Effective and appropriate follow-up is also important to generating a good business relationship. You don't want to smother your clients with a flood of communications, but a few, well-timed communiqués can be sincerely appreciated. For example: As we mentioned above, a brief "thank you" letter after a service has been rendered is altogether appropriate. Remembering special occasions is also a good time to relay a short message: a birthday, an anniversary, a holiday, a graduation, a promotion, or even a note after having come back from a vacation. Also, if you come across an article or piece of information that relates to a client's profession, hobby, or side interest—and you think he or she may enjoy receiving it—then pass it along.

These are just a few suggestions, but if you use your imagination, you will certainly think of others. The point, however, remains the same: Enhancing the quality of your service will go a long way to developing long lasting and mutually satisfying business relationships. Your client base will return year after year, and with word-of-mouth recommendation, your client base will increase in number as well. And to reiterate: this is one crucial area in your practice where you can easily excel over the large "assembly line" firms.

## In Closing

So there you have it: the essential ingredients needed to start and develop your own successful tax practice. But bear in mind: A text of this sort can never really exhaust the subject at hand primarily because so many important aspects of the work are constantly undergoing changes. Nevertheless, with the knowledge and information put forth in this book, you can transform your own vision of a successful business career as a tax professional into a practical and thriving reality.

You are the architect of your dreams. You have acquired the technical knowledge you need to provide the public with a much needed professional service. You have the ability and wherewithal to continue building upon that fount of knowledge. With this text you have, at your fingertips, a range of tools that will enable you to more fully develop your professional business capacity.

The rest is up to you. We wish you much success in all your worthwhile endeavors.

# Appendix

# Average Tax Return Fees

In previous editions of this book we included a more comprehensive listing of fees. For this edition it was decided to limit the list to some sample forms. The reason for this is that fees charged vary, influenced by many variables, especially by which region of the country you are located.

The figures below are based on a 2011-2012 survey by the National Society of Accountants. We highly recommend that those looking to start a tax practice and who want a comprehensive study of tax preparation fees review this survey. As mentioned in Chapter 17, you may wish to consider becoming a member of the National Society of Accountants (NSA). A copy of the complete survey is included with your NSA membership, in addition to a plethora of other useful information, data, and access to a tax discussion forum. Following is a general list of the average fees for the some common tax forms:

- Form 1040 (Not Itemized)    $128
- Form 1040 (Itemized)    $233
- Form 1040 (Schedule C)    $236
- Form 1040 (Schedule E)    $215
- Form 1040 (Schedule F)    $238
- Form 1065    $524
- Form 1120 (C Corp)    $695
- Form 1120 (S Corp)    $660

As noted above, fees vary based on a number of variables. The full NSA survey report breaks down the survey results based on firm type, region of the country and even the size of the city. In any case, the fees you charge need to be worthwhile to you! The National Association of Tax Professionals (**www.natptax.com**) also publishes a study containing information on tax preparer fees.